. . . .

THE THEORY AND INTERPRETATION
OF NARRATIVE SERIES

Misreading
Jane Eyre

A POSTFORMALIST PARADIGM

Jerome Beaty

OHIO STATE UNIVERSITY PRESS

COLUMBUS

This research was supported in part by the University Research Committee
of Emory University.

Library of Congress Cataloging-in-Publication Data
Beaty, Jerome, 1924–
    Misreading Jane Eyre : a postformalist paradigm / by Jerome Beaty.
        p.   cm. — (The theory and interpretation of narrative series)
    Includes bibliographical references and index.
    ISBN 0-8142-0692-1 (cloth : alk. paper).
    1. Brontë, Charlotte, 1816–1855. Jane Eyre.   2. Narration
    (Rhetoric)   I. Title.   II. Series.
    PR4167.J5B36   1996
    823'.8—dc20   96-2288
                                                                        CIP

Text and jacket design by Cynthia M. Brunk.
Type set in Palatino by Tseng Information Systems, Inc.,
Durham, North Carolina.
Printed by Edwards Brothers, Inc., Ann Arbor, Michigan.

9 8 7 6 5 4 3 2 1

For
Elaine
Meaghan *and* Caelin

Application [is] always of necessity a sort of vulgarization, a smaller thing than theory.

—Henry James, *The Tragic Muse*

Kristeva's work reminds us that theory is inseparable from practice—that theory evolves out of practice and is modified by further practice. . . .

—Leon S. Roudiez, introduction to Julia Kristeva, *Desire in Language*

No theoretical problem can be resolved without concrete historical material.

—M. M. Bakhtin, "The *Bildungsroman* and Its Significance in the History of Realism"

CONTENTS

. . . .

Acknowledgments

My wife, Elaine, has put up with this other woman in the house for lo, these many years, and it has been at her urging and with her aid, comfort, and support that we have finally managed to get rid of plain, saucy Jane. My daughter, Meaghan, and son, Caelin, have been equally supportive—and impatient. Caelin says he can hardly remember when the small ghostly presence was not in the house, and especially in my study.

For encouragement, assistance, and perceptive comments and suggestions, I am particularly grateful to Jim Phelan of Ohio State University and Peter Rabinowitz of Hamilton College. Charlotte Dihoff, Ruth Melville, Ellen Satrom, and Victoria Althoff of Ohio State University Press have been most attentive and helpful.

The detailed comments of Barbara Hardy, of Birkbeck College, University of London, and George Levine, of Rutgers University, helped me clarify and strengthen my argument, though of course they are not responsible for what I might have failed to do in the end. Paul Hunter, of the University of Chicago, and the late Barry Wade read an early draft and pointed out new directions. My Emory colleague Walter Reed was invaluable in checking out my Bakhtinizing, and the Emory University Research Committee supported the late stages of the study.

Versions and variations of some of the material in chapter 1 appeared in *Victorian Literature and Society: Essays Presented to Richard D.*

Altick (Ohio State University Press, 1983); of chapter 3 in *Genre* 10 (1977); and of chapter 5 in *Narrative* (1996).

Students and colleagues have been patient and helpful in hearing me try out my ideas and arguments over the years. They are legion and anonymous, but I am grateful indeed for their stimulating comments and hope they will be pleased to see to what degree I have been able to benefit from them, and not too distressed at what I have missed or distorted.

. . . .

On Postformalism

There is a text in this gloss. Thanks to thirty years of theory, it is not so monolithic as the stone that Dr. Johnson kicked, but *it* is *there* and it is the object of our scrutiny, surrounded though it may be by the haze of time and the aura of language, and refracted by these and by the situation and subjectivity of the reader.

The text is *Jane Eyre*—its precise words in their fixed order beginning with "There was no possibility of taking a walk that day . . ." and ending with " ' "Amen; even so come, Lord Jesus!" ' " That text was written by Charlotte Brontë, published by George Smith in October of 1847. Well, not exactly. The text is the Clarendon edition of *Jane Eyre,* edited by Jane Jack and Margaret Smith, published by Oxford in 1969, using the first edition as the copy text but recording "all verbal variants in the MS and the first three editions" (Clarendon xx).

These words in their fixed order determine the overall structure and sequence of this paradigmatic reading of *Jane Eyre.* Such temporal formalism in the hands of a Meir Sternberg *(Expositional Modes and Temporal Ordering in Fiction)* brilliantly illuminates the structure and strategies of novel texts. His definition and demonstration of such temporal factors as the "primacy" effect—how the temporal position of the early portions of a text powerfully programs the reading of that text and how other strategies can modify or subvert this influence— have proved invaluable in my attempt to explore the structure and

. . . .

narrative strategy of *Jane Eyre,* and ultimately to help explain the consequent and inevitable "misreadings" of *Jane Eyre* and, by implication, of novels in general.[1]

Formalist, sequential reading, however, encounters practical problems that Sternberg does not explore. Almost immediately, for example, one is confronted with the question of what constitutes the narrative unit. Such a pragmatic and relatively innocent question raises a theoretical question that challenges the formalist assumption of the sufficiency of the text: how or by what is the narrative segmented? Sooner or later, too, the reading of the text, no matter how intentionally sequential, is deflected from the unilinear by recollection of what went before, which raises questions not only of the form but of who or what does the deflecting.

One of the "answers" to these and similar questions introduces "the reader" and the theoretical issue of whether a text falling in the forest without anyone present makes a meaningful or affective noise. Those more interested in the receptive eardrum than in the textual wavelengths argue that the text until it is read is only an inert object, a material book, and that when it is read it is no longer the same text, for a new subject, the reader, has been introduced and the result is realized dialogically.

A literary text then becomes more or less equivalent to a musical score: the notes are fixed and in a fixed order, but until it is read/performed it is an unheard melody; and each performance of the text is different, for notation/language is not fully determinate. So once performed the text is no longer merely Charlotte Brontë's or the pseudonymous Currer Bell's text, but "*Jane Eyre* (the Clarendon text) as read/played by ———." It is now one performance of what Wolfgang Iser calls the "work," which, he says, "cannot be identical with the text or with the concretization, . . . cannot be reduced to the reality of the text or to the subjectivity of the reader." It is "virtual," "situated somewhere between the two" (*Act* 21).

The reading, or performance, of the text immediately deflects it from its formal unilinearity, for the reader (with—or without?—signals) looks forward from the words being read, projecting a future

. . . .

text, and glances backward to pick up clues not only of what is to happen next but of what kind of fictional world this is. The work has, then, a second dimension. The text is linear, the reading "spatial" (bringing present, past, and future into the moment of reading). Moreover, this fluid, dynamic, multidimensional, indeterminate reading is unstable even in the reader's mind, for the aesthetic effect (or affective "meaning") "constantly threatens to transmute itself into discursive determinacy— . . . it is amphibolic: at one moment aesthetic and at the next discursive. This transmutation is conditioned by the structure of fictional 'meaning,' for it is impossible for such a meaning to remain indefinitely as an aesthetic effect" (Iser, *Act* 22). Though this discursive meaning or determinacy is engendered by the act of reading the text, it "translates" the text through frames of reference external to the text.

Are the spatializing of the text and the transmutation of the reading experience and the "translation" into discursive meaning the reader's doing, or is the reader simply following the "instructions" of the text? This is one of the key points at which modern critical theorists diverge. Even those who are considered reader-response critics differ widely, some situating the work (as we shall continue to call it) closer to the reader, so close at times as to override historical, semantic, or syntactical limits. This path can be loosely designated the poststructuralist or postmodernist (the terms themselves are subject to complex debate).[2] Iser, however, grants much more authority to the text, situating the work closer to what he calls the "artistic" or author's pole than to the "aesthetic" or reader's pole. Though he still maintains the text is not a work until actualized, Iser's valorizing of the text distinguishes him from the poststructuralists, situating him closer to what may be called "postformalist."

This is a term inferred from Mikhail Bakhtin and applied to him and to her own early work by Julia Kristeva (Roudiez 2). It suggests not only the historical development of their position from an early engagement with and critique of Russian formalism but also a residual prioritizing of the text—and formalism—and a literary-historical and sociohistorical view uncharacteristic of traditional formalism.

At first Russian formalists renounced historical knowledge and

. . . .

virtually ignored the "historicity of literature." Ultimately, however, many, like Viktor Shklovsky, were forced

> to rethink the principles of diachrony. The literariness of literature is conditioned . . . diachronically by the opposition to the givens of the genre and the preceding form of the literary series. When the work of art is "perceived against the background of other works of art and in association with them," as Viktor Shklovsky formulates it, the interpretation of the work of art must also take into consideration its relation to other forms that existed before it did. (Jauss 17)

Medvedev/Bakhtin considers such movements of formalism into the area of literary history "personal development[s]" which were inconsistent with the system of formalism itself but which were necessary "in order to move forward again" (75), that is, to move toward "postformalism." The formalists' tentative historicizing tried to keep history at least within the bounds of literary history. The concept of "literary evolution," for example, envisioned historical change only in terms of the interaction, the growth and decay, of literary schools:

> According to Viktor Shklovsky and Jurij Tynjanov, there exists in each period a number of literary schools at the same time "wherein one of them represents the canonized height of literature"; the canonization of a literary form leads to its automatization, and demands the formation of new forms in the lower stratum that "conquer the place of the older ones," grow to be a mass phenomenon, and finally are themselves in turn pushed to the periphery. (Jauss 17)

Even within this limited view of "history," we can see that, without recourse to "sub"-literary (folk) or "extra"-literary cultural and social forces, the "not-quite-post"-formalists approach such Bakhtinian areas as carnivalization and official language.

This study concentrates on the temporal form of *Jane Eyre* and the dialogic relationship of Brontë's novel to anterior and contemporary novels. In its formal and intraliterary focus, therefore, it may appear to be more "neoformalist" or "pre-postformalist" than "postformalist" tout court. However, not only do I reach out explicitly from time to time to extraliterary history—the condition of the governess, for

. . . .

example—and, especially in the later chapters, to extraliterary ideology, but the clash of novel species detailed here is dialogically related to the contextual struggle of cultural and social forces. Each of the genres carries social, political, philosophical ideologemes—domestic realism is radical in the nineteenth-century sense, individualistic, frequently feminist, yet bourgeois and laissez-faire; the Gothic romance essentially patriarchal and aristocratic, and so on. Indeed, literature often anticipates the development of such ideologemes, Bakhtin suggests, though "in an undeveloped, unsupported, intuitive form" (Medvedev/Bakhtin 17). From the late-capitalist, gender-conflicted position of our late twentieth-century reception, realism and romance, the bourgeoisie and aristocracy, are all "official," centripetal voices, so the most relevant and significant centrifugal aspect of *Jane Eyre* we can hear is the feminist quarrel with patriarchy. The voice of early feminist criticism was often essentialist or "formalist," in that it was decontextualized, oversimplifying the complexity of the struggle of social forces and the heteroglossia of the social—and of the literary—discourse. More recent feminist criticism, including its criticism of *Jane Eyre*, has resituated its voice historically, within the contemporary social context. This has greatly facilitated my attempt to blend that voice into the chorus (and babble) of voices in the text so that it might resonate in the "concrete heteroglot conception of the world" (Bakhtin, *Dialogic* 293) of *Jane Eyre*. That this study of *Jane Eyre*, despite its concentration almost exclusively on the texts of novels, is *post*formalist in its implied relation of literary to social forces may best be illustrated, perhaps, by interpolating "the novel," "narrative elements," and "literary" in a passage from Bakhtin that treats language, the word, and the social:

> language [/the novel] is not an abstract system of normative forms but rather a concrete heteroglot conception of the world. All words [/narrative elements] have the "taste" of a profession, a genre, a tendency, a party, a particular work, a particular person, a generation, an age group, the day and hour. Each word [/narrative element] tastes of the context and contexts in which it has lived its socially [/literarily] charged life; all words [/novels] and [narrative] forms are populated by intentions. Contextual overtones (generic, tendentious, individualistic) are inevitable in the word [/narrative element]. (*Dialogic* 293)

. . . .

(And one would of course want to add "gender" to "profession," "genre," etc.)

This study initially tries as rigorously as possible to read *Jane Eyre* sequentially, with no other intentional ulterior motive or theory.[3] Very quickly and ineluctably it is deflected from the unilinearly sequential, and ultimately into the literary—or novel—context of the 1840s. Driven by issues thus raised by its inability to sustain the "natural," sequential reading of the text, it explores the causes and the theoretical and methodological implications of the deflection. In due course, then, this study situates itself somewhere in postformalist territory, between the more relentlessly temporal formalism of Meir Sternberg, who follows the novel text linearly; and Iser, who follows the reader following the text; and Bakhtin, within whose comprehensive view of language, of genre, and of the novel as a culture- and occasion-specific (and thus historical and intertextual) utterance this study takes its place. While it explores only the occasion-specific particularities of Brontë's novel, it will also serve as an example of, if not a paradigm for, the reading of novels.

Intertextualities

The text of a novel is formally linear, and it is read or performed sequentially. The first section of this study attempts to read sequentially the first volume of *Jane Eyre,* and in doing so encounters and entertains the practical and theoretical issues engendered by such a reading.[1]

One of the earliest issues that arises in reading the text of a novel linearly but critically is segmentation: what constitutes the narrative unit, the hunk of the novel that can be temporarily excised and submitted to critical attention? The text is formally segmented by chapter and volume endings, which serve as marks of punctuation and indications of intentional structure. Indeed, it is here that Bakhtin sees most clearly the hand of the author: "We meet him (that is, we sense his activity) most of all in the composition of the work: it is he who segments the work into parts (songs and chapters and so on)" (*Dialogic* 254; see also Stevick). There are also scenes or suites of scenes, sometimes coinciding with chapters and sometimes not, that seem to constitute narrative units. Chapters and volumes, despite Stanley Fish—"formal units are always a function of the interpretive model one brings to bear (they are not 'in the text')"—are formal units marked "in the text," the activity of the author, as Bakhtin would have it, not of the interpreter, as Fish would. Scenic units, however, though to the critical reader they appear discrete, definable, and intentional units, may not be marked by the author's hand. Perhaps they "do not lie innocently in the world;

. . . .

1

rather, they are themselves constituted by an interpretive act . . . that has called them into being" (Fish, *Class* 13). Perhaps we need a critical quantum theory that dialogizes the formalist attribution of authority—indeed "reality"—to the text and the postmodern, reader-response attribution of authority only to the interpreter or, rather, his or her community. Whether part of the text or part of the interpretive act, the scene will here be considered a fundamental narrative unit of, if not the text, at least the performed literary work that is *Jane Eyre.*

If the novel is formally linear it is also, in the Bakhtinian sense, an "utterance." It is unique and occasion-specific, part of an ongoing dialogue. It speaks into the novel discourse of its time, engaging in dialogue with that body of fiction, making its statements in terms of what has already been or is being said and staking its claims within that dialogue for its new vision or response: "Something created is always created out of something given. . . . What is given is completely transformed in what is created" (Bakhtin, *Speech* 120).

A first novel by an unknown writer, like "Currer Bell's" *Jane Eyre*, is even more dependent on the context of contemporary novels, on "what is given," than are novels by an established author. It enters fictional discourse without the context of the author's previous work. One of the signals that orients the reader to an authorial context, the known author's name, is missing. The new work does not therefore stand alone, however. It takes—or must make—its place in the dialogue of the novels of the day or among the species of contemporary or traditional novels. Contemporary readers—and reviewers—are therefore likely to be unusually attentive to early signals of kinship claims, curious about just what this new work is, what dialogue it is entering, where it fits, and what it has to offer. Though later readers, like ourselves, will know who "Currer Bell" is, what she will write, and how *Jane Eyre* relates to her canon and her life and to the subsequent history of the novel, that novel will still have about it the benchmark of its origins.

> The contemporary reader will find himself confronted with familiar conventions in an unfamiliar light, and, indeed, this is the situation that causes him to become involved in the process of building up the meaning of the

work. However, readers from a later epoch will also be involved in this process, and so, clearly, a historical gap between text and reader does not necessarily lead to the text losing its innovative character; the difference will only lie in the nature of the innovation. For the contemporary reader, the reassessment of norms contained in the repertoire will make him detach these norms from their social and cultural context and so recognize the limitations of their effectiveness. For the later reader, the reassessed norms help to re-create that very social and cultural context that brought about the problems which the text itself is concerned with. (Iser 78)

It is, then, more important than with subsequent novels by known novelists for the critic, contemporary or modern, to situate first novels like *Jane Eyre* in the context of the novel as it existed at the time. It is even more important in reading such novels sequentially to attend to the new novel's very earliest signals, even those before the very first words—the title and subtitle, for example. Therefore I begin with the title page of *Jane Eyre* and proceed sequentially through the early portions of the text. Paradoxically, however, instead of focusing narrowly and intensely on the text and its one-dimensional linearity, in order to comprehend the text the sequential reading is at the very beginning derailed from the linear and taken outside the text to the fictional context, the dialogue to which the text is responding and within which it seeks to make its way and its world.

The first chapter in this section focuses initially on the subtitle of *Jane Eyre. An Autobiography*, exploring the kinds of plot and epistemological expectations which that generic signal engendered, expectations soon strategically complicated by other generic signals—of the foundling novel and the Gothic, for example. There are other conventional signals, scenic rather than generic, in these first chapters of *Jane Eyre*. In the very first chapter Jane strikes her cousin John, who is mistreating her, and she is taken away to be locked in the red-room. The scene of a child who fights (or lies) and is punished by being confined is common in early nineteenth-century fiction and is not limited to a single genre: it can be found in Byronic novels, sentimental novels, foundling novels, governess novels. Rather than pinned down or identified, the Brontë scene is refracted (to use the Bakhtinian term

. . . .

PART I

[*Dialogic* 299–300]) by all the contexts in which a similar scene occurred, the scenic topos complicating expectations of plot and theme.
Latter-day critics can recognize such topoi only by reading widely
in the novels, and particularly the minor or forgotten novels of the
period. Though such recognition does not insure a "definitive" interpretation of the meaning of the text, it does enrich the reading
affectively, generating and informing multiple expectations at given
moments in the reading and enhancing the reader's appreciation of
the strategies of the text. Awareness of the conventions or topoi may
also prevent facile literary-historical conclusions that a resemblance
between this in *Jane Eyre* and that in Novel X must indicate that X was
a "source" of or an "influence" on Brontë's novel.

Intertextuality itself may be somewhat problematized in chapters
5 through 9 of *Jane Eyre*, which are set in Lowood Institution and
are the subject of the second chapter of this study. If any portion of
Brontë's novel may be said to be literally autobiographical it is in these
chapters. The "originals" of Lowood (Cowan Bridge School) and of
Brocklehurst (the Reverend William Carus Wilson) and the similarity
of the situation at the fictional and the real school are well known
and were even attested to by Charlotte Brontë. Both her older sisters,
Maria and Elizabeth, came home from that school to die. She believed
the school was responsible for their deaths and that the picture she
presents of the conditions at Lowood were essentially true of Cowan
Bridge School (Clarendon, Appendix II 615–21). Yet even though many
reviewers found much in *Jane Eyre* that was highly original, ironically
more than one saw in Lowood only a female version of Dickens's
Dotheboys Hall in *Nicholas Nickleby*.

Though this is the most dramatic and documented instance of art
imitating both life and, apparently, art, there are others in *Jane Eyre*.
The Clarendon notes quote Mrs. Gaskell's version of "the probable origin of the idea of giving Mr. Rochester a mad wife" as "an event [that]
happened in the neighbourhood of Leeds," and cites as a second possible source "a tradition associated with Norton Conyers, which seems
to have served as a partial model for Thornfield Hall. . . . A low room in
the third story used to be called 'the mad-woman's room'" (600–601).
Yet, as later chapters here will bear out, this "deserted wing" motif,

. . . . . .

4

often the place of a mad woman's or wife's confinement, was already not so much a convention as a cliché in Gothic fiction. So prevalent is the device, indeed, that Brontë seems to be borrowing (without parody) from Jane Austen's parody of the device in *Northanger Abbey*, a novel which, indeed an author whom, *she had never read* (see below, ch. 3, n. 5).

These coincidental resemblances of Brontë's text to those of others suggest the exercise of the utmost caution in attributing "influence" of one author or text on another. The coincidence of "reality" and fiction as "sources" not only problematizes the search for "origins" but, I would venture, suggests a solution to the apparent paradox of the most real being the most conventional, and that is the principle of "narratability." Why are we tempted to put an experience—first-, second-, or third hand experience into a novel we are writing or are about to write? Because it is "a good story"; that is, though we may not be conscious of a novel with such a story, it sounds like the kind of thing that novel stories are made of.

Such are the concerns of my first two chapters; the third chapter of part 1 traces the alternating foregrounding of two popular contemporary genres—the governess novel and the Gothic—that engender bewildering plot expectations and problematize the nature of the fictional world of *Jane Eyre*. The governess novel is identified in subject and tone with the feminine, the domestic, the middle class, the religious, the everyday, and—though its plots, situations, and views may, within limits, vary—it seems to have a distinct ideological voice that will resonate within the bourgeois, early capitalist, realist Victorian novel. Popular and "low," it thus nonetheless seems "capable of penetrating into the social laboratory where . . . ideologemes [('developments in philosophy and ethics')][2] are shaped and formed. The artist has a keen sense for ideological problems in the process of birth and generation" (Medvedev/Bakhtin 17).

The Gothic novel is perhaps even more varied than the governess novel, though its variety does not extend to the domestic or everyday, and generally it is ideologically "aristocratic" rather than middle class, romantic rather than realistic. Though seemingly retrograde, the genre continues through the century and is even revived

· · · · · ·

dramatically toward the end of the century, just as the British aristocracy and its values continue to have what seems an inordinate residual power within the capitalist expansion. These two disparate fictional kinds—and others that are also interpolated here—are so insistently, if intermittently, evoked by *Jane Eyre* they constitute alternative voices to that of the narrator, mystifying for the reader the course the novel is to take and the world as it is constituted in this novel. These voices are truly dialogic. That is, though they alternate they are not alternatives, one of which will prove "correct"; nor do they represent a thesis and antithesis that are to be resolved in some final synthesis. While maintaining their ground and ontological grounding, they influence and interact with, "speak with," each other—and with the voice of the narrator. They also reflect and contribute to the definition of the ideological moment of the novel's utterance, when aristocratic and middle-class, patriarchal and feminist, heroic and domestic, hierarchical and democratic assumptions and values simultaneously struggle for hegemony and dialogically coexist. The ideological ferment outside the novel and its narrative counterparts within the novel make the "meaning" of *Jane Eyre* problematic, the texture rough and deep, and the emotional impact intense and powerful.

The final chapter of this first section treats the emergence of the Jane-Rochester love story. A love story is not so much a genre or species of fiction as it is a transgeneric topic. Like the scenic topos, it can fit modularly into a fictional kind such as the governess novel or the Gothic novel, or almost any other kind of novel. It is polysemic, not exclusive to or even necessarily constitutive of any particular genre. Chapter 4, then, serves as a transition between the contextual and the textual sections of this study. Here the self-reflexive or recapitulatory ("spatializing") element of the novel structure begins to assert itself (the early portions of the text serving as the context of the later), while the generic, contextual element still strongly influences expectation and interpretation. This chapter begins also to concern itself with intratextual devices or strategies such as the ignis fatuus (or false lead), permanent and temporary gaps, implication (true or false) by juxtaposition, the function of volume endings, and double-voicedness and hybridization. It also is driven to consider such issues as second readings, the relation of plot to ontology, and the role of "wrong guesses."

Throughout this study, as in all criticism that entertains notions of reader response, the question of who, precisely, "the reader" is hangs over the discussion. Indeed, why imagine a reader at all, when the reader is, as Father Ong puts it, always a fiction? If this is so, why not shift our focus from inference to implication, from reader to text (as any pre-postformalist would)? Such a shift—or retreat—would first of all bring back with it a good deal of baggage that, while not necessarily inherent, historically accompanies such a perspective. Focusing on the text suggests a model of communication—encoding-decoding—that implicitly shifts the focus to the author and reintroduces almost inevitably rather simplistic notions of intention and influence and, perhaps most important, a conception of the literary text as monologic and monovalent. Defining the reader as dynamic performer rather than as passive recipient and the text as an utterance within a dialogue rather than as a message does not erase the text or the author. They remain significant but not the only factors determining the intellectual and affective meaning of the text. Notions of neither intention, strategy, nor influence are dispensed with. Their role is merely narrowed and delimited within a wider conception of the total communication.

The text as encoded message is frozen in its historical moment; it can only mean what the author meant at the moment of composition, a position analogous to that of the strict constructionist view of the Constitution. To avoid such a restrictive view, formalists have traditionally turned to the notions of transhistorical meaning or potential meaning, but especially the former. The issue of historicity and meaning is complicated here by "the reader" sometimes being referred to as "the Victorian novel-reader" but at other times as "we" or even "you." Who are these readers, "the Victorian novel-reader," "we"?

Occasionally I cite a Victorian critic or reviewer who recognized a scene, character, or plot element of *Jane Eyre* as having a novelistic precedent, but generally I use the term "Victorian novel-reader" not to suggest that there were readers in the late 1840s who had read, remembered, and recognized the relevance of each and every one of the novels I cite as in some way related to *Jane Eyre:* s/he (like this neo-logistic pronoun) is a composite, a fictional creation based on many "originals." I do not even assume that Charlotte Brontë knew and con-sciously referred to these novels. The novels here cited, therefore, are not necessarily "sources" but are representative of elements of con-temporary fictional conventions that would be consciously or uncon-sciously familiar to Victorian readers (including Brontë), conventions that defined the genre as it existed or was deemed to be at the time. Because I am dealing with conventions and not particular sources, allusions, or parodies, I often cite four or five precedents to demon-strate the ubiquity and commonplace nature of the element, scene, or concept that is common to *Jane Eyre* and its predecessors.

If the Victorian novel-reader is a composite, so, paradoxically, are "we." This is not the royal "we," for though it always includes "I," it is not restricted to that single "original," and that, not modesty or rheto-ric, is the reason for the use of the plural. "We" sometimes embraces Fish's "informed reader," Culler's "competent reader," Iser's "implied reader," Booth's "made" or created reader, or Rabinowitz's "authorial audience." The "we" is not subsumed by these, however; the singular "I" still remains to some degree outside the author's or the text's cre-ated reader (and the "thou" exists outside the plural, generalized "you" that I sometimes alternate with "we"). Without going too deeply into the matter here, let me say that I believe "the reader" is, as Iser says of the work, "virtual." Just as I do not believe Brontë deliberately encoded all the references to all the novels that I cite in my study but that those cited are representative of the genre of the novel as it was in 1847, so I do not believe any one reader recognized each and every one of those novels. The only one who did, up until the moment you read my text, is me (or, as English professors say, "I"). But a reader in 1847 would share to a greater or lesser extent the ideology of the novel of the day, would recognize both its mimetic and synthetic elements (and I must here add to Phelan's distinction the mimesis-of-the-synthetic or the "novel-istic" elements). We cannot now become a reader of 1847, who more or less unconsciously holds that particular occasion-specific "ideology of the novel." We may, however, recover a representative portion of the repertoire by working backward through the text and through delib-

. . . .

erate or unconscious allusions in *Jane Eyre* and gather a sense of what "the novel" must have been and therefore what, in Brontë's hands, it now becomes. In doing so, however, we do not erase (though we may try to bracket out) the century and a half since *Jane Eyre*. We are not 1847 readers but reconstructers of 1847 readers, historians, those who, as Collingwood says, merely try "to think past thoughts."

Reading, or, as I suggest, "misreading," *Jane Eyre* may dramatize the role of the critical "I," the reader who is not limited to the role Brontë assigns to or expects from her reader. As Rabinowitz says, "Were I teaching . . . Brontë, I would be disappointed in a student who could produce an authorial reading but who could not in Terry Eagleton's phrase, 'show the text as it cannot know itself' [*Criticism* 43]" (32). Rabinowitz's reader, after all, stands apart from the "authorial audience," but this does not invalidate the attempt, indeed the necessity, first to identify with that audience: "Authorial reading—in the sense of *understanding* the values of the authorial audience—has its own kind of validity, even if, in the end, actual readers share neither the experiences nor the values presented by the author" (36). Indeed, even understanding, or "com-prehension," is response, just as agreement is as much dialogue as is debate, for understanding and agreement "translate" in subsuming the text within the reader's frame of reference.

Species and Scenes:
Fictional Autobiography and the
Confined Child

Readers as a rule pause for a moment in anticipation as they open a new novel and glance at the title page, and even before they read the first word of the text they know, within limits, what kind of fiction to expect and what questions to raise. Many of these early signals are generic, alerting the reader to social and literary conventions that precede the text, and, indeed, "some preliminary generic judgment is always required even before we begin the process of reading. . . . 'reading'—even the reading of a first paragraph is always 'reading as'" (Rabinowitz 176). Recognizing this "reliance of reading on conventions that precede the text," Rabinowitz insists, "has enormous consequences for the processes of interpretation and evaluation" (29). Some of the signals that precede reading are embodied in format. The three-decker, the single-volume novel, the monthly part, and the serial installment all have more or less specific and loosely generic implications, not only, as Rabinowitz would have it, to help readers "recover the meanings of texts" but, perhaps more important, to channel their expectations. The title page, though it does not literally precede reading, does precede the text, and there the title, subtitle, author's name, publishing house or periodical, all map areas or limits of reader expectation even before the first word of the text itself is read.

The first readers of *Jane Eyre. An Autobiography* were informed on the title page that it was edited by Currer Bell. The term *edited by* was familiar in 1847 but polysemic, its descriptiveness refracted by the variety of uses to which it had recently been put.[1] It had been

used in the previous three years for comic novels and rogue or Newgate novels as well as fashionable, domestic, and historical novels, for
example. Among the novels of 1844 were *Martin Chuzzlewit*, "edited
by Boz," and *Memoirs of a Muscovite*, "edited by Lady Bulwer Lytton,"
while *The Luck of Barry Lyndon. A Romance of the Last Century*, "edited
by Fitz-Boodle" (i.e., William Makepeace Thackeray), was appearing
monthly in *Fraser's Magazine*; among those of 1846, *Lionel Deerhurst; Or,
Fashionable Life Under the Regency*, "edited by the Countess Blessington," one of the leading writers of fashionable or "silver-fork" novels;
and in the same year as *Jane Eyre*, 1847, *Bellah, a tale of La Vendée. From
the French*, "edited by the Author of 'Two old men's tales,' etc.," that is,
by the popular and respected "domestic" novelist Anne Marsh.

Thus, though "edited by" would not necessarily have indicated the
kind of novel being presented, what it might have been expected to indicate was a work by a well-known novelist, acknowledged by name,
pseudonym, or the titles of that novelist's other works. In 1847, however, "Currer Bell" was virtually unknown: *Poems by Currer, Ellis and
Acton Bell*, published the previous year, had sold but *two* copies (Gérin,
Brontë 335). There was another "edited" autobiography by an uniden-
tifiable author in 1847, *The Autobiography of Rose Allen*, "edited by a
Lady"—published at about the same time as *Jane Eyre*[2]—but there the
purpose of the device seemed clear: the lower-class fictional narrator
might be expected in the name of realism to require a more educated
pen to help tell her story. Jane, who is reading when we first meet
her and later teaches school and serves as a governess, does not need
such help.

In the novel itself there is no trace of an editor—no preface, foot-
notes, afterword, or interpolation of any kind, no single word that is
not "Jane's." The fiction of an editor nonetheless puts the entire text
in boldface quotation marks, makes the first-person autobiographer
into a "third person" to the first person of the "invisible" editor, and
raises the question of how we are to take these words by this person
called Jane Eyre. That the editor was an unknown, that there was no
trace of editing, no likelihood of parody, and no necessity to provide
a more educated narrator than Jane Eyre, made the tone even more
problematic than if it were a novel by such familiar names as "Boz,"

. . . .

"Fitz-Boodle," or the Countess Blessington. Such uncertainty may have contributed to the immediate speculation—for example, in the *Jerrold's* for October 1847 (6:474)—that this first-person narrative was not a fictional but a thinly disguised, actual autobiography.

Whatever the effect, the fiction of an editor, which was, indeed, irrelevant in a text without signs of "editing," was dropped from the second (January 1848) and all subsequent editions. The device had, in any case, been the publisher's, not the author's, idea (Pollard 100), perhaps intended to capitalize on the association of the device with such authors as Dickens, Thackeray, Anne Marsh, and the Countess Blessington. If so, the immediate success of *Jane Eyre* made such identification no longer necessary.

The publisher's other contribution to the title page, the subtitle *An Autobiography,* clearly more appropriate to Brontë's narrative strategy, was retained. The suggestion of that subtitle and the emotional intensity of the narration have led readers, reviewers, and critics ever since to conjecture about the literally autobiographical dimension of the text. Brontë, unaware that Thackeray's wife, though no Bertha Rochester, was in an asylum, dedicated the second edition of the novel to him. Elizabeth Rigby, in her infamous review in the *Quarterly,* while protesting that she has "no great interest in the question at all," repeats the "rumor" that the author is the original of Becky Sharp, is Thackeray's discarded mistress, and is now seeking her revenge (174–75). Modern readers, though they know the identity of Currer Bell and know the differences between Brontë's life and Jane's, still find it difficult not to think the novel autobiographical, a disguised version of Charlotte's strong attachment to her married Belgian employer-teacher, Heger, perhaps. Even modern readers who have never heard of Heger frequently identify Brontë with her creation, and especially with the young, passionate, and rebellious Jane. Fictional or actual, it is as an autobiography that *Jane Eyre* was first read and reviewed and has been read and discussed ever since.

In 1847 the term *autobiography* was a relatively new one, having first appeared in the language, according to the second (1989) edition of the OED only in 1797, yet it already had a variety of meanings and associations clinging to it. Though one survey of 119 autobiographies

. . . . . .

13

finds only five published before 1850 and suggests that "the term was not firmly established until the 1860's" (Rinehart 177), fictional autobiography seems to have had a somewhat earlier start. In 1829 the first pages of Bulwer Lytton's *Devereux. A Tale* were designated "The Auto-Biographer's Introduction." At his publisher's insistence, Disraeli allowed the first edition of *Contarini Fleming* (1832) to be subtitled *A Psychological Auto-biography.*[3] References inside the novels of the period suggest that in public discourse, if not yet in published life stories, the term was so common as to be a sign of the times. As early as the 1830s Carlyle was referring to "these Autobiographical times of ours" in his own embedded fictional autobiography, *Sartor Resartus* (bk. 2, ch. 2), and the Countess Blessington's fictional elderly gentleman in *Confessions of an Elderly Gentleman* (1836) observes, "This is an autobiographical age" (1). The word *autobiography* itself, however, seldom appeared in the titles of books until midcentury. Though the subtitle *A Psychological Auto-biography* appeared in the first, 1832, edition of *Contarini Fleming*, it was abandoned in 1834 in favor of *A Psychological Romance* and was restored only in the 1846 edition. In 1846, too, *Margaret Russell: An Autobiography* was published anonymously. Soon thereafter, nonfictional self-told life stories also began to be called autobiographies: *The Autobiography of Benjamin Franklin* is the title of the 1850 edition; earlier editions were called "Memoirs" or "Life of. . . ." So when *Jane Eyre* appeared, *autobiography* was relatively rare on the title page but was already polysemic.

It is difficult to draw a firm line between fictional autobiographies and fictional memoirs, confessionals, or stories "told by himself" or "herself." Memoirs, perhaps, more often deal with outward, even historical events; confessionals with overt acts, often stressing reform. Autobiography tended toward the internal and analytical or psychological. This may help explain its growing popularity, for internality, self-analysis and introspection had become a keynote—some said a sour note—of the times: "Introspection as a 'note' of the thirties and forties has never been duly recognized; yet contemporaries regarded the 'diseased habit of analysis,' 'the ingenious invention of labyrinth meandering into the mazes of the mind,' or in nobler phrase, 'the dialogue of the mind with itself' as characteristic of the times" (Tillotson

131). These phrases, from *Fraser's* in March 1848, *Blackwood's* in April 1846, and Arnold's preface to his *Poems*, 1853, are all, in varying degrees, depreciative, a critical judgment typical of the period despite the increasing internality of fiction and poetry. The *Blackwood's* critic, John Eagles, specifically referring to a fictional autobiography, Anne Marsh's *Mount Sorel*,[4] states emphatically that this internal meandering is not the way to write a proper novel: "Such was not the mode adopted heretofore by more vigorous writers, who preferred exhibiting the passions by action, and a few simple touches, which come at once to the heart, without the necessity of unravelling the mismazes of their course" (413). "Vigorous" is a code word suggesting "masculine," and internality is often associated with the feminine or effeminate, the "weak."

Private introspection in diaries and journals has a long history in England, especially in Dissenting or Low Church circles. These, which we proleptically call "spiritual autobiographies," contributed markedly to the emergence of the modern novel, beginning in the eighteenth century, and it is difficult for us to imagine the novel without such internality. What is being testified to here, however, is that even in the middle of the nineteenth century the "public display" of introspection was not yet an expected or accepted element of "real novels," though there was a generic mutation taking place about the time of the publication of *Jane Eyre* to accommodate such meanderings into the mismazes of mind and feelings.

A cool early review of *Jane Eyre*—in the *Spectator* for 6 November 1847—depreciatively identifies it with "that school where minute anatomy of the mind predominates over incident; the last being made subordinate to description or the display of character" (Allott 74). Even a favorable reviewer—A. W. Fonblanque in the *Examiner* for 27 November 1847—insists that *Jane Eyre* is not really a novel at all, and that it would be a disservice to it to judge it as one: "Taken as a novel or history of events, the book is obviously defective; but as an analysis of a single mind, as an elucidation of its progress from childhood to full age, it may claim comparison with any work of the same species" (Allott 77).

The novel in the late 1840s as defined by reviewers, then, is a history of events in which incident predominates and the passions are exhibited by action. There is another "species" of fiction, reviewers acknowledge, but it is not to be identified with the novel and is of an inferior kind. The "note" of introspection, Tillotson points out, had been sounded in the novel well before the 1830s and 1840s, but it was muted by the louder chorus of novels of action and of society: "Despite the precedent of *Caleb Williams*, it was slower to establish itself in the novel, partly because it was obstructed in different ways by the dominance of Scott, of the 'silver-fork' novels, and of Dickens" (132). And, she might have added, by the general expectations as to the proper subject and mode of the novel. The precedent of Godwin that Tillotson cites is acknowledged by contemporary reviewers, either as an exception to the general inferiority of the type, or as the keynote of another, if slightly inferior genre of long fiction. John Eagles can remember "but one tale in which this style of descriptive searchings into the feelings is altogether justifiable—Godwin's Caleb Williams" (414). Fonblanque cites the same novel as the model of the type. *Jane Eyre*, he says, "is not a book to be examined page by page, with the fiction of Sir Walter Scott or Sir Edward Lytton or Mr. Dickens, from which . . . it differs altogether. It should rather be placed by the side of the autobiographies of Godwin and his successors, and its comparative value may be then reckoned up, without fear or favour" (Allott 77).

Though *Things as They Are, or the Adventures of Caleb Williams,* as it was first called, was published in 1794, more than fifty years before *Jane Eyre* and before the word *autobiography* was introduced into the language, and Godwin's fictional "autobiographies" *St. Leon* (1799) and *Fleetwood* (1805) were published only a few years later, Godwin's work was still very much part of the literary scene in the 1840s. His last novel, *Deloraine,* had appeared as recently as 1833—after the death of Sir Walter Scott—and *Caleb Williams* (no. 2), *St. Leon* (no. 5), and *Fleetwood* (no. 22), all reissued in the long-lived Bentley's Standard Novels series in the 1830s, were not only in print but were still being advertised in the late 1840s (see, e.g., the 17 July 1847 *Athenaeum* [no. 1029:776]). Author of the radical political treatise *Enquiry Concerning Political Justice* (1793), husband of the radical feminist Mary Wollstonecraft, father-in-law of Percy Bysshe Shelley, and grandfather,

. . . .

as it were, of *Frankenstein*, Godwin was identified with revolutionary Romanticism, the Gothic, and feminism. In his fictional autobiographies, he characteristically pits the individual against society; in *Caleb Williams* the repressive power and injustice of privilege is so great it achieves almost supernatural or Gothic dimensions. Thus Godwin and his daughter preempt that high Romantic, aristocratic Gothic form for political radicalism and feminism. Fonblanque, editor of the radical *Examiner*, no doubt knew what he was doing when he tried to co-opt the startling new novel of the year 1847 for his cause. *Autobiography*, too, had somewhat radical connotations, not only in its scientific sound but in its suggestion of the autonomy of the individual, the celebration of self. Many contemporary readers thus may have expected *Jane Eyre* to conform to the Godwinian pattern and the radical implication of autobiography, especially when the term has the power of primacy in its place as subtitle and when the opening episode treats rebellion so memorably and sympathetically.

Fictional autobiography was not the sole property of the Godwin "school," however; other influential novelists had tried their hand at the form. It is unlikely to occur to us immediately to associate Bulwer Lytton with William Godwin either in politics or in literature. Though no Radical, Bulwer had been a reasonably active Liberal early in his parliamentary career, and his candidacy had been approved by Godwin. Though by 1847 his last dozen or so novels had been in the third person, and many, like *The Last Days of Pompeii* (1834), were quite literally histories of events and thus "real" novels, Lytton's early novels had been in the first person: *Falkland* (1827), an epistolary novel; the others—*Pelham* (1828), *The Disowned* (1829), and *Devereux* (1829)— fictional autobiographies. The last of these began with "The Autobiographer's Introduction" that has already been cited. Though these novels do not markedly resemble Godwin's except in first-person narration, Lytton's character names echo Godwin's and suggest a generic continuity: Falkland is the name of Caleb Williams's persecutor; Lytton's Falkland seduces a Lady Emily Mandeville, and Mandeville is the eponymous hero of another of Godwin's fictional autobiographies; a Tyrrel appears both in *Caleb Williams* and *Pelham*.[5] But by 1830 Lytton had apparently abandoned first-person narration for fashionable and

. . . . . .

historical fiction, and he did so for reasons that anticipate the judgments of Eagles and Fonblanque. In the dedicatory epistle prefacing the 1836 edition of *Devereux*, he says of that novel and *The Disowned*, "The external and dramatic colourings which belong to fiction are too often forsaken for the inward and subtle analysis of motives, characters, and actions" (vi). Nonetheless, *Devereux* had appeared in a new edition in 1841, that novel and *Pelham* both being in Colburn's Modern Standard Novelists series, and the Cheap Edition of his novels and tales was being advertised in the 21 August 1847 *Athenaeum* (1034:875), less than two months before the publication of *Jane Eyre*. Lytton's fictional autobiographies and his prefatory comments on the genre were thus part of the literary dialogue within which a new first-person novel in 1847 would take its place.[6]

The author of *Margaret Russell* in 1846 defended fictional autobiography for its internality, which paradoxically led outward to authentic universality: "One life, however varied in its scenes and outward acts, is, in its more essential and internal character, but the reflex of all" (*Russell* 4). Reviewers in the 1840s were still depreciative, however: aside from "meandering into the mazes of the mind," and lacking (masculine) vigor, fictional autobiographies were radical, antisocial, and displayed "an unhealthy egotism; a Byronism of personal feeling" (Eagles 413). It is, indeed, the radical dandy Byron, not the radical feminist Godwin, who is Lytton's chief master, as he was Disraeli's (Stone 197). It is not difficult to find the egotism, Byronic or otherwise, in Lytton; it is impossible to miss it in Disraeli—at the very beginning of *Contarini Fleming*, for example:

> When I turn over the pages of the metaphysician, I perceive a science that deals in words instead of facts. Arbitrary axioms lead to results that violate reason; imaginary principles establish systems that contradict the common sense of mankind. All is dogma, no part demonstration. Wearied, perplexed, doubtful, I throw down the volume in disgust.
>
> When I search into my own breast, and trace the development of my own intellect, and the formation of my own character, all is light and order. The luminous succeeds to the obscure, the certain to the doubtful, the intelligent to the illogical, the practical to the impossible, and I experi-

ence all that refined and ennobling satisfaction that we derive from the discovery of truth and contemplation of nature.

I have resolved, therefore, to write the history of my own life, because it is the subject of which I have the truest knowledge. (4)

In the preface to the 1846 edition of *Contarini*, Disraeli anticipates Eagles's objections to the genre and justifies his use of the autobiographical form as Eagles a few months later would justify that of *Caleb Williams:* "When the author meditated over the entireness of the subject," Disraeli says, "it appeared to him that the autobiographical form was a necessary condition of a successful fulfillment. It seemed the only instrument that could penetrate the innermost secrets of the brain and heart" (ix–x). After writing the Byronic *Contarini Fleming* in 1832, however, Disraeli had abandoned fictional autobiography and by the mid-forties had in *Coningsby* (1844), *Sybil* (1845), and *Tancred* (1847) transmuted the fashionable and the Byronic into the political novel. The new edition of *Contarini* thus appeared amid the publication and acclaim of the three political works.

In 1847, then, though the novel was still for many readers and reviewers "a history of events," the autobiographical genre was defended for the very reason it had been criticized — its internality, introspection, and subjectively authenticated "truth." And though some of the "autobiographies" were by women and of a domestic kind, there were others that were swashbuckling or Byronic, by authors more associated with the fashionable, the historical, or the political. The term *autobiography* was thus both familiar and strange: rare enough still in fiction to call up particular contexts and expectations yet not confined to a genre or gender. It was a term, then, that from its novelty and varied appearances was dialogically refracted.

Victorian readers or reviewers like Fonblanque or Eagles seeking to anticipate or comprehend the relevance of the subtitle of *Jane Eyre. An Autobiography* might understandably look past Lytton and Disraeli and back to Godwin and his radical (and feminist) circle, especially after they had read the first sentences of the new novel. Disraeli's name in particular would seem strange linked to that of Currer Bell, as would, in the same way and for similar reasons, the linking of the names of the two fictional autobiographers: Contarini Fleming, the eldest son of "Baron Fleming, a Saxon nobleman of ancient family [and the] daughter of the noble [Venetian] house of Contarini" (4); and Jane Eyre, the plain, small, poor, orphaned daughter of a clerical father and disinherited mother. Nothing could be more different from the exotic cosmopolitanism of Disraeli's setting than the mundane provincialism of Brontë's. Nothing could be more different from the Byronic self-aggrandizement of Childe Contarini in a world that responds to his emotions and imagination than the shivering but resilient self of little Jane in her hostile and unresponsive world. Nothing could be more different from the situations and settings of the two autobiographies unless it is the prose in which they are realized.

Ten-year-old Jane, an alien and unwelcome presence in the mundane household of her deceased uncle's wife, having been banished from the fireside and the company of her aunt and three cousins, is curled up in the curtained window seat in another room looking at a book with pictures, the scene prefaced by prose as raw and somber as the weather on that northern English November day:

> There was no possibility of taking a walk that day. . . . I was glad of it; I never liked long walks, especially on chilly afternoons; dreadful to me was the coming home in the raw twilight, with nipped fingers and toes, and a heart . . . humbled by the consciousness of my physical inferiority to Eliza, John, and Georgiana Reed. (3)

Contarini Fleming, on the other hand, opens with the young narrator "wandering in those deserts of Africa that border the Erythraean Sea" (1), arriving at the "halls of the Pharoahs," and musing on the vanished past. Then, the

> wind arose, the bosom of the desert heaved, pillars of sand sprang from the earth and whirled across the plain; sounds more awful than thunder came rushing from the south; . . . I knelt down and hid my face in the moveable and burning soil, and as the wind of the desert passed over me, methought it whispered, "Child of Nature, learn to unlearn!" (2)

Despite their differences, however, both *Contarini Fleming* and *Jane Eyre* belong to the then rare genre of fictional autobiography, and their opening incidents, despite their radically different prose styles, are so

. . . . . .

similar as to suggest that Brontë's novel may be a response to Disraeli's or that its scenic and situational "utterance" must force its way through the narrative territory already occupied by the opening of *Contarini Fleming* if it is to make its own statement. The ostracized orphan Jane, we all remember, is discovered by her bullying cousin John, who strikes her, insults her, and throws a book at her. She has been mistreated by him before, but now, for the first time, she fights back, furiously, and it is this act that destabilizes the situation and sets in motion the action of the novel. Resisting all the way, she is carried off by the servants and locked in the red-room. When, in the second chapter, Contarini's autobiography begins, he is a motherless and "melancholy child" (4) in a household he hates. His father had remarried, moved north, and sired two blond and wholly Saxon sons. The dark, southern child feels alienated from his new family in the "rigid clime whither I had been brought to live" (5). In the first dramatized incident, which takes place when Contarini is about eight years old, nearly the same age as Jane, one of his half brothers calls him stupid, and Contarini strikes him. As a consequence, "[I] was conducted to my room, and my door was locked on the outside" (6). Defiantly he bolts it on the inside and all day long refuses to open the door. The servants finally break it down, but he gnashes his teeth and growls at them. His step-mother summons his father, whom he allows to enter: "I burst into a wild cry; I rushed to his arms. He pressed me to his bosom. He tried to kiss away the flooding tears that each embrace called forth more plenteously. For the first time in my life, I felt loved" (7).

The sense of dialogue between these very different novels is intensified when the initial commonplace and realistic opening scene is immediately followed in both novels by the unexpected appearance of what seems to be a ghost. While confined in the red-room, as it begins to grow dark Jane begins to think of death and ghosts:

> I lifted my head and tried to look boldly round the dark room: at this moment a light gleamed on the wall. Was it, I asked myself, a ray from the moon penetrating some aperture in the blind? No; moonlight was still and this stirred: while I gazed, it glided up to the ceiling and quivered over my head. . . . I thought the swift-darting beam was a herald of some coming vision from another world. My heart beat thick, my head grew

. . . .

hot; a sound filled my ears, which I deemed the rushing of wings: something seemed near me; I was oppressed, suffocated: endurance broke
down; I rushed to the door and shook the lock in desperate effort. (15)

In *Contarini Fleming*, the young culprit has already been released from
confinement, and the apparition is a separate, yet immediately sequential incident. Still a child, Contarini falls in love with a young lady
eight years or more older than he, his cousin Christiana. Despite the
expression of love he won from his father in the first episode, Contarini
tells his cousin that no one loves him. She assures him that everyone
does, that she herself does, "and she kissed me with a thousand kisses"
(11). At a children's ball, however, she seems to be wholly absorbed
by another partner, a boy two years older than Contarini. The despon-
dent Contarini steals away to his dark bedroom and throws himself
on his bed:

> My forehead was burning hot, my feet were icy cold. My heart seemed in
> my throat. I felt quite sick. I could not speak; I could not weep; I could
> not think. Everything seemed blended in one terrible sensation of deso-
> late and desolating wretchedness.
>   . . . there was a sound in the room, light and gentle. I looked around;
> I thought that a shadowy form passed between me and the window. A
> feeling of terror crossed me. I nearly cried out. (14)

The voice of the older Jane, the narrating Jane, rarely interrupts
the action in the early scenes of the novel, but it does so at the critical juncture in the red-room scene to explain away the ghost: "I can
now conjecture readily that this streak of light was, in all likelihood, a
gleam from a lantern, carried by someone across the lawn" (15). Contarini's visitant too is no ghost; it is Christiana come to fetch him back
to the ball and to reassure him of her love. It is her visit rather than
his father's expression of love that the autobiographer calls "the first
great incident of my life" (12). Once again, Contarini gains love, Jane
only more hostility.

Though the opening scenes of childhood fights and the forcible
confining of the prideful autobiographers suggest a homologous relationship between these two internalized narratives, and the prior
presence of *Contarini* dialogizes the opening of *Jane Eyre*, the similarity

. . . .

of scenes helps define *Jane Eyre*'s difference. Though both children feel marginalized in their household, the privileged Contarini, unlike the dependent Jane, is the older child, strikes the first blow, and, though locked in a room initially against his will, the room he is locked in is his own room and it is he who prolongs the incarceration. Most important, his rebellion succeeds: for the first time he is assured of love, parental love. Jane's violent rebellion does not succeed. She tries to escape the room in which she is imprisoned, begging her aunt to release her. But her aunt pushes her back into the room, and Jane faints. Love-starved like Contarini—"You think I have no feelings, and that I can do without one bit of love or kindness; but I cannot live so," she later tells her aunt —pride and rebellion earn her not assurance of love but further banishment; she loses even this poor substitute for a family and a home.

The coincident opening suite of scenes in *Jane Eyre* and *Contarini Fleming* makes Brontë's scene polysemic. Though the novels thereafter go almost diametrically different ways,[7] and for Brontë's reader Disraeli's novel is backgrounded, because of the primacy effect it is not entirely lost. The aura of Byronism is now part of the world of the novel. *Contarini Fleming* in its fashion prepares the way for *Jane Eyre*'s own Byronic hero, Rochester. More important, the narrative outcome and moral vision of Brontë's fictional autobiography is problematized: Godwin's rebellious hero Caleb Williams is victimized, Disraeli's Contarini triumphs. Whither Jane?

The dialogue of *Jane Eyre* with its contemporary fictional context through its opening incidents is not limited to *Contarini Fleming*. Scenes like those in Brontë's and Disraeli's fictional autobiographies also appear in a number of other novels that, though not precisely autobiographies or even analyses of a single mind, are at least fictional biographies or "histories." Such scenes are so frequent as to be narrative commonplaces, or what I shall call "scenic topoi."

One novel with a strikingly similar incident, or scenic topos, like *Contarini* appeared in a new edition in 1846. It is a novel few readers were (or are) likely to have missed: *Oliver Twist; or, The Parish Boy's Progress*. Neither an autobiography nor Byronic, this "history" of a foundling seems, in its sympathy for the underdog and antipathy for entrenched authority, Godwinian, if not particularly radical. Though

. . . . . .

crime is treated in a totally different fashion, even the Newgate aspects of *Oliver Twist* may recall *Caleb Williams*. In its faith in human innocence, its foundling theme, and its stereotypes—such as "the outcast waif and benevolent gentleman" (R. Colby 120)—*Oliver Twist* seems in the sentimental or "low" (as opposed to the Byronic or "high") Romantic mode. In its Bunyanesque subtitle and tendency toward moral as well as social allegory (Lankford 20–31), it is related to a still "lower" tradition, the religious, didactic, and domestic novel, which will figure significantly in the grounding of *Jane Eyre* and as a major element in the new species of novel Charlotte Brontë is evolving.

Its early situation and scenes further refine and refract the opening of *Jane Eyre*. Oliver, like Jane but not like Contarini, is poor and "diminutive"; he is not only an orphan like Jane but, worse, a foundling. He is locked up not once but twice in the early (though not the first) chapters of his "history." The first time, on his ninth birthday, he is confined with two other boys; the second time, like Contarini and Jane, he is confined alone, for fighting. The second occasion is introduced by Dickens as the true beginning of Oliver's "progress," just as the similar incidents were the true beginnings—the destabilizing events—of Jane's and Contarini's life stories: "And now I come to a very important passage in Oliver's history; for I have to record an act slight and unimportant perhaps in appearance: but which indirectly produced a most material change in all his future prospects and proceedings" (35).

The ten-year-old Oliver (Jane is ten when we first meet her, Contarini eight) has been apprenticed to an undertaker and, like Jane, is the unwelcome intruder in the household. A fellow worker, Noah Claypole, taunts the younger and smaller Oliver and pulls his hair and ears. Like Jane on earlier occasions, Oliver endures the mistreatment. When Noah insults the memory of Oliver's mother, however, Oliver "[grabbed] Noah by the throat; shook him, in the violence of his rage, till his teeth chattered in his head; and, collecting his whole force into one heavy blow, felled him to the ground" (32).

The undertaker's daughter and wife come to Noah's rescue, dragging "Oliver, struggling and shouting, but nothing daunted, into the dust-cellar, and there locked him up" (32). Jane found that "four

· · · · · ·

hands were immediately laid upon me, and I was borne upstairs," and she too "resisted all the way" (8–9). Jane screams violently in panic; Oliver kicks violently in anger. The beadle is summoned; he suggests that part of Oliver's conduct must come from his bad family. At this point, Oliver, believing his mother is being insulted again, recommences kicking. When Sowerberry returns, he releases Oliver, scolds him, shakes him, and boxes his ears, as Aunt Reed does to Jane when the child challenges her (28). Oliver protests that Noah has brought his punishment on himself by insulting Oliver's mother, but Mrs. Sowerby says his mother deserved Noah's insults. Oliver says Mrs. Sowerby is lying; she bursts into tears (41–42). Jane, too, brings her guardian to the verge of tears by accusing her Aunt Reed of deceit: " 'People think you a good woman, but you are bad; hard-hearted. *You* are deceitful! . . .' Mrs. Reed looked frightened; . . . twisting her face as if she would cry" (39–40).

There are other significantly similar episodes in *Jane Eyre* and *Oliver Twist* in the earlier portions of each novel, though the sequences of the events are different. It is as a consequence of her behavior leading to and during her incarceration that Jane is sent to Lowood Institution, a charity school. Oliver has already been confined in a "charitable" institution, a workhouse, indeed was born there. After his punishment—he has been beaten by the undertaker and Bumble as well as having been locked away—he escapes Sowerberry and begins his odyssey. Jane is frightened by what she believes may be a ghost while confined in the red-room, where her uncle died nine years before; Oliver has been confronted by the ghostlike earlier, on the first night he spent in the undertaker's workshop:

> An unfinished coffin on black tressels, which stood in the middle of the shop, looked so gloomy and deathlike that a cold tremble came over him, every time his eyes wandered in the direction of the dismal object: from which he almost expected to see some frightful form slowly rear its head, to drive him mad with terror. Against the wall, were ranged, in regular array, a long row of elm boards cut into the same shape: looking, in the dim light, like high-shouldered ghosts with their hands in their breeches-pockets. (25)

. . . .

Oliver is too depressed by the loneliness, gloominess, and strangeness to be terrified; he falls asleep.

Oliver, like a Godwinian hero, is persecuted because he is a victim—an orphan, poor—as Jane is. Though Jane is not a foundling, she might be better off with fewer Reed relatives, and like Oliver, she searches throughout her story for a home, a hearth like the one from which she was banished on the first page of the novel. Neither Contarini nor Oliver, different as they are, need to change or grow morally, though Contarini must learn a good deal more about the world, and Oliver about evil and about his own heritage. Both are blameless but besieged by a hostile world. The text of *Jane Eyre,* in a rare allusion to literature, reinforces the contextual assumption of innocence by referring to two other fictional innocents: *Pamela* and *Henry, Earl of Moreland* (5). The reference to *Pamela* is not immediately relevant, but it is now part of the text's and the reader's repertoire—and indeed it will be foregrounded later and discussed at some length at that time. But here it is *Henry Moreland,* John Wesley's 1781 abridgment of Henry Brooke's *The Fool of Quality* (1766-70)—a version frequently reprinted early in the nineteenth century—that is immediately relevant, for its opening chapter too involves a childhood fight and punishment by separation (though not physical confinement). The young hero, Henry, bloodies the nose of his older brother, Richard, who has insulted their foster mother, and Henry's own mother banishes him. He is raised by simple foster parents and has a healthful, vigorous, unspoiled childhood, much unlike that of his pampered brother. He is a "fool" in that he is innocent. This is a sentimental tale in which man is naturally good, goodness is innocence, and the world is not so much hostile as corrupt and corrupting. Jane may well have seemed to the contemporary reader early in the novel an innocent in a hostile and corrupt world; many readers then and now continue to see her so. The power of contemporary fictional precedents seems to reinforce such a monologic view.

So, too, does the power of primacy. The opening scenes of a novel are crucial. They establish the tone, genre, and something of the development of the narrative, its outcome, and the nature of the fictional world. Meir Sternberg, attempting to define the signifying power of

. . . .

the early portions of a novel, cites a psychological experiment in which
blocks of character description of identical length but opposite meaning were presented to subjects in their entirety but in different order.
As a rule not only did that which was presented first determine the
interpretation but, despite explicit instructions to respond in terms of
the passage as a whole, "the overwhelming majority of subjects did not
even notice the glaring incompatibility of the information contained
in the two successive segments":

> Due to the successive order of presentation, the first block was read
> with an open mind, while the interpretation of the second—in itself as
> weighty—was decisively conditioned and colored by the anterior, homo-
> geneous primacy effect; the leading block established a perceptual set,
> serving as a frame of reference to which the subsequent information was
> subordinated as far as possible. (94)

Sternberg finds this central in the analysis of the temporal ordering of
fiction, and it does explain a good deal about the effect and interpretation of *Jane Eyre*, including the reading of the opening scenes.

Though ego and innocence are valorized by all the novels mentioned so far, encouraging a degree of monologic comprehension and
projection, they vary enough to refract the narrative utterance of the
opening chapter of Brontë's novel into a polysemy that problematizes
its outcome. Contarini is a successful "superior" rebel; Jane, so far, is
not. Oliver finds home and family but is a child still when his narrative closes; Jane is no "fool," not the sentimental innocent of *Henry
Moreland*, but a witty, skeptical, and challenging child.

Disraeli and Dickens are canonical novelists, and even Henry
Brooke has a place in standard histories of the novel. There are novelists, however, immensely popular in their day, now all but forgotten,
who also served as a refracting context for the reading—and perhaps the writing—of *Jane Eyre*. Many of these popular novelists, often
women, were identified with a particular fictional genre that would—
in part through the power of *Jane Eyre*—come to dominate Victorian
and early twentieth-century fiction. Generically we have been moving, from *Contarini* and *Caleb Williams* through *Oliver Twist* to *Henry,
Earl of Moreland*, down from the high Romantic toward that kind of low
Romantic novel known in the early nineteenth century as "the domes-

· · · · · · ·

tic novel." This is not a tag we would readily attach to *Jane Eyre*, but that is how Brontë's novel was characterized at the time.[8] The *Atlas* on 23 October 1847 calls it a "powerful domestic romance" (Allott 67), and the *People's Journal* for November 1847 deems it "[a] notable domestic novel" (Allott 80). Eugène Fourçade, in his highly favorable review in *Revue des deux mondes* for 31 October 1848—a review approved of by Brontë herself—identifies *Jane Eyre* in a similar, if almost ludicrously Pari-centric fashion, as "a novel of country life" (Allott 102). "Domestic" seems to have meant British, familiar, of the present or very recent past, of private life as opposed to the public, social or "fashionable," and "realistic" in the sense of the everyday.

Here we encounter something of an historical paradox: the domestic novels of the period before *Jane Eyre* (except for those of the anomalous and Inimitable Dickens) are largely unremembered, but "domestic realism" triumphs in the novel from about 1850 and brings with it the sentimentality, interiority, bourgeois morality, and, often, religiosity of the earlier domestic novels. From our vantage point the language and moral vision of young Jane, the romantic rebel, is centrifugal, carnivalistic, and modern (i.e., good); that of the mature Jane, the domestic realist and moralist, represents monologic narrative language and ideology, the "Victorian," the official, the centripetal. In fact, it was domestic realism that challenged the hegemony of the patriarchy and the aristocracy, the centrality and autonomy of the ego common in romantic literature, and the very concept of the novel as "a history of events" with its accompanying elevated style. These novels (and the mature Jane's narrative) certainly do not seem "carnivalistic" in the Rabelesian or Bakhtinian sense, but they are in their quiet way subversive.

In domestic novels, too, we find topoi familiar to us from the early chapters of *Jane Eyre*. One eighteenth- and early nineteenth-century tributary flowing into the main stream of the domestic novel was the moral didactic tale, often intended for children. Such a tale is Barbara Hofland's long-popular *Ellen, the Teacher. A Tale for Youth* (1814)—a new edition is advertised in the 6 March 1847 *Athenaeum* (1010:251)—which further dialogizes the opening scenes of *Jane Eyre*. This "story . . . about a poor orphan girl who suffers miserably in boarding school, eventually makes good as a governess and ultimately marries her cousin,"

. . . .

Inga-Stina Ewbank suggests, "may have been one of the germs from which *Jane Eyre* grew" (21).⁹ There are striking resemblances between the early chapters of the two novels. Though the scene does not open the novel, and though the occasion is not fighting, but a false accusation of lying at school (Jane, too, will be falsely accused of lying at Lowood), young Ellen Delville is, like Jane, Contarini, Oliver, and Henry Moreland, punished by being locked away in a room. Though no "ghost" appears or seems to appear while she is confined, she does faint during her punishment and does fall ill afterwards, just as Jane does. The physician called in to treat Ellen's badly infected finger befriends her, and, like the apothecary Mr. Lloyd who comes to treat Jane, he seems to be the only sympathetic soul in the poor girl's hostile environment.

When Mrs. Reed decides to send Jane to Lowood Institution, a charity school, the director, the Reverend Mr. Brocklehurst, arrives to interview his new charge. He seems to the young Jane Eyre "a black pillar" (33). His imposing size, his harsh, prim appearance and bullying manner, intensify our sympathy for the beleaguered Jane. Most of us are delighted by her frank, honest, unintimidated answers to his unctuous, pietistic questions. When Brocklehurst asks her what she must do to avoid hell, she says, "I must keep in good health, and not die" (34). When he asks whether she reads the Bible with pleasure, she says that though she likes some parts, she does not find the Psalms "interesting." Even in our more secular age, Jane's responses may make us fear for her future. More than a few Victorian readers may have been not only made fearful for her future but also less certain of her moral probity. It is one thing to parry the thrusts of the Pharisee, another to be flippant about religion or critically selective about Scripture. With the "supernatural" scene in the red-room and the hint of blasphemy here, the place of religion, of orthodoxy, is at least problematized.

Jane is not naive. Is she innocent? It was not an assumption of Calvinists or evangelicals. Though childhood in *Oliver Twist* and *Henry, Earl of Moreland* is pure, childhood in Hofland's novel is not a period of prelapsarian innocence protected for a time from a world that inevitably corrupts. Young Ellen Delville, though she has our sympathy, is a fiery little girl. She protests that she is "not passionate—I mean

. . . .

not *very* passionate; I never go into a rage, like Betsy Burns" (Hofland 4). Her mother (who will soon die, leaving Ellen, like so many of the young heroes and heroines of the period, an orphan) accuses her of often getting excessively angry with too little cause. She warns her that shame always follows passion. In Brontë's novel it is not Jane's friend *Helen* Burns who is the passionate child, but the protagonist herself: "You are passionate, Jane, that you must allow," her aunt tells her (40). Most readers find Jane's fiery anger justified, but Jane discovers that passion is akin to madness and its aftermath often unpleasant:

> A child cannot quarrel with its elders, as I had done; cannot give its furi-
> ous feelings uncontrolled play, as I had given mine; without experiencing
> afterwards the pang of remorse and the chill of reaction. . . . half an hour's
> silence and reflection had shewn me the madness of my conduct, and the
> dreariness of my hated and hating position. . . . Willingly would I now
> have gone and asked Mrs. Reed's pardon. (40–41)

The "rhetoric of anticipatory caution"—in which "the primacy effect itself—and hence our attitude to the protagonist, whose information or view largely gives rise to it—is perceptibly qualified from the beginning" (Sternberg 129)—in this passage serves to warn us that Jane's rebellious independence, delightful and satisfying as it is at the moment, may lead her into moral difficulties. The reader of contemporary novels like *Ellen* is doubly warned. But other contemporary novels, such as *Oliver Twist*, that valorize the child and his or her innocence, as does the primacy effect of Jane's justified rebellion in the text, create considerable polysemic static around such scenes and problematize the informed reader's expectations and projected configurations.

The "sad Effects" of a child's "Rage and Anger" are shown in another influential moral didactic tale. Sarah Fielding's *The Governess; or, Little Female Academy* was first published in the mid-eighteenth century but was still so popular in the nineteenth that the best-selling writer of moral tales for children of the time, Mrs. Sherwood herself, rather ruthlessly redacted it for her own audience and purposes. Though it is not nearly so close to *Jane Eyre* on the whole as *Ellen*, its first narrative incident is familiar: "An Account of a Fray, begun and carried on for the sake of an Apple. In which are shewn the sad Effects of Rage and Anger." And it immediately thereafter sets up autobiog-

. . . . . .

raphy as a moral mode, as example, or, at least, as a means of introspection. After the "fray," one of the students recommends love, not
fighting, and friendship, not revenge; then she promises to tell something morally instructive about her own life.

> "And after I have given you the Particulars of my Life, I must beg that
> every one of you will some Day or other, when you have reflected upon
> it, declare all that you can remember of your own; for, should you not
> be able to relate anything worth remembering as an Example, yet there is
> nothing more likely to amend the future Part of any one's Life, than the
> recollecting and confessing the Faults of the past." (Fielding 121)

Introspection and example are the traditional functions of what we
now call the spiritual autobiography, common in the seventeenth and
eighteenth centuries. That tradition wends its way into fiction through
Bunyan and Defoe and into fictional autobiographies such as Mrs.
Sherwood's *Caroline Mordaunt; or, The Governess* (1835)—didactic, religious, domestic, written by a female for a female audience. Like the traditional spiritual autobiography, it is an apologia, the story of growing
awareness of God's Providence and of deliverance. Its nature and narrative mode suggest an alternative autobiographical tradition to that
of Godwin and his successors, not to mention that of the Byronic Disraeli and Lytton, and therefore would necessarily complicate the contemporary readers' expectations, and would thus dialogize *Jane Eyre.*

A significant portion of *Jane Eyre*'s audience must have read or
known of most of the novels we have been discussing, and it is likely
that a substantial number would have read more than one. From the
very beginning of *Jane Eyre,* then, such readers would have felt the
world of that novel familiar and would have been alerted to a range
of expectations generated by the conventional scenic topoi with which
Jane Eyre opens. But some of the most eclectic readers may have been
puzzled, for the expectations were overdetermined. The opening episodes, while commonplaces in contemporary narrative, had been put
to such a variety of uses by such different fictional kinds they were
generically polysemic.

The function of such conventions, however, is not to assure "right"
guesses about what will happen next, nor, just yet, to define exactly
what kind of moral and consequential universe is being embodied,

· · · · · · ·

but, through the refractive or dialogic interaction of the novels and their generic kinds, to generate a number of narrative, moral, and epistemological expectations, to enrich the reading by offering alternative possibilities that are sometimes alternative visions of reality, and to keep the reader's mind actively engaged in creating the work by projecting its "future" and therefore its shape and meaning. *Jane Eyre* is not merely what it "says" when the final temporary gap of indeterminacy is closed; it is also all that it projects and rejects along the way.

For modern readers in particular, it is important to take the anticipatory cautions seriously and to recover at least some of the relevant representative novels of the period in order to experience the dialogic nature, the ambiguous signals, and thus the suspense with regard to outcome and ontology of *Jane Eyre*. Not only is the primacy effect of Jane's isolation and John Reed's cruel treatment of her very strong, and not only have the literary conventions to which Brontë appeals been forgotten, but the religious and behavioral values that underlay them have faded as well. "Our" Jane, the rebellious one, is undeniably in the text, but her shadowy domestic and religious sister is there too, and in *Jane Eyre* shadows have substance just as voices calling across vast spaces have valid messages.

2

Reality and Narratability:
Dothegirls Hall and Child-Deaths

When Jane enters Lowood Institution it is an environment strange to her but familiar to the Victorian novel-reader. The school as setting and teachers as characters were common in nineteenth-century fiction (see R. Colby 15–16), and no other portion of *Jane Eyre* has been so specifically and frequently identified with literary precedent as has the Lowood section. Yet, ironically, nothing in the novel is taken more directly from Brontë's own experience. Cowan Bridge School, the Reverend Carus Wilson, and the death of her own sister Maria supplied Charlotte Brontë with all the material she needed for the creation of Lowood Institution, the Reverend Mr. Brocklehurst,[1] and the poignant presentation of the last days of Helen Burns ("Lowood School, and the Rev. Mr. Brocklehurst," Clarendon 615–21). Brontë's narrative, however, was already heteroglossically occupied—by other school novels, the scandal surrounding Yorkshire schools, and, in particular, *Nicholas Nickleby*. These scenes are made to seem familiar and "highlighted" while at the same time their originality and personal force are "dimmed" by a fictional precedent, by the contemporary social and fictional context, by what Bakhtin calls a prior "alien word" (*Dialogic* 277). This prior "occupation" is most obvious in the relation of Lowood to Dickens's Dotheboys Hall. G. H. Lewes in the *Westminster Review* (48 [January 1848]: 297) was not the only one to call Lowood Institution "in some respects a second edition of Dotheboys Hall" and more than one reviewer compared Brockle-hurst to Squeers.[2]

We meet Brocklehurst before his Institution and Squeers before the Hall. Wackford Squeers is not, like Brocklehurst—and Carus Wilson—a man of the cloth, though he seems to want to appear so: he is "clad in sombre garments, and long black gaiters, and bear[s] in his countenance an expression of much mortification and sanctity" (*Nickleby* 2:34). He behaves in a kindly fashion to the boys when a prospective client is present, cruelly when no one is watching; he spouts morality and piety, and denies the flesh—of others—to fatten his own wallet. When, in the first scene in which Squeers figures, a Mr. Snawley approaches to dispose of his stepsons, the two men seem to understand each other immediately. Squeers stresses the beautiful morality that Mrs. Squeers instills in the students, and Snawley says he is particularly interested in having the boys' morality attended to—though morality prevents neither man from haggling over money. Squeers understands perfectly when Snawley says that he fears their mother might squander money on them and spoil them if they were to remain at home:

> "And this," resumed Snawley, "has made me anxious to put them to some school a good distance off, where there are no holidays—none of those ill-judged comings home twice a year that unsettle children's minds so— and where they may rough it a little—you comprehend?"
>
> "The payments regular, and no questions asked," said Squeers, nodding his head.
>
> "That's it, exactly," rejoined the other. "Morals strictly attended to, though."
>
> "Strictly," said Squeers. (2:35)

Mrs. Reed also wants her charge's morals strictly attended to:

> "Mr. Brocklehurst, . . . this little girl has not quite the character and disposition I could wish: should you admit her into Lowood school, I should be glad if the superintendent and teachers were all requested to keep a strict eye on her, and, above all, to guard against her worst fault, a tendency to deceit." (35)

. . . . . .

She, too, makes it clear that she does not wish to be encumbered by
Jane during holidays: "I should wish her . . . to be made useful, to be
kept humble: as for vacations, she will, with your permission, spend
them always at Lowood" (36). He finds her decision and desires "perfectly judicious." Brocklehurst brags of having "mortified the worldly
sentiment of pride" in the Lowood girls and teaching them humility
by dressing them as if they were "poor people's children," while his
wife and daughter wear silk gowns. Squeers, breakfasting on coffee,
hot toast, and a round of cold beef, serves five boys two pennies'
worth of milk, watered, and divides bread and butter for three among
them: " 'Conquer your passions, boys, and don't be eager after vittles,'
he says. As he uttered this moral precept, Mr. Squeers took a large bite
out of the cold beef" (2:45).[3]

Very good advice this, morality aside, for those who are to live
at Dotheboys Hall, where, if not burnt as it is at Lowood, the ubiquitous and universally reviled porridge is scarcely more appetizing
or sustaining: "Into these bowls, Mrs. Squeers, assisted by the hungry
servant, poured a brown composition which looked like diluted pin-
cushions without the covers, and was called porridge" (2:89). Porridge,
even when neither burnt nor diluted, seems to have been the bane of
school or nursery diet, at least in novels; Mrs. Sherwood's Caroline
Mordaunt describes porridge as "a sort of mess which is generally
loathed by English palates, and which I presently perceived that nothing but excessive hunger could have compelled these young people to
swallow" (Caroline 285). At Dotheboys Hall, when the boys finished
their porridge and "a minute wedge of brown bread, . . . Mr. Squeers
said, in a solemn voice, 'For what we have received, may the Lord
make us truly thankful'—and went away to his own" (2:89–90). The
burnt porridge at Lowood is also followed by thanksgiving: "Thanks
being returned for what we had not got, and a second hymn chanted,
the refectory was evacuated for the school-room" (51). Jane's irony in
the context of prayer, though justifiable, further dialogizes the religious discourse of Jane Eyre; given Jane's rebelliousness and skepticism
and our sympathy for Jane, the irony directed toward religious hypoc-
risy spills over onto religion itself, ambiguating the moral nature of

the novel's universe, particularly since the irony is that of the mature, narrating Jane and so seems to have full authorization.

Though there is no such ambiguity in *Nicholas Nickleby,* the school portions of the two novels are remarkably parallel. Florence Dry finds not only the food but the entire institutional regimen in Lowood and Dotheboys similar:

> Morning comes too soon for Nicholas and Jane; each dresses in bitter cold by candlelight. Morning prayers and Bible study at Lowood School take the place of brimstone and treacle at Dotheboys Hall, after which both schools breakfast on porridge which is equally distasteful. When Mr. Squeers in *Nicholas Nickleby* calls up the first class, "half-a-dozen scarecrows out at knees and elbows" range themselves in front of his desk. When Miss Miller in *Jane Eyre* does likewise, "eighty girls sat motionless and erect: a quaint assemblage they appeared. . . . [Their] costume suited them ill, and gave an air of oddity even to the prettiest." This suggests the "singular dress" of Smike in *Nicholas Nickleby.*
>
> Similar are the dinners at both establishment, the one of "stir-about and potatoes and hard salt beef" the other of "indifferent potatoes and strange shreds of rusty meat, mixed and cooked together." Frozen water, unpleasant lessons, and distasteful and insufficient food are the order of the day at Dotheboys Hall and Lowood School. (12–13)

Dry also sees a significant similarity between the friend Jane makes at Lowood, Helen Burns, and the abused and somewhat retarded grown-up pupil Nicholas Nickleby befriends, Smike: they both die of consumption; their dying words are not dissimilar; they both welcome death and die quietly in their sleep (15).

Though the context of the Yorkshire schools does juxtapose Smike and Helen, there is heteroglossic refraction or static around Helen Burns from other directions. There is in the contemporary fictional context, for example, a similar pairing of the rebellious young heroine with a pious young friend or sister, occasioning a scene of moral or religious debate. In Rachel McCrindell's *The English Governess* (1844), a new edition of which was advertised in the *Athenaeum* of 17 April 1847 (1016:412) just six months before *Jane Eyre* was published, there are two sisters (like Charlotte and Maria) who more than somewhat resemble

. . . . . .

Helen and Jane in their physical and moral conditions: pride and passion dominate the features of Maria Neville, the elder sister, while the eighteen-year-old Clara has "a complexion, delicate almost to transparency, [that] announced a weak and precarious state of health"; sunshine both confirms "the idea of early death . . . [and] . . . surrounds her with a kind of celestial radiance, prophetic of angelic glory" (9). When the delicate, celestial Clara tells Maria to endure mistreatment from the man their widowed mother wants to marry and to be guided by Scripture, Maria retorts,

> "Clara, you are a dear good little girl, but you know I cannot think as you do on the subject of religion. You may have a great deal of scripture, and even reason on your side; but I cannot believe that it is my duty to sacrifice my feelings, my interest, my happiness, and every thing that is dear to me, merely because my mother [wants to remarry]. Your principles of passive obedience and non-resistance may lead you to bear it patiently; [but I will not]." (10–11)

When Helen instructs Jane to eschew violence and revenge and to love her enemies as the New Testament tells us to do, Jane is no more moved to such behavior than is Maria:

> "If people were always kind and obedient to those who are cruel and unjust, the wicked people would have it all their own way. . . . When we are struck at without a reason, we should strike back . . . so hard as to teach the person who struck us never to do it again." (65)

Despite appearances, Clara lives, becomes the English Governess, and leads a happy (though not unperilous) life; Helen Burns dies while still a schoolgirl. For the reader of McCrindell, then, Helen's early death, so clearly foreshadowed in the text of *Jane Eyre,* is not inevitable. The fate of the proud and passionate Maria does not bode well for Jane; sick and abandoned, Maria comes to Christ only on her deathbed. The eponymous heroine of *Ellen the Teacher,* on the other hand, who was, like Jane, proud and passionate as a child (though not so passionate as her friend *Betsy* Burns), does not die an early death but grows into a paragon of patience and control. Jane's future as well as the moral register of Brontë's novel is thus problematized by the fictional context, by the heteroglossically occupied scenic topoi.

. . . .

Helen's early death at Lowood, we know, was based on the death of Charlotte's sister Maria at Cowan Bridge School, but the death of a child was all too familiar in the Victorian reader's experience. In 1828 Brocklehurst's original—though he may be exaggerating just a little to make his moral point—the Reverend William Carus Wilson, claims that "the greatest part of the human race die in infancy" (Clarendon 621). Brocklehurst's story of the good child who died at five years of age and his Child's Guide with its story of the sudden death of a "child addicted to falsehood and deceit" (37) are faithful to the tone and content of Carus Wilson's *The Children's Friend* (Clarendon 621). Though Brontë's source was no doubt Wilson, Wilson himself was only using a common subject for tracts, sermons, and religious exempla. The *Methodist Magazine,* for example, a complete run of which graced Haworth Parsonage (Gérin, *Brontë* 35; Leyland 105), was full of deathbed scenes, including those of children. The 1803 volume, for example, lists some twenty-three entries in the index under "Experience and happy Death of." One scene of "happy Death" is that of "A Boy belonging to the Sunday-Schools in London." This presumably factual account of the death of Isaac Eke, who had been suffering for long months from fever, could have come from one of any number of novels of the early Victorian period, for the child deaths in Victorian novels are as common as explicit sex in modern novels.

The most famous child-death scenes, of course, are those in Dickens, who establishes the scenic topos. Helen's death in *Jane Eyre* most resembles not that of the childlike Smike in *Nicholas Nickleby* but of the child Dick in *Oliver Twist*, a novel reissued not long before *Jane Eyre* was published and already conjured up in the reader's memory by earlier episodes. If Smike is, like Helen, part of the Yorkshire school scene, Oliver is closer to Jane than is Nicholas, his plight closer to hers than to that of Nicholas, and his relationship to Dick more like Jane's to Helen than Nicholas's to Smike.

As suggested in the first chapter of this study, many episodes in *Jane Eyre* and *Oliver Twist* are similar, though the sequence varies. Jane fights, is locked in the red-room, and is later sent to Lowood Institution; Oliver was raised in parish institutions, and his fight and punishment take place afterward. So it is with the episodes surrounding the deaths of the young friends of Oliver and Jane. Fleeing from Sower-berry's, Oliver passes the workhouse where he grew up and sees in the garden his pale-faced friend: "They had been beaten and starved, and shut up together, many and many a time" (96). Oliver tells Dick he is running away, then expresses some anxiety about his friend's pallor:

> "I heard the doctor tell them I was dying," replied the child with a faint smile. . . . I know the doctor must be right, Oliver, because I dream so much of Heaven, and Angels, and kind faces that I never see when I am awake. Kiss me," said the child, climbing up the low gate, and flinging his little arms round Oliver's neck. "Good-b'ye, dear! God bless you!" (96–97)

Toward the end of the novel, when Oliver returns, Dick is dead. What Dick sees as dreams peculiar to the dying—heaven, angels, kind faces—Helen believes surrounds everyone, everywhere:

> "Besides this earth, and besides the race of men, there is an invisible world and a kingdom of spirits: that world is round us, for it is everywhere; and those spirits watch us, for they are commissioned to guard us; and if we were dying in pain and shame, if scorn smote us on all sides, and hatred crushed us, angels see our torture, recognise our innocence . . . , and God waits only the separation of spirit from flesh to crown us with a full re-ward." (81)[4]

She believes that "by dying young I shall escape great sufferings. I had not qualities or talents to make my way very well in the world: I should have been continually at fault" (96). Dick, too, is glad to die young, so that he and his sister can be children together in heaven (173).

The third-person narrator of *Oliver Twist* had already leaped for-ward in time to describe the effect of Dick's dying blessing: "Through the struggles and sufferings, and troubles and changes, of his [Oliver's] after life, he never once forgot it" (97). Jane also takes a rare leap for-ward in narrative time from Helen's death-scene: "Her grave is in Brocklebridge churchyard; for fifteen years after her death it was only covered by a grassy mound; but now a grey marble tablet marks the spot, inscribed with her name, and the word 'Resurgam'" (97).

The brief scene of Dick's death in *Oliver Twist* is followed in Dickens's canon by a similar scene involving an equally minor char-acter, Harry West, in *Old Curiosity Shop,* and later in that novel by the

. . . .

famous death of the heroine, Little Nell. In February 1847 (perhaps in time to trigger Charlotte Brontë's memories of her sister Maria while she was writing the Lowood chapters of her novel), Paul Dombey dies. Just as Helen Burns dies in her sleep in Jane's arms, so Paul Dombey lies dying in the arms of his sister. At the last, Paul lets her go only long enough to clasp his hands in prayer.

Helen Burns believes that the invisible world of spirits surrounds us here on earth, but that other world is never made visible to her in the novel, nor does Jane as narrator specifically confirm Helen's belief at this point. The real child Isaac Eke whose death was recounted in the *Methodist Magazine* sees pretty things with white wings; Dickens's Paul Dombey sees the light around the head of Christ shining upon him. Not so reticent as Brontë's, Dickens's narrator tells us flatly that Paul has become one of the host of "angels of little children" (*Dombey* 298).

Dickens's were not the only fictional children dying in the 1830s and 1840s. In 1835 the eponymous heroine of Mrs. Sherwood's governess novel *Caroline Mordaunt* "is brought back into religion by a pious little pupil who, like Jane Eyre's Helen Burns, dies in her arms" (V. Colby 165). Like Helen Burns—and like Maria Brontë—Emily Selburn dies of consumption. Like Helen Burns, Emily Selburn seems to be preternaturally informed on religious matters. Mrs. Sherwood maintains that such knowledge can be attained at a very early age only "in cases resembling that of this most lovely one, where the time is short, and that which is to be done must be done quickly" (280). What young Emily preaches is not Helen's Arminianism, and not merely her mother's Evangelical doctrine of faith over works, but predestinarianism.

Rachel McCrindell's *The English Governess*, published just three years before *Jane Eyre* and the death of Paul Dombey, also offers us consolation out of the mouth of a dying child (but of a less exclusive kind than Mrs. Sherwood's). Clara Neville first attends the deathbed of her sister Maria, who comes to Christ during her lingering illness and consoles her children with the thought that death is the "bright herald of everlasting blessedness" (256). Not long thereafter, Clara has the sad duty of attending her four-year-old nephew Charles, who is fatally ill with measles, but he too knows he is going to Christ and

. . . . . .

that Clara and his sister Emma will eventually join him there. He is dying as he says this, but he does not expire before a minister appears and reads over him the latter part of I Corinthians and Hebrews 5–6, promising resurrection and finding in suffering a sign of God's favor.

In the same year, in another governess novel, Elizabeth Sewell's *Amy Herbert*, little Rose Harrington lay dying attended by her mother and governess:

> A momentary strength had been granted her, and with a clear though feeble voice, she followed the [Lord's] prayer to the end; and then, stretching out her little hand, she said, "Mamma, it is bright now. They are come to take me." And with a faint smile, as she half repeated Emily's [the governess's] name, her head once more sank upon the pillow, and the innocent spirit was at rest. (309)

Mrs. Harrington seeks consolation in believing, like Helen Burns, in an ambient world of invisible spirits and finds "inexpressible comfort" in the possibility—neither confirmed nor denied by the Bible, she says—"that those whom I have loved might still be near, though I could not see them" (321–22). The night before Rose's death, Emily Morton, the governess, was sitting by Rose's bed praying when Rose awakened and assured her that "God is near, and the angels, though you cannot see them" (309). Emily was resigned to the death of her charge, for she recognized that death "for Rose . . . would be an escape from all the dangers of the world to the enjoyment of rest and peace forever" (307). Long before Rose's fatal accident, a cottager had observed that she "had an angel's face, and that it was fitter for heaven than for earth" (299).

Thus to multiply instances of child-death scenes may seem the purposeless piling on of pious Pelions merely to demonstrate what might be accepted with fewer lengthy examples: that is, the ubiquity of such scenes in early nineteenth-century fiction. But the multiplicity of instances also demonstrates that no matter how closely the character of Helen and the nature of her death are related to Maria Brontë and her early death, and no matter how important they were to Charlotte Brontë personally, they are "novel-worthy" for author and reader not necessarily because of their "truth to experience" but rather because

. . . .

41

of their conventional nature in the novel of the period. And in considering literary history and the interrelation of texts, it is important to recognize that the source, the authorization of "narratability," is the convention, not necessarily the particular scene or situation in some other single work or author. Attribution of "influence" or accusation of "borrowing" rather than recognition of a convention is particularly tempting when precedent is found in a major writer like Dickens. It would indeed be convenient for us if major writers wrote within conventions embodied only by the other Lowells and Cabots of literature, but such is not the case. Elements, scenes that we find common to Dickens and Charlotte Brontë, are more often than not discoverable as well in more than one minor novel of the time: they are scenic topoi or commonplaces, conventions of the period and novel genre, or of the genre as it manifests itself in that period. To recognize this is of some significance not merely in terms of historical accuracy but in understanding the dynamics of literature, of literary creativity, and of the nature of the novel as a constantly developing period-specific genre.

What also should emerge more clearly from these multiple examples is that despite the commonplace nature of the scenes, and what may seem to us their identical nature, the topos of the dying child is heteroglossic, with varying signification—from Helen Burns's Arminianism to Caroline Mordaunt's Calvinism; from the textual verification of angels and spirits in Dickens and Sherwood to Helen's convincing but narratively unauthorized belief and Jane's shaken and puzzled skepticism; from the melodramatic and sentimental in Dickens and McCrindell to the cool, understated, realistic, almost secular presentation in *Jane Eyre*. Placing *Jane Eyre* in the context of the novels of the time thus does not define its monologic "meaning" but instead opens up the text dialogically to other voices, complicating expectation of event and meaning and intensifying by rendering more active the anticipatory, participating experience of reading it.

Schooled in expectations conditioned by the novels of the time, and reading with rigorous sequentiality that brackets out certain knowledge of what is to come gained from previous readings of *Jane Eyre*, we may be able to comprehend the relationship of Helen and Jane, their religious discussions and Jane's doubts, and Helen's early death

. . . .

as dialogic: the indeterminacy—the heroine's religious doubt in the face of the most pious of scenes—forces the reader to entertain multiple possibilities of what the novel is up to, what it is "saying" about death and dying, the soul and the afterlife, and consequently about human conduct. There are different voices, whispers of other novels, novels of various species or kinds, that speak of different worlds in different languages, a heteroglossic echo chamber surrounding the reader with a labyrinth of sounds and senses. There is, moreover, a kind of cosmological gap, creating, for the alert and informed reader, a thematic as well as narrative suspense.

Knowledge of the contemporary genres and conventions is a key to perceiving the strategy of and the diverse responses to a novel like *Jane Eyre*, and therefore is a key to the fullest possible experience of reading such a work. The signifiers are on the page, but there is a great deal of affective significance in what is off the page, in the medium or context in which *Jane Eyre* made its way. Because of the plethora of diverse generic signals and conventions, the scenes and "words" of *Jane Eyre* refract and recombine the conventional in such a way as to be simultaneously hailed as the most original of works and brilliantly traditional. While the "Opinions of the Press" excerpted by the publisher for inclusion in the third edition naturally include only those reviews that stressed the novel's originality—such as the comments in the *Atlas, Economist, Jerrold's Newspaper, Jerrold's Magazine, Morning Advertiser, Scotsman, Liverpool Standard,* and *Westminster Review* (Clarendon 631–35)—there were those that recognized its conventional materials, including favorable reviews like that in the *Athenaeum,* which speaks of its "exciting strong interest of [an] old-fashioned kind" (1043:1100–1101). Brontë subsumes disparate Romantic traditions and transforms them, creating a new species, the Victorian novel, but the overdetermination of the scenic topoi even within a familiar frame makes that new original-traditional novel apparently univocal but ultimately dialogic.

The ninth chapter of *Jane Eyre* ends with the death of Helen Burns and with a momentary leap forward in narrational time to what is to happen fifteen years later, when a tablet is put in place to mark Helen's grave. The last word of the chapter is "Resurgam." It is clearly a

· · · · · ·

punctuation mark in the novel, a heavy pause less than one-fifth of the way through a three-volume novel. The pause invites the reader to conjecture about the direction that the novel is to take. Is Jane to be a victim until near the end—as the first few scenes may suggest—an object of our sympathy and pity, recipient of our loyalties and cheers? Or is she to ride heroically over the oppressions of petty tyrants, leaving them disdainfully in the dust? Or is she to lose heroically and romantically, secure in her moral superiority? Is she the moral measure of the world of the novel, or is she a fallible creature who must suffer in order to grow into moral maturity? Knowledge of a number of contemporary novels—such as *Oliver Twist, Henry, Earl of Moreland, Contarini Fleming, Ellen the Teacher, Caroline Mordaunt, Amy Herbert*—and their scenic topoi and varying outcomes and worldviews raises these questions, and, on their own or reinforced by subgenres or kinds of novels, these novels offer alternative possibilities or expectations. Each of them or their generic counterparts when foregrounded projects a whole scenario of Jane's future, and even when backgrounded or almost forgotten that scenario does not entirely fade: it can be brought forward again with the slightest of allusions or suggestions.

At this point in *Jane Eyre, Oliver Twist* and the foundling novel, modified and reinforced by the school scenes in *Nickleby*, give strong indications of the direction in which Brontë's novel will develop. But there are forks in the road to Jane's future: will she stay on at Lowood? Will other children die? Will Jane be subjected to more indignities, more suffering? Though the children's deathbed scenes are for modern readers strongly linked to Dickens, in the novels of the second quarter of the nineteenth century such scenes often indicated a didactic, moralistic, religious novel, perhaps even more particularly, a governess novel. Will Jane grow up to be a teacher, like Ellen Delville, or a governess, like Emily Morton and Caroline (or even Clara) Mordaunt? These possible futures are part of the dialogue of the novel not explicitly in the text, but implicitly in the context to which *Jane Eyre* is responding. There are many voices clamoring for our attention.

At this point, expectations associated with the foundling and governess novels, and domestic novels in general, are foregrounded, but there remain faint traces of other expectations that have been aroused

· · · · · · ·

earlier. Too often we think of expectations in binary terms, as rather simple either/or alternatives, but if we note the workings of our own minds carefully as we read, we will find whole batteries of expectations, some strong, some faint, some still fainter, with their relative intensity modified as each new detail or event crosses the line of our vision as we read. Everything put in our minds by the text is part of the work, in a sense is the work. Once in the work none of the potential eventualities ever entirely disappears, though it may fade or be overtaken by later fictional events. Too often when we speak of expectations—narrative or thematic—we treat them as temporary gaps which, once filled, cease to be part of our experience of the novel. All possibilities but one, the "right" one, are eliminated; that one alone remains in the reader's mind and is an actual part of the novel. But even the overtaken expectations are in the text, linger in its shadows, and are a permanent part of our reading experience and of our configurations of the future in the work we are reading. Indeed, this final, gap-closing "making of sense" not only leaves one or more of these alternative voices as "part of the 'meaning experience,'"[5] but at times is itself drowned out by the primacy and power of one or more of the other voices, opening the way for one kind of "misreading" of the text, a reading of the text "as it cannot know itself" (Eagleton, *Criticism* 43). Such, as we shall see, is the fortunate dialogic fate of *Jane Eyre*.

. . . . . .

Dialogic Genres:
The Governess and the Ghost

C hapter 10 of *Jane Eyre* begins eight years after the end of chapter 9.

> Hitherto I have recorded in detail the events of my insignificant existence: to the first ten years of my life, I have given almost as many chapters. But this is not to be a regular autobiography: I am only bound to invoke memory where I know her responses will possess some degree of interest; therefore I now pass a space of eight years almost in silence: a few lines only are necessary to keep up the links of connection. (98)[1]

The "future" is upon us. Oliver and the foundling novel no longer figure prominently in our projected version of Jane's future, for in the interval she has become a teacher. The governess novel now moves to the forefront—for a time. For it is characteristic of the structure of expectations in this novel that readers are never left fully certain for long of just what specific species of novel they are reading, and as a result each scene and narrative move is occupied by "alien words," by scenic topoi and generic conventions that refract the Brontë text.

Our projection of Jane's future and our perception of the nature of the novel, refracted by other narrative utterances, frequently focus on our view and judgment of Jane's character. At this point there seems to be a gap between the reader's perception of Jane and the Jane that the narrator describes. Jane as narrator claims she was always naturally obedient, even submissive, but for these past eight years, she says, under the influence of Miss Temple, she has been tranquil as well. Though we are told there was such a Jane, we do not see her, for the time of tranquility is just the period that Jane has decided to skip. The obedient and submissive Jane, the Jane who never struck back or answered back—Jane before the opening of the novel—we also have never seen. The Jane we now see once more—or still—is therefore that less-than-tranquil Jane of the opening chapters, reinforcing the primacy of that characterization of the heroine (see above, ch. 1). There were, however, anticipatory cautions which the narrator's description of Jane's character may retrospectively reinforce. On the dreary day on which the novel opened, for example, she seemed content to go forth only in her imagination. She seemed to yearn primarily for the fireside, home, acceptance, and love; she did not absent herself from the hearth but was banished. True, she finally rose up in passionate rebellion against John Reed's persecution, but her outbreak in the red-room was terror, not rebellion. True, she confronted Aunt Reed and accused her of deceit, but her sense of triumph was brief and her repentance swift, and would have been followed by an apology had she thought there was any chance of its being accepted.

Nonetheless, the eighteen-year-old Jane of the tenth chapter seems more like the "uncautionary," rebellious, saucy, and self-reliant Jane of the early chapters. On the afternoon of the very day Miss Temple left Lowood, Jane discovers that she feels once more "the stirring of old emotions," the desire "to seek real knowledge of life amidst its perils" (100). Such a quest, especially for one young and poor and unprepossessing and female, may very well seem to reinforce our first impressions of Jane and of the potential Godwinism of the novel. Is this Jane's "true" character authorized by the mature narrator? Or has the mature narrator allowed young Jane to speak here so that we can understand and sympathize with her unenlightened state? The utterance here seems a mixture of both, double-voiced or hybridized. First-person narration frequently suggests moral growth, the immature "I" becoming through the recounted experience the mature narrator. The major fictional autobiographies of the middle of the nineteenth century—*Jane Eyre* and *Villette, David Copperfield* and *Great Expectations, Henry Esmond*—all seem to function in this way and are thereby

. . . . . .

period-specific, reflecting the transition from Romantic egocentricity to Victorian sociocentrism. But when, as in *Jane Eyre,* the mature narrator is reticent and the young heroine compelling, the result is dialogic: the primacy of the virtually unqualified experience of the heroine and the reader's experience of those chapters claim equal or greater authority than the "hindsight" of the narrating voice or even the ultimate revelation of the moral universe of the novel. This dialogism between the experience of the novel (both young Jane's and the reader's) and the interpretation of that experience (both by the mature narrator-Jane and the configurative final structure of the narrative) mark the special nature of Brontë's novel and its contribution to the development of the genre. Indeed, a narrator who is reticent but not without didactic purpose is appropriate to that period between the hegemony of authority and order and that of subjective or intersubjective relativism. The reader is allowed, indeed invited, by the narrator's reticence, to share young Jane's experience as if her self-reliant secularism were as viable as any other worldview, even though that narrator has earned a knowledge of another truth and seeks by the narration to lead the reader to that truth just as she, Jane, was led. The personal and the providential, experience and meaning, are in a dialogue of contradiction without confrontation. A narrative with this epistemological, experiential ambivalence is the prose equivalent of what Robert Langbaum some years ago defined as the Victorian "poetry of experience," embodied chiefly in the dramatic monologue, a form suitable to a period in which traditional values were everywhere questioned but not yet jettisoned. The equivalent form to the dramatic monologue in the novel is the fictional autobiography, in which an author/editor of authority, acknowledged or unacknowledged, is hidden behind a speaker. *Jane Eyre* is just such a "novel of experience."

If the narrator has been reticent, however, her surrogates both in text and context have been cautioning the reader. Not only Miss Temple but Helen Burns has intervened between the Jane of the first chapters and Jane in chapter 10. The generic and contextual signals have also shifted—by the foregrounding of Dickensian radical sentimentalism and even of the pious and didactic governess novel—so that for some time now we have been in the world of "domestic" fiction. To

. . . .

a contemporary reader more familiar with that world, Jane's thoughts and intentions might have seemed more puzzling—or suspect—than they might to us: not powerful enough, perhaps, to overcome the primacy of the opening scenes or the Godwinian and Byronic signals, but strong enough to make the outcome and the nature of the moral world of the novel more problematic than they may appear to a modern reader, thus refracting the words, intensifying the suspense, and dialogizing the moral universe of the novel.

That Jane is no longer tranquil, is restless, and yearns to "go forth" into the world to "seek real knowledge of life" arouses expectations of a less domestic order than those of recent chapters. Jane's first entry into the world, however, will be as a governess, domestic enough but with some promise of adventure. For, whether they sought it or not, governesses outside the world of fiction were getting "real knowledge of life," often "amidst its perils." Representation of the life of the governess is refracted not only by the literary but by the social repertoire as well. The plight of the governess was a matter of some concern in the 1840s. With the burgeoning middle class entering the market as employers, by midcentury there were some 27,770 governesses in England, and their problems were serious and widespread enough to occasion the founding of the Governesses' Benevolent Institution in 1841. Appeals to the new Institution revealed such misery that the Christian Socialists set about to improve the governesses' status by improving their education. In the year in which *Jane Eyre* was published, a series of Lectures to Ladies began in London, their popularity leading immediately to the founding of Queen's College for Women in 1848 and Bedford College in 1849. "It is easy," then, "to understand the popularity of the governess with the Victorian novelist," Patricia Thomson tells us. "An allusion to a governess in a novel was . . . sure to arouse a stock emotional response in the minds of readers" (39).

The popularity of the issues surrounding governesses and of the fictional genre they had spawned is evident, for example, in Elizabeth Rigby's reviewing *Jane Eyre* in the *Quarterly* along with another new novel that she saw as concerned with the governess issue, *Vanity Fair*, and with the annual report of the Governesses' Benevolent Association. Thackeray's novel is seldom treated as a governess novel,

. . . . . .

nor is Becky Sharp discussed primarily in her role as a governess, but Rigby—soon to be Lady Eastlake—wants to score a point against *Jane Eyre*. She clearly does not think much of governesses, especially those who aspire to marry "above themselves," to marry, if they can, their gentlemen masters. Both Becky and Jane are just such governesses, she contends, but at least Becky is honest about it, and Thackeray, unlike Currer Bell, makes no claims for his "heroine's" morality.

Most of the public and novelistic concern about governesses, however, came from a different direction. A genteel, educated, unmarried woman living in a household not as a servant, not as an equal, but as a dependent is in a situation with great potential for exploitation, in reality and in narrative. The situation was not brand new but was exacerbated in the second quarter of the nineteenth century by the confusing reversal of class and power, when the governess was quite often genteel, and an increasing number of the masters and mistresses were newly rich and newly empowered bourgeoisie. Governesses were not new to fiction either, but the new social conditions revived and altered the form, and the character type of the governess as she would appear in Victorian fiction was becoming increasingly familiar in the early decades of the century. There are, for example, a number of governesses in Jane Austen's novels. Those who are currently governesses (like Miss Lee in *Mansfield Park*) are minor and shadowy, and those who have important supporting roles (like "poor Miss Taylor" and Jane Fairfax in *Emma*) are either no longer or not yet governesses. Mrs. Sherwood's *Caroline Mordaunt* (1835),[2] apparently the first novel to exploit the new situation in a full-length work, seems also to have established the pattern. Thomson indicates that the fictional governess of the period had "conventional attributes. She was bound to be a lady—preferably the daughter of a clergyman; she was always impoverished, unprotected, and, by virtue of her circumstances, reasonably intelligent and submissive" (39). Jane fits the description (at least Jane the narrator tells us she is naturally submissive). Ewbank adds that the conventional governess is usually orphaned (as is Jane), that she is subjected to some form of social humiliation, and that where she is the heroine she marries either a gentleman (if not a lord) or a clergyman

. . . .

(Ewbank 59–63). The convention, then, not only refracts our reception of *Jane Eyre* but channels our expectations.

This is the kind of novel that has been threatening to emerge and control the reader's expectations from its early chapters. Jane is to be a governess. This announcement reflects on all the details of the novel to this point, elevating the ordinary and obvious to new referentiality and polysemy.

The potentially Godwinian Jane, wanting to go out into the world "to seek new knowledge amidst its perils," prays, as might be expected, for "liberty." Her prayer "seemed scattered on the wind then faintly blowing." Does the wind scatter the prayer or does it only seem to do so? Though it is difficult to know for sure, the consciousness here seems to be monologically young Jane's, the mature narrator having withdrawn. Young Jane must take the possibility of the wind's dispersal of her prayer as meaningful, as sign or some sort of intervention, for she tries again with a judiciously altered request: " 'Then,' I cried, half desperate, 'Grant me at least new servitude!' " (101). This more modest request will, it turns out, be granted, but not before Jane racks her brain to figure out how to go about getting a position. Without family or friends, she must rely on herself. But how to manage? A "kind fairy" drops the suggestion to advertise on her pillow.

Is this "fairy," though archly introduced, a response to her desperate prayer? Young Jane does not stop to conjecture. Nor do most modern readers, reading monologically from the experiential perspective of young Jane, without guidance from the narrator and with a literary, social, and moral repertoire that dismisses even the prayers and the wind, considering them, like the fairy, as metaphor or "stage business." How "kind" was the fairy? And why does the suggestion come from the fantasy of a fairy and not some more authoritative voice if we are to take these messages seriously? The incident here is refracted by its counterpart in other governess novels. Most fictional governesses get positions through friends or relatives, but Jane has already dismissed that possibility—she has neither. Others answer advertisements from prospective employers who seem respectable and safe; they do not themselves advertise. When Clara Neville, Rachel

· · · · · · ·

CHAPTER 3

McCrindell's English Governess, decides to seek a position and "began seriously to consider what would be the best means of accomplishing her purpose," she, like Jane, proposes to act for herself, and, as in Jane's case also, the suggestion seems to come from outside herself: "The idea of advertising in a newspaper presents itself" (48).[3] This seems reasonable enough, we would think, but the rector's wife "entertained a decided objection to this method, and she [Clara] therefore, for the present, relinquished it. She did not see, however, much probability of her obtaining a situation in any other way" (48). Not if one needs to rely on oneself, but if one has faith, a lady requiring a governess will providentially soon appear. And so she does to Clara.

A reader aware of the conventional way governess positions were obtained in novels, and especially if aware of the McCrindell episode—or of the convention, social or fictional, behind it—such a reader might fear for the consequences of what might be conventionally considered Jane's indecorous act. Jane herself betrays a little apprehension—perhaps a slight anticipatory caution—and is quite relieved when her advertisement is answered by a "Mrs. Fairfax," who writes in a hand

> old fashioned and rather uncertain, like that of an elderly lady. The circumstance was satisfactory: a private fear had haunted me, that in thus acting for myself and by my own guidance, I ran the risk of getting into some scrape; and above all things, I wished the result of my endeavours to be respectable, proper, *en règle*. (105)

Without the McCrindell episode or its equivalent in our repertoire or consciousness, we are liable to pass over Jane's apprehension rather blithely or attribute it to her youth, inexperience, excessive scrupulosity, or timidity. If so, we miss some of the suspense in this relatively quiet portion of the novel.

Another faint echo, audible only to those whose ears are tuned to the voice of the governess genre, involves the awkward bit of scene-shifting with which chapter 11 of *Jane Eyre* begins:

> A new chapter in a novel is something like a new scene in a play; and when I draw up the curtain this time, reader, you must fancy you see a room in the George Inn at Millcote . . . and I am warming away the numbness and chill contracted by sixteen hours' exposure to the rawness of an October day. (112)

. . . .

Such a shift is not unique or even highly unusual in eighteenth-
or early nineteenth-century novels. The narrative device or space is
occupied and polysemic, but there is a strong echo of a passage in
Mrs. Sherwood's *Caroline Mordaunt*. The popularity of that novel and
the other echoes of it in *Jane Eyre* make this otherwise trivial resemblance audible and noticeable: "And now, my readers, if they please,
must follow me again to the stage [coach], hear my cousin's parting
advice, and accompany me till I am set down at the White Hart, in the
beautiful city of Bath, where I arrived about six in the evening" (227).

The coach and inn, the address to the reader, the specification of
the time and place seem notably parallel, and the similarity is height-
ened by the contrast in the young travelers' reception: Caroline is
met by a sedan chair and carried off to her new place of employ-
ment in the "beautiful city of Bath"; there seems to be no one to meet
Jane, and when, a half-hour later, she finds that there is transporta-
tion, it is not a sedan chair but "a one-horse conveyance . . . a sort of
car" driven by a plain and rather abrupt servant. The Sherwood passage, compounding the implications of the McCrindell allusion when
we are already alerted to the governess-novel context by Jane's new
career, makes Jane's reception, or lack of one, foreboding, ominous,
antiromantic, and both narratively and thematically significant. Without the governess-novel context or guidance from the narrator, we are
as inexperienced as Jane. The episode seems dull and drab; uncomfortable and boring for Jane, just boring or unpromising for us. Just as we
were excited into indignant sympathy with Jane in the opening chapters, so here we are lulled into a state analogous to Jane's.

It is reassuring to Jane (and to the reader of governess novels) to
find that Mrs. Fairfax is elderly and ladylike but not haughty or domi-
neering, as so many mistresses are in governess novels. It is also somewhat disappointing: what adventures, what interest can we anticipate
in so ordinary a household? By the middle of the chapter, however,
there are some promising developments: Thornfield has a master,
one Mr. Edward Rochester; Jane's charge is a ward of Mr. Rochester.
She is, alas, French and sings songs unsuitable to her tender years,
having been trained by her mother, an actress and a "dear friend" of
Mr. Rochester's.

. . . .

53

An unmarried gentleman-master is sure to arouse expectations in the novel-reader familiar with the contemporary conventions, for governess-marries-gentleman is one of those bournes to which governess novels eternally return. His name, his ward, and his relationship to the ward's mother suggest he might be dangerous to an unprotected young lady living in his household as a dependent, however, and the conventional scene of humiliation may not be far off. Jane may be especially vulnerable. Her religious convictions were never too strong. Her sauciness to Brocklehurst was delightful, but is it quite right for a child not to like the Psalms? (Surely we do not want to identify Jane with another "selective" reader of the Bible, one who hated Solomon and wrote that, "I made it a condition with my tutor . . . that I would not read my Bible at all, if he would not excuse me one of the wisest books in it: to which, however, I had no other objection than that it was called The Proverbs"—for that reader was Lovelace [*Clarissa*, Letter 191, 611].) Was she not still expressing serious religious doubt at Helen's deathbed? We have heard nothing of her religion since. Where religious conviction is not deep and strong, can moral strength suffice? Jane has already proved just a bit too confident in her own powers, a bit too self-reliant, too unaware that at times human resources alone may not be enough. Can it be that Rochester will be or will seek to be The Vile Seducer? And will Jane be strong enough to resist his blandishment? It is, perhaps, difficult to recapture the naïveté of what we assume was that of the Victorian reader, though I suspect the adolescent and preadolescent readers of *Jane Eyre* in our own time also thrill to the possibility of danger from Rochester. This openness to an alternative outcome is obviously not "essential" for the understanding of *Jane Eyre*, but it is essential to the full experience of the novel's effect.

The locus classicus of sociosexual harassment in fiction is, of course, *Pamela*. We have just had occasion to refer to Richardson's *Clarissa*; *Pamela*, mentioned in the very first chapter of the novel, is the fountainhead of the governess novel. Janet Spens, among others,[4] has pointed out that "Jane is a nursery governess and her social position as such is nearly indistinguishable from that of Pamela as a waiting-woman to Mr. B.'s mother. Both habitually talk of the hero as 'my Master' and are sent for to his presence. . . . Mrs. Fairfax corresponds closely to Mrs. Jarvis—the housekeeper who befriends Pamela" (5). But if we remember our *Pamela,* we recall that there was an evil housekeeper (Mrs. Jewes) as well as the kindly Mrs. Jarvis, so we cannot be too confident about Jane's safety. Knowledge of predecessors, fortunately, does not rob the narrative of suspense but, on the contrary, multiplies possibilities.

Part of the success of both novels, too, was due to the titillating episodes leading up to "the rise of the heroine in social position" and the nature of the "perils" the heroine faced. Sexual harassment was, of course, a delicate subject for Victorian novelists, and it is seldom free of concern with class. The Countess of Blessington's Clara Mordaunt, for example, is herself a lady and feels socially superior to most of her employers, many of whom are quite vulgar. Even the titled can be vulgar, however. The Ladies Meredith gossip unreservedly and insensitively in Clara's presence. Lady Elizabeth rattles on from one bit of gossip to another:

> ". . . Have you heard about Lady Fanny Elton's *femme-de-chambre?* O! it is a horrid affair, I assure you; but, if people will take beauties into their families, they must take the consequences; it is not every woman who has the good fortune to possess such a husband as Lord Axminster [Clara's employer]." (2:155)

Not all Clara's employers or their friends are as decent as Lord Axminster, and they are all worse when they are socially and even culturally "inferior." The Marsdens, West Indian friends of Clara Mordaunt's parvenu mistress, Mrs. Williamson, are, in their "half-caste" way, even crasser than their hostess. West Indian blood is conventionally "hot" (Bertha Rochester, of course, is from the West Indies), and so is that of Hercules Marsden, the vulgar son of the vulgar family:

> "How much do you pay miss for looking after your piccannies?" asked Mrs. Marsden [in Clara's presence].
>
> "I pay her twenty-five guineas a year," replied Mrs. Williamson.
>
> "Just what I pay my maid," remarked the creole.
>
> "And what I have agreed to pay my tiger [groom or footman]" said her hopeful son. "Faith! I think I shall take a governess for myself . . . but I shall bargain for her being as young and pretty as miss," looking

impudently at Clara, who felt indignant at being made the object of his indelicate remarks.

"Single gentlemen do not keep governesses," said Mrs. Williamson.

"O! that, I suppose, is a privilege reserved for the married men, and a devilish agreeable privilege it is, eh,—my old boy!" turning to his host, "do you find it so?" (1:93–94)

Blessington, like Richardson, makes explicit the vulnerability of the governess/employee to humiliating sexual exploitation—the capitalist version of the *droit du seigneur*—that is very near the surface in *Jane Eyre* and implicit, even if in some instances unthinkable, in the governess novel as a kind. Mrs. Ryals, in Mrs. Hall's "The Governess, a Tale," finishes her litany of the sins of governesses with this: "Another [governess]—really the world is very depraved—occasioned a painful difference between Mr. Ryals and myself; and let that be a warning to you, my dear friend, not to admit any pretty quiet sentimental young ladies into your domestic circle . . . men are but men" (53). In an embedded tale in *Margaret Russell,* Ruth, a governess, is a victim to all sorts of nameless indignities, including "dishonorable pursuit" by the ward of the owner of the house in which she is employed (255).

Governesses, however, at least fictional governesses, do sometimes marry aristocrats, whether the master, the son, or a distinguished guest. In *The Governess; Or, Politics in Private Life* (1836), Mrs. Ross's Gertrude Walcot marries Sir Herbert Lyster, her mistress's brother, but Ross makes clear that this is not a case of social climbing: "The candid reader will not fail to have observed," she tells us, "that it was as the intimate friend of Lady Trevor, Sir Herbert Lyster first loved Gertrude Walcot,—as his sister's governess, he never had,—most likely never would have thought of her in any other light" (310). Not all the governesses are so well-born or so pure, even in this same tale. Lady Carhampton was governess to the daughter of Lord Carhampton and, Ross tells us, "acquired the title of wife by the most disgraceful preliminaries" (247). In another tale, "Our Governess," the employer of Miss Pierrepoint, the governess, feels obliged to "check her mildly, and in private, for some forwardness with one of our male guests" (Hall 180).

The stage seems set for the appearance, for better or worse, of the "master," Edward Rochester, who will apparently enter into the conventional complications of a governess novel. That is the fictional world foregrounded here in the middle of the eleventh chapter of Jane Eyre's autobiography. All thoughts of Contarini Byronism and false, ghostly apparitions have long since faded into the background. The complicating factor, the center of interest, seems to be in what I have been calling the novel's "Godwinism," though it, too, seems subsumed by the domestic or governess tale, Jane's rebellious character offering only an interesting variation on the species, placing her in greater danger and the outcome in greater doubt. It seems possible that strong-willed Jane will have some sort of confrontation with this master —perhaps a sexual one. Or, she may begin with him a series of confrontations between her and subsequent masters and mistresses, a kind of pilgrimage common in governess novels, including Anne Brontë's *Agnes Grey*, which Charlotte had read but which had not as yet been published, as well as *Caroline Mordaunt*. We can settle down to a familiar, but not too familiar, domestic tale.

But almost immediately another voice (literally) is heard: the Gothic, a voice that for a number of chapters has been silent, suddenly echoes through Thornfield Hall. Mrs. Fairfax is showing Jane through the Hall when they come upon several rooms on the third story.

> "Do the servants sleep in these rooms?" I asked.
>
> "No; they occupy a range of smaller apartments to the back; no one ever sleeps here: one would almost say that, if there were a ghost at Thornfield Hall, this would be its haunt."
>
> "So I think: you have no ghost then?"
>
> "None that I ever heard of," returned Mrs. Fairfax, smiling.
>
> "Nor any traditions of one? no legends or ghost stories?"
>
> "I believe not. And yet it is said, the Rochesters have been rather a violent than a quiet race. . . ." (128)

The last "ghost" that threatened to appear was in the red-room, and this scene and its generic baggage are once more foregrounded from the repertoire of the reading. Then, Jane was a child and was overwrought, and the older Jane, the narrator, conjectured (but only conjectured) that the "ghost" was surely just the gleam from a lantern. Now Jane is grown—if not quite mature—yet she keeps pumping Mrs. Fairfax about a Thornfield ghost or ghost story and does not want

. . . . . .

to take no for an answer. Surely there is no ghost. The narrator is silent, the novel at this point once more monologic. Does Jane simply want to conjure up the fiction of a ghost to break the boredom? Did she—before she reached the maturity of the narrator—still believe that a ghost had been about to appear in the red-room? Some mature novelists and readers in the 1840s did believe in ghosts. Catherine Crowe, known for her realistic fiction, in 1848 published a collection of supposedly authentic stories of ghosts, apparitions, and supernatural events, and the volume was respectfully referred to in the *North British Review* within months of the publication of *Jane Eyre* (see above, ch. 2, n. 4).

Jane and Mrs. Fairfax go out onto the leads to survey the grounds. Jane then precedes Mrs. Fairfax down the staircase to the attic and waits there while Mrs. Fairfax fastens the trapdoor.

> I lingered in the long passage to which this [garret staircase] led, separating the front and back rooms of the third story: narrow, low, and dim, with only one little window at the far end, and looking, with its two rows of small black doors all shut, like a corridor in some Bluebeard's castle. (129)

References both serious and facetious to the eponymous villain of Charles Perrault's fairy tale, in which the innocent young wife is forbidden entrance into one room in the castle (because the bodies of his former wives are buried there), are fairly common in the early nineteenth century. They crop up in Austen's *Northanger Abbey*[5] and Sheridan LeFanu's *A Chapter in the History of a Tyrone Family*; in Thackeray's *Barry Lyndon* and the first (January 1847) number of *Vanity Fair*; and, a few months after the publication of *Jane Eyre*, in a serial appearing in Douglas Jerrold's *Shilling Magazine*, entitled *The Gallant Glazier; or, the Mystery of Ridley Hall*.

Fatherless Fanny (1819) perhaps deserves special mention. Louis James says its popularity "may well have brought it, [*sic*] potentialities to the notice of novel-writers; it[s Cinderella theme] is the theme of many domestic romances, including *Oliver Twist*" (130). Even more important for our purposes is that its preface, with its claim to realism, its justification of the marvelous, its protestation of morality and the healthy depiction of passion, and its claim to be something new in the novel genre, might well have been the preface to *Jane Eyre*:

> This Novel is one of the newest and most modern now extant, and is out
> of the common track of Novel writing: it is an attempt to unite the vari-
> ous merits and graces of the ancient romance and modern novel; and, like
> history, represents human nature as real life. To attain this end, there is
> required a degree of the marvellous to excite the attention and real man-
> ners of life to give an air of probability to the work, and to engage the
> heart in its behalf. . . . the whole [is] so closely connected, as to keep the
> imagination of the reader continually alive to the subject before him.
>
> . . . The passion that awakens and gives energy to life, is alone painted
> in those colours which Aurora gives to the morning . . . when all is ec-
> stasy, harmony and joy. ([Reeve] iii–iv)

The fifth chapter of *Fatherless Fanny* is entitled "A Modern Bluebeard."
Lord Bellafyn, the Bluebeard of Ireland, accusing his wife of infidelity,
has shut her up in the castle, allowing no one to see her and reportedly abusing her. She is later reported dead, poisoned by her husband,
and her ghost is said to have been seen on a rock overlooking the sea,
though other reports say she has escaped to England and her funeral
was a sham, staged so Lord Bellafyn could marry his longtime mistress.[6]

At this point in *Jane Eyre*, following upon the heels of the reference to Bluebeard, the Gothic leaves its indelible rubric upon the text:
"While I paced softly on, the last sound I expected to hear in so still a
region, a laugh, struck my ear. It was a curious laugh: distinct, formal,
mirthless." Mrs. Fairfax says she often hears that laugh, but it is only
Grace, one of the servants. She calls her.

> I really did not expect any Grace to answer; for the laugh was as tragic,
> as preternatural a laugh as any I ever heard; and, but that it was high
> noon, and that no circumstances of ghostliness accompanied the curious
> cachination; but that neither scene nor season favoured fear, I should have
> been superstitiously afraid. (130)

The narrator's silence continues, but the action itself de-
emphasizes for Jane thoughts of the supernatural. The squarish figure
and hard, plain face of the servant appears: "Any apparition less
romantic or less ghostly could scarcely be conceived" (130). It is the
"lantern" explanation but without the narrator's intervention. The
novel-reader knows that there are possible reasons for terror other

than ghosts, and the appearance of the servant does not necessarily eliminate even the possibility of a ghost. Jane's monologic description of her own responses and conclusions may not suffice. Brontë's narrator knows when to remain silent.

At this point readers even remotely familiar with the Gothic are likely to readjust the configuration of the novel as they have been piecing it together from what has already been presented and projecting it forward toward what is yet to come. The governess novel will be pushed into the background while a series of details that have lain more or less dormant in the mind will be brought once more to the fore, the fullness and clarity of the recall depending on the reader's original perception and present retention. From the very opening pages we may recall the pictures in Bewick's *History of British Birds* that Jane pored over as she sat in the window seat before John Reed so rudely interrupted her:

> I cannot tell what sentiments haunted the quite solitary churchyard with its inscribed headstone. . . .
>
> The two ships becalmed on a torpid sea, I believed to be marine phantoms.
>
> The fiend pinning down the thief's packet behind him, I passed over quickly: it was an object of terror.
>
> So was the black, horned thing seated aloof on a rock, surveying a distant crowd surrounding a gallows.
>
> Each picture told a story . . . as interesting as the tales Bessie sometimes narrated on winter evenings. (5)

The Gothic, at least implicitly, thus preceded the rebellion motif; it also preceded and now overwhelms the generic indicators of the governess novel. But neither of these is erased; both hover in the near background, waiting to come once more to the fore. The "rebel-novel" (Jacobin and/or feminist) and the Gothic are comfortable bedfellows (in Godwin, for example). The rebellious heroine and the governess novel, a somewhat less familiar grouping, do sometimes appear together: Ellen was tempestuous as a child, and Caroline Mordaunt had to undergo a moral education or reeducation. The governess and the ghost? Not a familiar mix, but once put side by side it is apparent that the Gothic heroine, captive rather than employee of the

. . . .

villain, is nonetheless, like the governess, defenseless in his house-hold/castle and subjected to the same threats as Pamela and Jane. The simultaneous presence of three voices, the polysemic refraction of the situation in the context and competing languages of the contemporary novel, makes it difficult for readers to know just what kind of novel they are reading but makes it equally difficult for them to ignore the generic signals. What is new in *Jane Eyre,* then, are the dialogic voices which not only complicate the reader's expectations but also prob-lematize—at least for a time—the moral universe of the novel. Despite the familiar materials, a new species of novel, an original, is before us.

But this is too static a description of the experience of reading this portion of the novel. The pacing here is extraordinary. Chapters 10 and 11 each began in halting fashion, shifting time and scene. The novel seemed to be floundering in search of a direction. The reader was searching for direction as well, but without the pressure of suspense, urgency, or even significance. Since there was little need to project for-ward, there was little need to recapitulate, to deduce from the earlier portions of the text a configuration that would predict what was to come. The reader was in a position similar to Jane's: there had been a tranquil, generalized summary of the eight quiet years at Lowood, a sudden move, and then the "promise of a smooth career" at Thornfield. We did not have much more to look forward to than did Jane. Then a series of generic signals and quick cuts in the action forced the reader to rapidly reassess the nature of the story, simultaneously recapitu-lating what has gone before in order to help identify the terms and strategies of the text. Both the forward-moving, horizontal/temporal movement and the recapitulatory, synchronic, vertical/spatial move-ment of the novel thus quicken. Now there is the master, Rochester, whose very name may suggest a sexual threat; his ward, who is French and of dubious background; and though there are no ghosts at Thorn-field, Jane is told, there is a preternatural laugh. Elements of governess novels, of Godwinian rebellion novels, and of Gothic novels are seri-ally recapitulated and juxtaposed in a new and puzzling configuration.

The two dimensions of the text—the temporal and the spatial—are not, as is often suggested, antithetical. The unusually hectic move-ment in these two chapters and the two that follow is only in part due

. . . . . .

to the action. There is a strange laugh, a meeting in the dark woods, the arrival of the master, and a somewhat bizarre interview with him. But what fully energizes the text and its language is its thickening texture, its picking up of generic stitches that have been dropped earlier, its blurring without erasing the governess-novel configuration. That model does not at present seem to serve even as an alternative possibility of the future development of the novel. The Gothic offers its own alternative possibilities, its own possible transformation into something else, most likely a Byronic love story. Though no longer in the forefront of the reader's imagination, the governess novel is still hovering in the background, even as the Gothic had been hovering for so long.

In chapter 8, at Lowood, Jane tells Miss Temple about Mr. Lloyd's having attended her "after the fit; for I never forgot the, to me, frightful episode of the red-room" (83). Since the episode was so memorable to Jane, we must remember it too, and it may be well for us to revisit that scene briefly now, even at the risk of some repetition, in order to give it its new emphasis in the new context of the strange doings at Thornfield.

In this seldom-used room where Mr. Reed had died, young Jane, having been locked in for punishment, sees her own white face and glittering eyes reflected in the mirror. She looks "like one of the tiny phantoms, half fairy, half imp, Bessie's evening stories represented as coming out of lone, ferny dells in moors" (112), she thinks. At first, she is too angry at the injustice of her treatment to be frightened. As the anger turns to depression and the room turns dark, she begins to think of her dead uncle, and as she glances from time to time toward the dimly gleaming mirror:

> I began to recall what I had heard of dead men, troubled in their graves by the violation of their last wishes, revisiting the earth to punish the perjured and avenge the oppressed; and I thought Mr. Reed's spirit, harassed by the wrongs of his sister's child, might quit its abode—whether in the church vault or in the unknown world of the departed—and rise before me in this chamber. . . . This idea, consolatory in theory, I felt would be terrible if realized. . . .

. . . .

A light shines on the wall and glides to the ceiling over her head.

> I can now conjecture readily that this streak of light was, in all likelihood,
> a gleam from a lantern, carried by some one across the lawn; but then,
> prepared as my mind was for horror, shaken as my nerves were by agita-
> tion, I thought the swift-darting beam was a herald of some coming vision
> from another world. (15)

The autobiographer explains the ghostly appearance away, but the explanation is hedged—"I can conjecture . . . in all likelihood"—and
her confession a few chapters later that she has never forgotten the
episode leaves in doubt just how the novel will resolve the issue of
supernatural appearances. Other Gothic elements have entered the
text and more will be introduced. Some are treated as superstitions—
as when Jane overhears the servants talking: " 'Something passed her,
all dressed in white, and vanished'—'A great black dog behind him'—
'Three loud raps on the chamber door'—'A light in the churchyard
just over his grave'—&c. &c." (18). Others are treated as jokes, as when
the "kind fairy" drops a suggestion to advertise on Jane's pillow. But
their very presence and frequency keep some sort of Gothic configuration a possibility. Though no reader can be expected to recall the past
text in its totality, and some readers will have made up their minds
whether Jane's world is naturalistic or Gothic, there would seem to be
sufficiently conflicting signals to ambiguate the issue, so that even the
convinced will recognize the possibility of the dialogic worldviews.

Rochester himself makes a Gothic entrance. One evening in January, Jane takes a walk. She rests on a stile. The sun goes down. She
hears a horse approaching.

> In those days I was young, and all sorts of fancies bright and dark ten-
> anted my mind: the memories of nursery stories were there amongst
> other rubbish; and when they recurred, maturing youth added to them
> a vigour and vividness beyond what childhood could give. As this horse
> approached, and as I watched for it to appear through the dusk, I remem-
> bered certain of Bessie's tales wherein figured a North-of-England spirit,
> called a "Gytrash;" which, in the form of a horse, mule, or large dog,
> haunted solitary ways, and sometimes came upon belated travellers, as
> this horse was now coming upon me.

. . . . . .

63

. . . close down by the hazel stems glided a great dog, whose black and white colour made him a distinct object against the trees. It was exactly one mask of Bessie's Gytrash. (135–36)[7]

The horse and rider appear and prove to be all too earthly: the horse slips, the rider falls. Jane helps him remount. Later she learns he is Mr. Rochester, master of Thornfield, and he admits, "When you came on me in Hay Lane last night, I thought unaccountably of fairy tales, and had half a mind to demand whether you had bewitched my horse: I am not sure yet" (149). He makes much of her having been seated on the stile, waiting, he suggests, for her "people . . . the men in green: it was a proper moonlight evening for them" (149). Stiles are associated elsewhere with the supernatural, not with men in green but with ghosts, as in Thomas Love Peacock's *Nightmare Abbey* (1818), which was republished in Bentley's Standard Novels and Romances as no. 57 in 1837:

> ". . . when I was in Devonshire," Mr. Flosky says, "the following story was well attested to me. A young woman, whose lover was at sea, returning one evening over some solitary fields, saw her lover sitting on a stile over which she was to pass. Her first emotions were surprise and joy, but there was a paleness and seriousness in his face that made them give place to alarm. She advanced towards him, and he said to her, in a solemn voice, 'The eye that hath seen me shall see me no more. Thine eye is upon me, but I am not.' And with these words he vanished; and on that very day and hour, as it afterwards appeared, he had perished by shipwreck." (177–78)

Jane as narrator, speaking from the vantage point of her maturity, excuses her momentary fears by reminding us of her youth and calls the nursery tales "rubbish." When a stile and ghost are introduced much later in the novel, the superstition is also dismissed, but it does testify, as perhaps the overtones do in the Rochester/Jane meeting, to a more-than-usual if not more-than-natural emotional experience. When, on that later occasion, Jane returns from her visit to her aunt unannounced, she comes upon Rochester sitting on the stone steps of a stile, and as on their first meeting, there is an air of the insubstantial or supernatural. The ghost "appears" in the text by negation: "Well," Jane says, "he is not a ghost; yet every nerve I have is unstrung"

(306). Bits of the supernatural or superstitious are being dropped into the reader's repertoire, casually populating the background, building, perhaps, to a critical mass.

The talk of ghosts at Thornfield occurs at the end of chapter 11; the appearance of Rochester occurs in chapter 12; at the end of chapter 13, after he and Jane have formally met, Jane challenges Mrs. Fairfax's earlier description of him as not "peculiar." The housekeeper admits that he may have "peculiarities of temper," but she says that allowances should be made because of "family troubles." His elder brother, Rowland, had done him some grievous and unforgivable wrong, had died without a will, and Edward Rochester has come into the property. Since that time, nine years ago, the new heir has been unable or unwilling to stay at Thornfield more than two weeks at a time. Why can he not abide the Hall? Mrs. Fairfax is evasive. It is a mystery even to her, she claims. "It was evident, indeed, that she wished me to drop the subject; which I did accordingly" (156).

Thus ends chapter 13. Jane does not at this point remind the reader of the preternatural laugh. But the end of the chapter strategically gives readers time to pause a few seconds, to reflect, to readjust their configuration of what had gone before, and to project that which might yet come. What evil lurks in Thornfield Hall? What kind of fictional world are we in?

Earlier fiction may help answer the questions. Shut-up rooms in a house or castle was a common device in Gothic novels of the early nineteenth century. In 1814 Scott, in his "Introductory" chapter to *Waverley; or, 'Tis Sixty Years Since*, suggests that the motif was already old:

> Had I . . . announced in my frontispiece, "Waverley, a Tale of other Days," must not every novel-reader have anticipated a castle scarce less than Udolpho, of which the eastern wing had long been uninhabited, and the keys either lost, or consigned to the care of some aged butler or housekeeper whose trembling steps, about the middle of the second volume, were doomed to guide the hero, or heroine, to the ruinous precincts? (63)

Watt calls the device "the deserted wing," and says that in the shilling shockers of 1818

. . . .

no Gothic castle, was complete without its "deserted wing." . . . We learn
early in the story that one of the lords of the castle has shut up the access
to a certain wing, for some reason, and we are immediately held in suspense about it. After reading a dozen [Gothic shilling] shockers, we begin
to realize that deserted wings are reserved for the explorations of curious
heroines or rightful heirs . . . bent on solving the mystery of a murder
perpetrated by the ancestors of the current usurper. (24–25)[8]

Is the laugh that echoes through the third story that of a ghost? If there
were, despite Mrs. Fairfax's insistence, a ghost in Thornfield Hall,
whose ghost would it be? Would it be that of "the rightful heir," Rowland? Perhaps, but there are other possibilities: "The deserted wing
is not necessarily the residence of the ghost of an unburied ancestor.
It often serves as the base of operations of villains and their female
counterparts [like Grace Poole, perhaps?]. In Mrs. Radcliffe's *Sicilian
Romance*, a Gothic husband found it a convenient depository for his
wife" (Watt 25).

Here the narratable is so narratable, such a fictional topos or cliché,
that it is not its narratability but its verisimilitude that needs defending.
A reviewer of Harriet Martineau's *The Billow and the Rock*, published
just a year before *Jane Eyre*, defends Martineau's depiction of the kid-
napping of a wife and the placing of her on an island, not only because
it was based on the actual case of Lady Grange, a drunkard with "an
ungovernable temper," but because a note to Maria Edgeworth's *Castle
Rackrent* reports an actual case in which a wife was imprisoned for
twenty years in the "upper room in an Irish country-house" where the
husband still entertained. Released when he died, she "scarcely had
clothes sufficient to cover her; and her understanding seemed stupe-
fied." When she recovered she said, "I have been three times married;
the first time for money; the second, for rank; the third, for love—
and the third was worst of all" (*Edinburgh Review* 85:247). Not a very
promising prospect if *Jane Eyre* is to become a love story.

Another reviewer, defending *Jane Eyre* in the *Athenaeum*, claimed
that he had heard of someone's actually having been confined in a
mansion house for years without public knowledge (Allott 71–72).
Brontë may have based her own novel on another such actuality or
at least on a tradition taken for actuality (Clarendon 588–89, 600–601)

. . . .

rather than directly on other novels. Actual or fanciful, the fictional topos was still alive a generation after the shilling shockers, *Waverley*, and Austen's satiric *Northanger Abbey*, which was meant to put it to rest. The same reviewer who defended its actuality in *Jane Eyre* recalls, "Some such tale as this was told in a now forgotten novel—Sketches of a Seaport Town." The reviewer gives no details of that "novel" and is, indeed, slightly inaccurate, since, as the title suggests, the cited text is not a novel but more like a series of sketches or novellas. It is strange that the anonymous reviewer would make that mistake, for the author of the "novel" was H. F. Chorley, and the anonymous reviewer was . . . H. F. Chorley.

The tale referred to is "Parson Clare," which appears in *Sketches* (1834) in three parts. The early portions of the story might almost be the prehistory of Rochester's marriage, except the greed motivating the marriage was not Rochester's own but his family's, and the seaport town is not in the West Indies. Wilson Herbert, a young clergyman, jilts Anna Oldacre, whom he has been courting for some time, in order to marry the ugly and base heiress of the fatally ill miser Parson Clare. After the marriage, Herbert tries for years to discipline and "feminize" his wife, but without success.

> Even during that short period of constraint, strange rumours of her eccentricities transpired. She was not one of those passive personages, conscious of their own deficiencies, whom you may persuade or terrify into whatever you please, for the time being. She was vain, vulgar and violent; incapable of being stirred to the task of amending herself by either shame or emulation. Many even went so far as to say that, during the course of that time, she had shown glimpses of more disgraceful propensities than the love of tawdry finery, or the distaste to everything polished and refined. (Chorley 199)

A year passes, a daughter is born, and Mrs. Herbert wallows in luxury and self-indulgence. There follows an episode that has a striking parallel in *Jane Eyre*, except that Rochester discovers that he is betrayed not by his wife but by his mistress: A "kind friend" enlightens Herbert as to certain aspects of his wife's conduct that the husband is always the last to know. He decides to become better acquainted with

· · · · · · ·

his wife's activities. One night he sits up to await her return from a party he had left earlier:

> At last the sound of wheels is heard;—not, as before, to die away into deep silence. The chariot stopped.—The drawing-room where Herbert had been sitting, was in darkness, the candles having burned their last. He ran out to the top of the stairs, and leaned over to listen. The lamp in the hall too was just expiring, so that he could see without being seen. He heard his wife's coarse voice, and that of a gentleman. He breathed short and thick, and clenched a small cane between his hands so violently, that the print of his fingers was seen on the bamboo next morning. There was some bidding of good-night, and the door closed upon the cavalier. (205)

In only his second conversation with Jane, Rochester recounts his "discovery," with interruptions, over the space of some six pages. There is a similar pattern: the betrayed man, sitting in the dark, listens to the carriages pass until one stops; he then rises and stands above the scene, invisible in the dark.

> "I recognized the 'voiture' I had given Céline. She was returning: of course my heart thumped with impatience against the iron rails I leant upon. . . . Bending over the balcony I was about to murmur, 'Mon Ange' . . . when a figure jumped from the carriage after her; cloaked also: but that was a hatted head which now passed under the arched *porte cochère* of the hotel." (174)

Rochester interrupts his narrative to describe the tumultuousness of jealousy, to comment on the weather, to look at and curse Thornfield—misleading the reader, perhaps, into believing Céline has something to do with the mystery therein—to shoo Adèle away. And then he continues: "When I saw my charmer thus come in accompanied by a cavalier, I seemed to hear a hiss, and the green snake of jealousy, rising on undulating coils from the moonlit balcony, glided within my waistcoat and ate its way to my heart's core" (176). He hides behind curtains to ambush them should they enter Céline's boudoir. When they do, he recognizes his "rival" as an unworthy young viscount. The conversation he overhears he finds "frivolous, mercenary, heartless, and senseless" (177). He hears Céline making fun of his "deformities." His jealousy, as well as other passions, dies. "Opening the window, I

. . . .

walked in upon them; liberated Céline from my protection; . . . made an appointment with the Vicomte for a meeting at the bois de Boulogne" (178). He wounds the vicomte in the arm and is quit of "the whole crew," except for Adèle, who had been given into his custody as his own daughter by Céline six months earlier.

Neither Wilson Herbert nor Rochester is alone in his betrayal, for the episode is a scenic topos of the period. Eustace Conway, the eponymous hero of a John Frederick Denison Maurice novel published in the same year as *Sketches*, is similarly victimized by his French mistress. He, like Rochester, has been leading a life of dissipation. Like Rochester, he visits one night to find his mistress not at home. He sits reading a novel while awaiting her return; he dozes; the candle burns out. The door opens, and his friend Mr. Morton enters with Louise, who tries to claim that Eustace has arrived uninvited. Morton believes Conway and they leave together, Eustace cured of Louise but not of dissipation (1:243–44).

Wilson Herbert is less resolute than either Eustace or Rochester. He has confronted the "cavalier," but he cannot decide what course of action to pursue with regard to his wife. She staggers away from him, heads up the stairs, falls, and strikes "her head against the sharp corner of a step. Her husband heard the fall, and the outcry of the assembled servants who pronounced her to be killed" (Chorley 205).

Eighteen years later, Herbert's daughter, Phoebe; her fiancé, Sir Thomas Dulwich; and his mother are out riding when they come to a house at what proves to be the back entrance to Herbert's estate, a site he had abandoned ever since his wife's accident. Sir Thomas and his mother playfully insist on visiting the house. They snatch the housekeeper's keys from her and explore half the house, opening all the long-locked doors but finding no more of interest than had Catherine Morland at Northanger Abbey or Jane at Thornfield in their extensive but incomplete tours.

> "And now, Madame la Concièrge," said Sir Thomas, "I think we are satisfied. We have seen nothing worth making such a fuss about; never a ghost, not a picture. Is there any thing precious on the other side of the house?"
>
> "No, Sir—I do not know, Sir," replied Markland, in great agitation, "I have never been in several of the rooms myself, Sir."

. . . .

Sir Thomas insists that they explore the "deserted wing":

> they were on the point of entering the corridor, when they were trans-
> fixed by a sound which made itself heard above the highest pitch of their
> voices;—an outcry, something between the yell of a terrified wild beast,
> and the shriek of a strong man in his death-struggle, rung from the fur-
> ther end of the right-hand passage, again and again. . . . a second scream
> was heard, and louder than the first,—a scuffling of feet,—the rattle of
> a chain;—and Markland was seen issuing from the passage crying out,
> "save me!—help!—murder!"—and pursued by a ghastlier figure than any
> of the party had ever before beheld.
>
> It was a strong middle-aged woman, of a herculean figure, upon
> whose face was stamped every bad passion, intensified by insanity. Her
> brilliant eyes were distended to their utmost;—her head was overgrown
> with a felt of shaggy black hair. Her attire was little more than a foul blan-
> ket, strapped round her waist; and a broken chain appended to this belt,
> and the rings about her wrists which had belonged to manacles, told how
> strictly she had been coerced, and how mighty had been the effects of her
> present paroxysm of frenzy. From the slight bedstead close outside the
> door of her prison-chamber, on which Markland had been accustomed
> to sleep, she had wrenched out a post, and was pursuing her dismayed
> keeper with the utmost fury, when her eye lighted upon the strangers.
> With a bound, and another inarticulate shout, she rushed toward [sic],
> brandishing her weapon, and aimed a violent blow at Sir Thomas, who
> vainly endeavoured to oppose her progress. It descended,—but not as
> she had directed it—upon the fair forehead of Phoebe. Then the maniac
> sprang down stairs, and in another instant, the fiendish sound of her law-
> less laughter was heard upon the lawn without. The unfortunate girl fell
> at her lover's feet, covered with blood.
>
> "What have I lived to see!" cried Markland. "Heaven have mercy
> upon us! she is killed!—and by her own mother too!" (211–12)

Austen's Mrs. Tilney, had she indeed been incarcerated, would
have been pure victim. Mrs. Herbert, though improperly imprisoned
and so a victim of sorts, is a dangerous and immoral creature, driven
mad by lust. She kills her own daughter, unintentionally, in her mad
rage. The upper story of Thornfield may, then, be populated by Rowland's ghost or Rochester's mistress or wife, and the incarcerated
woman may be a helpless victim or a lustful, murderous madwoman

· · · · · · ·

(could it be Céline?) who kills her daughter (is Adèle in danger?). The ghosts of many possibilities haunt the third story of Thornfield Manor.

That Chorley, reviewing anonymously, did not take the opportunity to claim his own story as the "source" for *Jane Eyre* but argued instead that both works were credible, based on or consistent with reports of actual incidents, may testify to his modesty or his credulity, but it may also suggest the invisibility of conventions. That is, conventional stories are accepted and enjoyed because they are familiar; the expectations aroused are familiar, and, though not always predictably, in one form or another they are fulfilled conventionally or meaningfully modified. The whole reading experience validates the convention and its "realism": it seems real because it is familiar, that is, like "everyday" events—or "everyday" stories.

New meaning, new views or versions or visions of reality, are therefore usually embodied in conventional narratives with a "twist": "Something created is always created out of something given. . . . What is given is completely transformed in what is created" (Bakhtin, *Speech* 120). The use of the convention is not necessarily a conscious strategy on the part of the author, an attempt from above to communicate with the rabble of readers. The author is also a reader. The "novel" is defined for the author by prior novels, and the genre is what it is at the moment, its "utterance" specific to the occasion. The world according to novels—"reality"—is also defined to a significant degree by the novels of that particular time. The original author, one who says, "It has been written [thus], but I say unto you [otherwise]," is therefore dependent for his or her ability to see and to say on the fact that "it" has been written. Charlotte Brontë can create *Jane Eyre* not in spite of conventions like the "deserted wing" but through them. Readers are surprised by this new species of novel and assent to its "realism" not because it is unlike anything they had read before but because it is like but unlike, strange but somehow familiar, shocking but recognizable. The recombined conventions are defamiliarized and, paradoxically, while they are accepted and found original in their new form, they call into question the old conventions themselves.

This procedure of using multiple fictional conventions to defamiliarize the familiar and make surprising what is commonplace, make

· · · · · · ·

71

new from the old, is analogous—if not identical—to the means by which Iser sees literature recombining societal conventions in new relationships, reorganizing them from their stable "vertical" arrangement of the past to a new "horizontal" combination, and thus forcing the reader to reexamine the conventions themselves:

> The fictional text makes a selection from a variety of conventions to be found in the real world [*for our purposes read* "in the fictional context"], and it puts them together as if they were interrelated. This is why we recognize in a novel, for instance, so many of the conventions that regulate our society and culture [*read* "our novels"]. But by reorganizing them horizontally, the fictional text brings them before us in unexpected combinations, so that they begin to be stripped of their validity. As a result, these conventions are taken out of their social [*read* "fictional"] contexts, deprived of their regulating function, and so become subjects of scrutiny themselves. (Iser 61)

In literature, however, the new combination replaces to a considerable extent the old conventions and effectively redefines the novel genre. By inbreeding and crossbreeding conventions and varieties of Gothic and governess novels with an admixture of still others, Brontë has created not a Frankensteinian monster but a new, heartier species of novel out of old varieties that will now be replaced. Indeed, in time the new hybrid will itself seem trite.[9] When the convention fades from memory, the familiar, conventional plots may seem less "realistic," and the new combination made of these old parts may seem so too (as do some social realism novels of the 1930s, for example). These once conventional, realistic, and new works may now seem arbitrary and even bizarre. Some of the quieter conventions with which a work like *Jane Eyre* is created virtually disappear. The more flamboyant recede but are readily recognizable once we run across them. So it is, then, that when we encounter one of these once conventional but now "unrealistic" yet recognizable plots in two separate works, we often identify the earlier as the "source."

One "source" for the Thornfield plot of *Jane Eyre* was suggested long ago by A. A. Jack in an appendix to the Brontë section of *The Cambridge History of English Literature:* Sheridan LeFanu's *A chapter in the History of a Tyrone Family, being a tenth extract from the Legacy of the Late Francis Purcell, P. P. of Drumcoolagh.* Later to appear in the *Purcell Papers*, it was first published in the *Dublin Magazine* for October 1839. By citing Brontë's letter to that periodical in which she thanks the editors for a good review of her and her sisters' *Poems* and identifies herself as a "constant and grateful reader," Jack establishes the likelihood that Brontë read LeFanu's work. Whether or not it is a true source for Brontë—and we have seen enough of the convention to recognize that Brontë's plot probably does not originate in any one specific work—Le Fanu's tale was certainly in the repertoire of a good many novel-readers of the period and offers situational and scenic topoi that appear as well in *Jane Eyre*. It is useful, then, to follow—and extend—Jack's comparison of the two works, not to demonstrate influence, but to help define further the fictional dialogue into which *Jane Eyre* was speaking.

LeFanu's narrator is a young Irish girl, Fanny Richardson, who, recently married to Lord Glenfallen, accompanies him for the first time to his country house, Cahergillagh Court. Calling himself her Bluebeard—a reference we have noted before—he mysteriously forbids her that portion of the castle accessible by the back door. A month after her arrival Fanny discovers a blind woman in her room. When, in response to the blind woman's question, Fanny says she is Lady Glenfallen, the intruder grows angry:

> The violence of her action, and the fury which convulsed her face, effectually terrified me, and disengaging myself from her grasp, I screamed as loud as I could for help. . . . I heard Lord Glenfallen's step upon the stairs, and I instantly ran out: as I passed him I perceived that he was deadly pale and just caught the words, "I hope that demon has not hurt you." (qtd. in Jack 461)

Glenfallen tells Fanny that the blind woman is out of her mind, but he assures her that he will not let her bother Fanny again. That very night, however, the blind woman appears in Fanny's bedroom. She insistently questions Fanny about whether the young girl is really married to Glenfallen, and after Fanny says she was married "in the presence of more than a hundred witnesses," the blind woman claims to be the first and the true Lady Glenfallen (LeFanu 3:88; Jack does not treat this episode fully). Fanny sees

> something in her face, though her features had evidently been handsome, and were not, at first sight, unpleasing, which, upon a nearer inspection, seemed to indicate the habitual prevalence and indulgence of evil passions, and a power of expressing mere animal rage with an intenseness that I have seldom seen equalled. (Jack 461)

The novel-reader's repertoire is stocked not just with the motif of the deserted wing, not even with the mere fact that one possible inhabitant of that wing—or third story—might be an imprisoned wife, but there is built up in the convention something of a taxonomy of clandestinely incarcerated wives. The first-time reader of *Jane Eyre* does not of course know that it is Rochester's wife upstairs, though the convention makes that a possibility, and of course Bertha herself is not known to the reader, so that any comparison with Lady Glenfallen is at this point proleptic. Still, some of these qualities of the blind woman may not only be stored for later recall but may condition the expectations. This is not to say that LeFanu's story is a prerequisite for the reader's repertoire, but it can serve as one instance of how that repertoire may be stored and how any earlier work in the convention may influence the reading (whether or not it has influenced the writing) of the text of *Jane Eyre* prospectively and retrospectively. Though not a lunatic, despite Glenfallen's charge, Lady Glenfallen, like Bertha, seems to have unsettled her nature by passion, though lust is not specified here as it is in Bertha's case. Like Bertha, too, she is not English—few passionate women in nineteenth-century English fiction are—but Dutch (not to my knowledge conventionally thought of as a passionate people). Passion, violence, insanity, and otherness—the wife upstairs at Thornfield, if there is one, is being described in absentia by her imprisoned sisters. Lady Glenfallen joins Mrs. Herbert and even the fancied poor Mrs. Tilney of *Northanger Abbey* in the attic (but not in Gilbert and Gubar's attic).

Unlike Austen's satire or Chorley's novella, LeFanu's tale, like *Jane Eyre,* is a first-person narration, and the horror is intensified because the narrator, Fanny, is at risk, as Jane might be. Fanny is twice mysteriously threatened, then attacked: The mirror in her room pivots away to reveal a concealed door,[10] through which the blind woman enters. The intruder stops, listening, finds a razor, and attempts to murder the fear-frozen Fanny. "A slight inaccuracy saved me from instant death; the blow fell short, the point of the razor grazing my throat" (Jack 462). The blind woman is seized and tried for murder; she then implicates her husband. She is sentenced and dies; Glenfallen is acquitted but goes mad and cuts his own throat.

Jack does not push the parallels, indeed may not push them far enough. Glenfallen, for example, like Rochester, is "neither young nor handsome" (LeFanu 3:51) and is capable of being gay and kind or gloomy and morose, though he seems to change from one mode to the other in the course of the story rather than vacillate back and forth as Rochester does. He is sensible, ironic, and disarming in describing his castle (which is as disappointingly modern and unmysterious as General Tilney's abbey was to Catherine Morland):

> "I much prefer a snug, modern, unmysterious bedroom, with well-aired sheets, to the waving tapestry, mildewed cushions, and all the other interesting appliances of romance. However, . . . if old Martha be still to the fore . . . you will soon have a supernatural and appropriate anecdote for every closet and corner of the mansion." (LeFanu 3:64–65)

Fanny finds the scene tranquil, and "a hale, good-humoured, erect old woman was Martha, and an agreeable contrast to the grim, decrepid [sic] hag which my imagination had conjured up" (3:67). Jane finds the scene at Thornfield tranquil, Mrs. Fairfax agreeable, and gets a whiff of the supernatural (or allows the reader to sniff tentatively at the must of the Gothic) despite, not because of, the housekeeper.

In *A chapter in the History of a Tyrone Family,* the false scent of the supernatural covers the real stench of crime and violence and the evil nature of the supposed hero. It is difficult to remember, perhaps, that first-time readers of *Jane Eyre,* particularly those in the 1840s, may not be sure for some time whether Rochester is Gothic villain or Byronic hero. His character seems unambiguous only in retrospect; there are numerous indications of his basic goodness, but there are other signs of his potential for less-than-admirable behavior, and neither one nor

. . . . . .

the other is given temporal primacy. No matter which configuration a reader might project, there are ample "anticipatory cautions" to keep the wary reader from being certain. Indeed, to be too certain of Rochester's character and intentions too soon is to miss a good deal of the tension, appeal, and significance of *Jane Eyre*. Reading other contemporary novels with Byronic/Gothic hero/villains can help us stay alert to the heteroglossic potentialities of the text.

The maiden alone, in a manor house or castle with a deserted wing (or section or upstairs room or suite of rooms) from which noises emanate or strange events originate; mysteries that might be ghosts; mysterious malefactors; incarcerated wives, dead or alive, blind or mad—these conventions dominate the early chapters of the Thornfield center of the novel. Though the mystery is never far from the forefront through much of the rest of this section of *Jane Eyre*, it is the possibly-Gothic/possibly-not puzzle of Rochester's character that sometimes moves front and center. Though Gothic novels are almost always love stories, that love usually takes place within the aura of the Gothic. Here the Gothic retreats from center stage, still haunting the dark recesses, but like a shadow. The spotlight of the reader's attention is focused not on the mystery of the third story but on the sweet mystery of love and its story—and on its narrative and moral suspense: What is the true nature of the enigmatic master of Thornfield? How strong is the moral fibre of the self-reliant, skeptical, unconventional heroine?

The Transgeneric Topic, Love:
A Tale of Incident, Fire, and Feeling

The final chapters of volume 1 of *Jane Eyre* describing Jane's first months at Thornfield offer a bewildering variety of clashing generic signals, as we have seen. These signals not only educate expectations but also evoke selective recollection of earlier details of the text. Jane is now a governess, which, for those familiar with the genre, generates the retrospective, centripetal pulling together of such incidents as the deathbed scene of Helen Burns, a scene common in such novels, and the prospective anticipation of what Jane is to find in her new career. Many such novels are didactic tours, showing how not to treat governesses and how not to rear a child; the heroine moves from one unsatisfactory position to another, sampling the ills of masters, mistresses, and children. Some governesses, like Caroline and Clara Mordaunt or Mrs. Ross's Gertrude Walcot in *The Governess; Or, Politics in Private Life* (or the fictional governess that Charlotte Brontë knew but readers of 1847 did not, Agnes Grey), are subjected to vulgar tyranny, sometimes, but not always, by the newly rich bourgeoisie. Many of the pupils are spoiled brats, protected by willfully blind and pampering parents. So Adèle (flighty, a bit spoiled, but redeemable) and Mrs. Fairfax (respectable, accommodating, and, most important, willing to leave the training of Adèle to Jane) do not seem likely to make their governess's life miserable: "The promise of a smooth career, which my first calm introduction to Thornfield-Hall seemed to pledge, was not belied on a longer acquaintance with the place and its inmates" (131). All of which is pleasant enough, but where is the real knowledge of life for Jane or the suspense and illumination for the reader?

The fact that there is a Mr. Rochester who is Jane's actual employer, the talk of ghosts, and especially the preternatural laugh, which incident immediately preceded this passage promising tranquillity, may have promised something else, perhaps something Gothic. However, the appearance of the apparent source of the laugh, Grace Poole—"any apparition less romantic or less ghostly could scarcely be imagined" (130)—seems to have satisfied Jane. The incident is not just passed over quickly, it seems to have been dismissed; and there is no hint of dialogical response or qualification by the narrator. If active readers expect something more, even something romantic or ghostly, from the third story, they must separate themselves from the consciousness of young Jane and reduce her authority. However, even if both the ghostly laugh and the existence of Rochester are, with Jane's assistance, pushed into the background of the reader's mind, they still lie there dormant, capable of being aroused by further developments.

One source of expectations that has been backgrounded for a time—what we have been calling the Godwinian motif—now comes forward again and pulls into the present past details of the text. Jane's story began in rebellion; her intractability caused her to be ejected from Gateshead and sent to Lowood Institution. When Miss Temple leaves, taking Jane's "reason for tranquillity" (100) with her, Jane's adventurous spirit urges her to enter the wider world, to gain experience, whatever the danger. Now, in the tranquillity of her new position, after the excitement of the change, she yearns for more "practical experience"; she wants to meet more people and encounter "more vivid kinds of goodness" than that exemplified by Mrs. Fairfax or Adèle:

> Who blames me? Many no doubt; and I shall be called discontented. I cannot help it: the restlessness was in my nature; it agitated me to pain sometimes. Then my sole relief was to walk along the corridor of the third story . . . and allow my mind's eye to dwell on whatever bright visions rose before it . . . ; to let my heart be heaved by exultant movement, while it swelled it in trouble, expanded it with life; and, best of all, to open my

. . . .

inward ear to a tale that was never ended—a tale my imagination created, and narrated continuously; quickened with all of incident, life, fire,
feeling, that I desired and had not in my actual existence. (132)

Jane strikes the Godwinian note, feminist, rebellious, perhaps morally
dangerous:

> It is vain to say human beings ought to be satisfied with tranquillity; they
> must have action; and they will make it if they cannot find it. Millions are
> condemned to a stiller doom than mine, and millions are in silent revolt
> against their lot. Nobody knows how many rebellions besides political
> rebellions ferment in the masses of life which people earth. Women are
> supposed to be very calm generally; but women feel just as men feel;
> they need exercise for their faculties, and a field for their efforts as much
> as their brothers do; they suffer from too rigid a restraint, too absolute
> a stagnation, precisely as men would suffer; and it is narrow-minded in
> their more privileged fellow-creatures to say that they ought to confine
> themselves to making puddings and knitting stockings, to playing on the
> piano and embroidering bags. It is thoughtless to condemn them, or laugh
> at them, if they seek to do more than custom has pronounced necessary
> for their sex. (132–33)

Such sentiments are "occupied utterances," commonplaces—ideological topoi, as it were—in the Godwin tradition. The eponymous
heroine of Mary Hays's *Memoirs of Emma Courtney* (1796), for example,
finds that since her inheritance is insufficient to support her, she must
support herself to remain independent. But how? She is dissatisfied
with life as a teacher or governess and yearns for freedom and a
wider world:

> I might, perhaps, be allowed to officiate, as an assistant, in the school
> where I had been placed in my childhood . . . [like Jane]; but this was a
> species of servitude, and my mind panted for freedom, for social inter-
> course, for scenes in motion, where the active curiosity of my temper
> might find a scope wherein to range and speculate. . . . Cruel prejudices!
> I exclaimed—hapless woman! Why was I not educated for commerce, for
> a profession, for labour? Why have I been rendered feeble and delicate
> by bodily constraint, and fastidious by artificial refinement? Why are we
> bound by the habits of society, as with an adamant chain? Why do we

. . . . . .

suffer ourselves to be confined within a magic circle, without daring, by a magnanimous effort, to dissolve the barbarous spell? (1:54–55)

The desire for freedom and rebellion against the servitude of women's roles such as that of teacher are analogous to those in *Jane Eyre*, but this is an even more overt call for rebellion against the constraints of gender in British society than is Jane's. That such frustrations of desire may break out in other channels, leading some women into moral disaster or turning back on the minds of strong women to destroy them—dangers implicit in the Brontë passage—is explicit in Hays:

> While men pursue interest, honour, pleasure, as accords with their several dispositions, women, who have too much delicacy, sense, and spirit, to degrade themselves by the vilest of all interchanges, remain insulated beings, and must be content tamely to look on, without taking any part in the great, though often absurd and tragical, drama of life. Hence the eccentricities of conduct, with which women of superior minds have been accused—the struggles, the despairing though generous struggles, of an ardent spirit, denied a scope for its exertions! The strong feelings, and strong energies, which properly directed, in a field sufficiently wide, might—ah! what might they not have aided? forced back, and pent up, ravage and destroy the mind which gave them birth! (1:169)

Comments restive or revolutionary are common in women's novels of the period. Geraldine Jewsbury, for example, thought of as an English disciple of George Sand, "particularly demands the enlargement of the sphere of women's activities" (*Jerrold's* 7 [1848]: 370, reviewing Jewsbury's *The Half Sisters*). The first-person narrator in *Margaret Russell: An Autobiography* (1846) cries out, as Jane does, for action, even duty: "My thirst, my longing, was for action: I yearned for some strong necessity to call me out of myself; some duty, some material for the capacities of my nature to work upon" (101). Jane's feminist yearnings are thus refracted by the already occupied "word," so that her projected future is endangered in new ways: she may be tempted by "the vilest of all interchanges," and though her spirit will make her resist, her religious skepticism may undermine such resistance; even should she resist, her strength, her very energy, may destroy her mind, for energy, strong passions, and madness are closely allied in the repertoire, as the Hays passage suggests.

There is another strong voice in the dialogue besides the Godwinian, however. The didactic, centripetal governess novel often chastises such Godwinian passions, as in the case of, among others, Ellen ("the teacher") Delville, who was a bit too "passionate," whereas the heroine of the centrifugal, Godwinian Hays novel rejects teaching and tutoring for passion and "life." Predicting Jane's future and defining the moral universe of Brontë's novel, however, is more complicated than merely anticipating one or the other of these outcomes, for other possibilities are foreshadowed by other generic signals. The Godwinian passages are immediately followed by two paragraphs concerning "Grace Poole's" laugh.

The "silent revolt" passage has now been refracted for us by considerable critical comment and ideological echoes. Virginia Woolf, in *A Room of One's Own,* feels there is an "awkward break" between that passage and Grace Poole's laugh because female rage wells up in Brontë and makes her move away from the topic. Later critics, like Elaine Showalter, wonder why such an innocent and commonplace abruptness so disturbed Woolf (and her answer, as Cora Kaplan puts it, is that the problem is not Brontë's but Woolf's "inability to come to terms with her sexuality, with sexuality itself" [172]). Kaplan for her part convincingly finds that, though seemingly incoherent, there is not so much a break as a submerged relationship between the passage and the laugh (170–73). She points out that the passage is not narrowly feminist but includes "human beings" and "millions," many of whom are men:

> it is a significant moment of incoherence, where the congruence between the subordination of women and the radical view of class oppression becomes, for a few sentences, irresistible. It is a tentative, partial movement in spite of its defiant rhetoric, a movement which threatens to break up the more general, self-conscious [conventional] class politics of the text. And it brings with it, inexorably, its own narrative reaction which attempts with some success, to warn us quite literally that the association of feminism and class struggle leads to madness. (173)

. . . .

This cogent and convincing reading is a splendid example of a view of the text that it cannot have of itself.

The scene is immediately followed—though three months have passed in the fictional world—by Jane's encounter in the woods with the stranger who falls from his horse. Though Jane sees in this incident no seeds of further developments—"The incident had occurred and was gone for me: it was an incident of no moment, no romance, no interest in a sense; yet it marked with change one single hour of a monotonous life. . . . it was yet an active thing, and I was weary of an existence all passive" (140)—the reader's dialogic response may be somewhat different.

After all, who is this Rochester? Maidens alone in castles (or manor houses) in which there is some mystery are often threatened by gentlemen of rank, masters, Gothic villains. There is also the threat of Jane's "morally suspect" feminism, rebellion, Godwinism: will these flaws let her play into the hands of The Vile Seducer? On the other hand, unprotected governesses sometimes marry gentlemen, even their masters. Though the scowling figure does not resemble the heroes of governess novels at this point, love, that topic present in virtually all genres and belonging to none, may in one form or another be entering the world of *Jane Eyre*.

There have been earlier intimations of that possibility inserted into the reader's repertoire which this new possibility may recall. Single notes on the theme of love have been sounded from the beginning of the novel. If the novel opens as it does because the initial episode marks Jane's first moment of rebellion and therefore the beginning of her independent life, the condition of that rebellion involves not only John Reed's cruelty but Jane's exile from the happy family group near the fire. The only outlet for her love at Gateshead is her doll: "Human beings must love something, and, in the dearth of worthier objects of affection, I contrived to find pleasure in loving and cherishing a faded graven image, shabby as a miniature scarecrow" (29). Giving love and happiness is some solace, but not enough. She tells her aunt, "You think I have no feelings, and that I can do without one bit of love or kindness; but I cannot live so" (39). Later, she tells Helen that even self-approval and a clear conscience are not enough if there is no love:

. . . .

> . . . if others don't love me, I would rather die than live—I cannot bear to be solitary and hated, Helen. Look here: to gain some real affection from you, or Miss Temple, or any other whom I truly love, I would willingly submit to have the bone of my arm broken, or to let a bull toss me, or to stand behind a kicking horse, and let it dash its hoof at my chest. (80)

Such willingness to suffer to gain love in so passionate, rebellious, and self-reliant a character may very well foreshadow transgression and suffering, as the Hays passage suggests. Love and rebellion are linked in Jane's passionate nature: "I must resist those who punish me unjustly," she told Helen earlier. "It is as natural as that I should love those who show me affection, or submit to punishment when I feel it is deserved" (65). Then Helen urged turning the other cheek; now she emphasizes the limits of self-reliance and human love: "Hush, Jane! you think too much of the love of human beings; you are too impulsive, too vehement; the sovereign hand that created your frame, and put life into it, has provided you with other resources than your feeble self, or than creatures feeble as you" (81). Regardless of how we perceive it, Helen's warning becomes part of the heteroglossic world of the novel, at the very least an anticipatory caution: In the world of *Jane Eyre*, "love of human beings" in all instances and circumstances may not be an altogether moral and happy affair. And yet it is a love story that seems to be building in the final chapters of volume 1.

Though at Lowood there was no intimation of romantic love, Jane did know human love there, at first for Helen, then Miss Temple. For Miss Temple she feels more awe than ardor (85) and receives more kindness and affection than love. She feels warmer and more protective toward Helen, but without the serenity of her feelings toward Miss Temple. Even so qualified, love makes bleak Lowood preferable to the bourgeois comforts of Gateshead:

> Well has Solomon said:—"Better is a dinner of herbs where love is, than a stalled ox and hatred therewith."
>   I would not have exchanged Lowood with all its privation, for Gateshead and its daily luxuries. (87)[1]

None of this, however, suggests a love story. Helen dies; Miss Temple marries and leaves Lowood; Jane grows up, and she too leaves

Lowood. It is on her first morning at Thornfield that the muted note of romantic love is struck. Jane awakens anticipating that her new life will provide "flowers and pleasures, as well as its thorns and toils . . . : not perhaps that day or that month, but at an indefinite future period" (118). She dresses as attractively as possible:

> I sometimes regretted that I was not handsomer: I sometimes wished to have rosy cheeks, a straight nose, and small cherry mouth; I desired to be tall, stately, and finely developed in figure; I felt it a misfortune that I was so little, so pale, and had features so irregular and so marked. And why had I these aspirations and these regrets? It would be difficult to say: I could not then distinctly say it to myself; yet I had a reason, and a logical, natural reason too. (118–19)

The placement of this passage is puzzling. The logical and natural reason for Jane's attention to her appearance would seem to relate, certainly in retrospect, to her desire for romantic love, yet the passage appears a page *before* she learns there is a master and a Rochester and thus a possibility of romantic love even in dull Thornfield. A dozen pages later, Jane paces the third-story corridor, listening with her inner ear to a "tale that was never ended—a tale my imagination created and narrated continuously; quickened with all of incident, life, fire, feeling, that I desired and had not in my actual experience" (132). If this tale is also the tale of love, it too would seem premature, for Mr. Rochester does not appear for three or four more pages. Of course the narrator knows what is coming—she is, indeed, now Mrs. Rochester—and she (or Brontë) may be manipulating the sequence to heighten suspense or prepare the first-time reader for what good things are to come. There is a more subtle narrative possibility: though these passages are immediately followed by reference to Rochester, he may be another ignis fatuus, a red herring smeared across the narrative line to misdirect the expectations of the reader away from what will be the true outcome; this doubt may be reinforced by the ambiguity of Rochester's character—is he Byronic hero or Gothic villain? Finally, there is the more "agnostic" function: placing Jane's desire for and openness to love first creates expectations of her finding it, but introducing it *before* the introduction of Rochester makes him only one possibility, an immediate but not exclusive possibility. The "tale" passage, for example, in the context of the paragraph in which it appears, could refer to ventures or adventures uncommon for women and unrelated to love. Or— a possibility we may have reason to remember later—there may be a rival romantic hero.

Though the "logical and natural reason" for Jane's concern for her physical appearance and the subject of the tale her imagination continuously told her may be inferred from what follows, neither is specifically addressed by the narrative; both are "permanent gaps" in the text. The gaps are at the whim or discretion of the narrator. She is here withholding not only the reason and the tale but also, as she does throughout, all the information we are anxious to learn about Jane's future—we have not been told who or what occupies the third story of Thornfield, nor have we been told that the narrator is Mrs. Jane Rochester. The obvious purpose of such withholding is the generation of suspense or mystification, an end critics deplore (Booth 255) but readers demand, and the popularity of *Jane Eyre* then and now is in no small measure dependent on its brilliant modulation of mystery. Manipulating suspense does not necessarily make a work second-rate, as Booth implies, however, nor does eschewing it necessarily make for better art. The plot of *Caroline Mordaunt* is in many respects quite similar to that of *Jane Eyre,* and its outcome and "message" are revealed in the first paragraph; yet it is significantly inferior to *Jane Eyre,* and the early demystification is part of the reason (see below, ch. 7). In *Jane Eyre* the narrator's reticence generates suspense, but it also shrouds a larger mystery: what kind of fictional world is here embodied? As we shall see, the reader's blind experience in the "middest," remaining as ignorant as Jane, is essential to the moral purpose of the novel. Mystery or suspense often operates in this fashion: it engages the reader in shaping the fiction and the world of the fiction, projecting first one, then another configuration, uncovering, questioning, challenging the reader's assumption about cosmic and human reality. Plot in such a novel, and *Jane Eyre* is one, is a function of the fictional ontology; plot is a trivial concern only when the ontological base of the fiction is insignificant.

The narrator knows what will happen next, or, more accurately, what has already happened in the narrational past that is in the fictional future, but she chooses not to say, choosing to take advantage of the convention of the narrative past tense to give the illusion that the action is unfolding even as we read. Occasionally, however, she will draw back from the younger Jane, as in generalizing that children cannot argue with adults without feeling bad afterward, or explaining that the light in the red-room was probably from a lantern, or telling us that fifteen years after Helen's death an engraved marble tablet was placed on her grave. Sometimes the narrator will indicate that there is a space between her consciousness and Jane's without specifying what her new knowledge is, as in the passage wherein she says that "then" she could not have defined the reason she was concerned about her appearance. The occasional direct intrusion of the narrator's voice, separating her consciousness from that of the younger Jane, paradoxically calls attention to the fact that the narrative language and consciousness is most of the time doubled or "hybridized," "a mixture of two social languages within the limits of a single utterance, an encounter, within the arena of an utterance, between two different linguistic consciousnesses, separated from one another" (Bakhtin, *Dialogic* 358). The difference between the consciousnesses of the two Janes lies not only in the elder's knowledge of what is to happen in the fictional future but also in their epistemological and ontological views. The hybridized narration is not the mixture of "two *impersonal* language consciousnesses . . . but rather a mixture of two *individualized* language consciousnesses . . . and two individual language intentions as well: the individual, representing authorial consciousness and will [i.e., here the narrator Jane], on the one hand, and the individualized linguistic consciousness and will of the character represented [i.e., the younger Jane], on the other" (Bakhtin, *Dialogic* 359). The intentional novelistic hybrid (hybridization also takes places unintentionally in real language) does not only mix two language consciousnesses but presents "the collision between the differing points of views on the world that are embedded in these forms" (Bakhtin, *Dialogic* 360).

The momentary separation of the voices of the two Janes makes us scan the possibilities, alerting us to the variety of signals. We do not

THE TRANSGENERIC TOPIC, LOVE

yet know what the elder Jane is like, from what vantage—or disadvantage—she is writing, so though we cannot say that we read such passages with full knowledge of their import, we know that there is some difference in the perspectives of the younger and older Jane. The text from time to time tells us as much, but it does not always specify just when either voice is speaking or whether both are, as it were, speaking at once, hybridized. Narrative complexity as well as mixed generic signals alerts us to the multitude of possibilities of future events and of interpretation, and undermines simple conventional or preconceived certainty as to outcome or meaning. Doubt on both scores propels us forward, but we are meanwhile experiencing—or, in effect, creating—other futures, other outcomes, other novels, other worlds, all of which remain part of our total experience of *Jane Eyre.*

The narrator presumably also controls the pacing, the timing not only of revelations (of who or what is upstairs, for example) but also of juxtapositions, such as the placing of the natural concern of appearances before the mention of Rochester, and the imagined tale of fire and feeling before his actual appearance. The narrator does not fully control, however, the intertextuality, the dialogue of the narrative with contemporary and other novels and the consequent refraction; but this does not necessarily imply that a third consciousness or source of construction, the author—Charlotte Brontë a.k.a. Currer Bell—is in total control: "The author (speaker) has his own inalienable right to the word, but the listener [reader] also has his rights, and those whose voices are heard in the word before the author comes upon it [the fictional context] also have their rights. . . . [The word] is performed outside the author, and it cannot be introjected into the author" (Bakhtin, *Speech* 121–22).

The first encounter between Jane and Rochester in the lane reverberates with a variety of fictional kinds, so that what we might think of as the "normal" anticipation—[somewhat long-in-the-tooth-] boy-meets-girl—is to a degree inhibited or retarded. Perhaps it is not just the films and fame of *Jane Eyre* that make less informed readers "know" from the beginning that Rochester is to be a romantic hero but also readers' deafness to the cacophony of generic signals and to the subtleties of the first-person narration. Guessing "right" sometimes

. . . .

87

may mean reading "wrong," that is, missing not so much the "meaning" as the participatory experiencing of the text.

If there is anything approaching a clear generic signal in the lane scene, it is the Gothic or pseudo-Gothic, a signal that may be loud enough at this point to mute the note of conventional romantic love. It was, after all, only at the end of the previous chapter (ch. 11) that the strange laugh broke the stillness, and, we have even more recently been told, Jane has frequently heard the laugh these past three months.

Since romantic love of the usual sort is not foremost in the reader's mind, we are better able to accept the fact that the appearance of "the master" does not inevitably arouse romantic thoughts in Jane's mind. At the beginning of the next chapter (ch. 13), the stranger in the lane has been identified as Rochester, and he is now in residence at Thornfield. What his presence means to her at first is not the possibility of love, but what Hays's Emma called "scenes in motion" (1:54), for Jane the welcome end of tranquillity:

> Thornfield Hall was a changed place; no longer silent as a church, it echoed every hour or two to a knock at the door or a clang of the bell; steps, too, often traversed the hall, and new voices spoke in different keys below: a rill from the outer world was flowing through it; it had a master: for my part, I liked it better. (144)

The narrator's voice stays doubled with Jane's and does not help us read that final clause. Jane was bored with the tranquillity of Thornfield as she had been with that of Lowood in her last days there. She is seeking knowledge of life, and whether that knowledge will be of love or from "new voices in different keys," we cannot as yet be sure.

That first evening, before she is summoned into the master's presence, she stares into the fire, where she sees something like a castle on the Rhine. The picture is broken up by Mrs. Fairfax entering with the summons, her entrance "scattering too some heavy, unwelcome thoughts that were beginning to throng on my solitude" (145). The narrator again does not separate her voice from Jane's, does not reveal what these thoughts were: Is Jane fearful that Rochester will never seek her company? that no one will? Is she hurt by Adèle's telling her that Rochester asked that day whether the governess was that small,

. . . .

thin, pale person? At the moment this unexplained gloom serves to darken the tone of the forthcoming scene, vaguely encouraging the notion that even if Rochester does pay her attention Jane would be well advised to curb her impetuosity: this "love," even if it comes, may be less than happy.

Like her earlier aspirations and regrets and the pictures her imagination made, the definition of these heavy unwelcome thoughts is also left blank, the narrator never returning to define them, and so they remain permanent gaps in the text. Though we can never fill them in with certainty, we do not know at this point that we cannot, and so we are urged, if we are reading intensively, to scan once more the textual and contextual horizon for interpretations of the narrative reticence and its implications, attending both to point of view and genre. This is not necessarily an emphatic or enduring pause in our reading. We may be scarcely conscious of the pause and retrospective/prospective action of our focus, so that when the gap is neither filled nor enlarged upon, we may forget its very existence. It would seem logical that on second reading, knowing that this gap will not be filled and so is inconsequential in the outcome of the novel, we would be less likely to pause, and so the gap would lose its functional control over our attention. Paradoxically, the opposite is more likely to be true: knowing that nothing will be made of this, perhaps a little less eager to turn the page and get to the bottom of the mystery than on first reading, we are all the more likely to pause here and explore the implications and function of the gap.

What is true here of the gap is more true than is usually recognized of the function of details and devices in the text: they continue to operate on the reader during subsequent readings, though perhaps with slightly different degrees of force and effect. The strategies of the text that may seem designed for suspense and other aspects of a first reading are a permanent part of the pattern of the text. A straight line and a maze with identical termini do not constitute identical patterns. A second reading that heads right for the exit does not improve, but impoverishes, our appreciation of the text.

As if to mark the gap or emphasize the pause and so to keep our mind hovering over the text, scanning back and forth—or per-

. . . .

haps to make us content to remain within the confines of young Jane's language and consciousness—the gloomy thoughts at the fire are followed by an interview with Rochester in which Jane is at her best. She is realistic but not materialistic. She expects no gifts and is not sure she would want one. She gives her honest opinion of Brocklehurst—he is a harsh, pompous, meddling man. Put at her ease by Rochester's gruff manner, which does away with the need for polite evasions, she is free to be her candid, forthright self. But if Rochester is as charmed by her as we are, and if he is not an honorable man, will honesty alone suffice?

Jane is loving, passionate, generous, direct, and honest; she is not greedy or grasping, cruel or mean-minded. Her need for love and her temper, however, may signal danger in her circumstances: Is she too passionate or tempestuous, too independent and self-reliant, especially for a young woman? Will real knowledge come at too high a price, the perils of her ego and ignorance being greater than the prize? Despite the first-person narration, we do not always know what she is thinking then, and because of the hybridization we do not know how the elder narrator views all of young Jane's thoughts and actions in these scenes. Unless we are reading "mono-aurally," listening only for the voice that is an echo of our own, we do not know for certain whether Jane is properly prudent, or excitingly, admirably independent; we do not know what to expect, what kind of novel we are reading, what kind of moral universe we are in. And so we are engaged in a dialogue of expectation with the text.

If what we anticipate depends largely on our view of Jane, it may depend even more on how we see Rochester: is he Byronic hero or Gothic villain? We must look at him more closely now as he half-reclines there on the couch. But what we see is only what the young Jane sees; the voice of the narrator is subsumed within young Jane's, and the voices "heard in the word before the author [came] upon it" are not conclusive. The initial physical description of him sends out mixed signals. He is not entirely attractive or attractively ugly. True, his nose is decisive and indicative of character, but beware: his nostrils denote, "[Jane] thought, choler; his . . . mouth, chin, and jaw . . . were very grim," and he was "neither tall nor graceful" (146). His actions

· · · · · ·

and words do little to clarify his moral character. His brusque manner is not entirely charming, and he is masterful to the point of being rude (even though he apologizes, explaining that he is used to command). We cannot be sure just what he thinks of Jane. He is grumpily pleased—"Humph!" he says—at Jane's sharp answer when he accuses her of false modesty; he admits she plays the piano better than "some" English schoolgirls; and he assumes that her drawing master did the best parts of the watercolors she shows him. Then he says brusquely, as if merely to show his power—or is it that he is too pleased by her forthrightness?—"There,—put the drawings away! . . . It is nine o'clock: what are you about, Miss Eyre, to let Adèle sit up so long? Take her to bed" (155).

This first acquaintance with Rochester is immediately followed by Mrs. Fairfax's sketchy history of his brother's injustice toward Edward, the brother's sudden death, and the present Mr. Rochester's brief and sporadic visits to Thornfield. The Gothic possibilities here, if they do not obscure, certainly overshadow whatever romantic possibilities there may be at this point. Romance from Rochester is more a threat than a promise.

If there is to be a love story, the next chapter (ch. 14) begins inauspiciously: Rochester is busy and sees little of Jane for several days. His excuse is hardly that of a would-be lover: "I have almost forgotten you . . . : other ideas have driven yours from my head" (162). Though tonight he wants to talk and listen and seems more pleasant, Jane suspects the change may merely be the effect of wine (159). The scene that ensues, however, is one of the most delightful in the novel. It is difficult to believe ill of Rochester, to resist his gruff charm and intriguing air of misery and mystery. We cannot feel Jane in danger either from him or from herself. She is at once her sauciest and most moral. She sees in his eyes something more than the glitter of wine: "He had great, dark eyes, and very fine eyes, too; not without a certain change in their depths sometimes, which, if it was not softness, reminded you, at least, of that feeling" (160). But when he asks if she finds him handsome, she cannot tell a lie: "No, sir." Nor does she find him benevolent, though he is no fool; her diagnosis is partly based on, partly confirmed by, phrenology:

. . . .

91

He lifted up the sable waves of hair which lay horizontally over his brow, and showed a solid enough mass of intellectual organs; but an abrupt deficiency where the suave signs of benevolence should have risen.

". . . No, young lady, I am not a general philanthropist; but I bear a conscience"; and he pointed to the prominences which are said to indicate that faculty—and which, fortunately for him, were sufficiently conspicuous. (161)

Phrenology is an "occupied" word. For us it is a pseudoscience, and we read this passage as quaint, even, perhaps, vaguely amusing. Phrenology early in the nineteenth century was not, however, associated with pseudoscience but with neurological science itself; its premise, that there was a connection between the body and psyche, was considered in some quarters sacrilegious, and Jane and Rochester's use of it thus may be dangerous. See, e.g., Captain Marryat's *Mr. Midshipman Easy* (1836), in which the eponymous moral hero (not to say, prig) flees his father's house because of his father's unholy experiments in changing the shape of the skull in order to change character (an early analogue of genetic engineering?). When the hero returns, having been successful within the more rigid and "moral" regimen of the Royal Navy, the old man has killed himself by having crushed his own skull. This novel gives the same warning as Mary Shelley's *Frankenstein; Or, The Modern Prometheus:* we should not mess with God's world. (See also Feltes.) This reliance on "science" rather than more conventional social and religious signs for the reading of character on the part of Jane and Rochester may have reinforced somewhat the radical, dangerous Godwinism that plays some part in the structure and strategy of *Jane Eyre* and so angered critics like Elizabeth Rigby. It seems to outradical a Wollstonecraft/Shelley. It may also serve as an anticipatory caution, warning us that all may not be morally well in the future relationship between Rochester and Jane.

Both Rochester and Jane recognize that their reading of the other's character may be wrong, that the other may have as yet unperceived "intolerable defects" (165). Rochester admits to defects, though he insists he is no villain, but only "a trite common-place sinner, hackneyed in all the poor petty dissipations with which the rich and worthless

· · · · · · ·

try to put on life," and like the other "defaulters" lays "half the blame on ill fortune and adverse circumstances" (165).

Jane takes the moral high ground, recommending repentance and reformation as the cures for remorse, and warning him that he cannot himself make up new moral laws no matter what the circumstances: "The human and fallible should not arrogate a power with which the divine and perfect alone can be safely entrusted" (169). Rochester insists that she is too inexperienced to judge such matters, and indeed it is difficult to imagine just where she came up with such views. Perhaps from Miss Temple or Helen? Are these earned insights or echoes of others? Jane herself has arrogated the power of vengeance and, though remorseful afterward, does not seem to have repented or reformed. Humility before a power greater than hers does not at this point seem one of Jane's most notable virtues. Is this moral voice the voice of the young Jane, of the narrator, or of conventional Christianity? Once more, narrative reticence makes unraveling the hybridized voice of young Jane here difficult. Her serene certainty may be reassuring (Jane has grown up to be a morally mature young woman) or paradoxically ominous (is she speaking out of the pompousness and pretentiousness of inexperience, as Rochester suggests?). We are by our questions or assumed answers in dialogue with young Jane and the text.

Uncertainty is in many way the keynote of the scene. Rochester seems to be making veiled allusions to past actions and present intentions that Jane has difficulty in following. At the height of her discomfort, when Jane wants to terminate the discussion, Rochester says, "Wait a minute: Adèle is not ready to go to bed yet" (171). The child is trying on her new dress, a present from Rochester: "In a few minutes she will re-enter; and I know what I shall see,—a miniature of Céline Varens, as she used to appear on the boards . . . my tenderest feelings are about to receive a shock" (171). As Adèle appears and the chapter ends, the possibility grows still stronger that Céline was the cause of Rochester's downfall, that Adèle is perhaps his own daughter, that they are the reasons for his remorse. Any marriage of the minds of Jane and Rochester seems to admit the impediments of Céline and Adèle. As the curtain comes down on chapter 14 we seem to be at the base of a love triangle, and that is what we are left to ponder during the space

. . . .

created by the chapter's end. Governess and Gothic and all genres and contexts other than that of the conventional love story have been for the moment pushed to the rear.

The gap in the final sentence of the chapter—"I'll explain all this some day"—proves to be a very temporary one. The explanation comes early in the next chapter; the "threat" of Céline as a rival seems blunted. But as that conflict recedes into the background, a new possibility based on a recently neglected configuration and concern comes to the fore. Even while telling Jane the banal story of his passion for Céline, her betrayal of him, his jealousy[2]—which seems to be building up to another triangle with Jane at the center—he looks up at the battlements of Thornfield with

> a glare such as I never saw before or since. Pain, shame, ire—impatience, disgust, detestation—seemed momentarily to hold a quivering conflict in the large pupil dilating under his ebon eyebrow . . . another feeling rose and triumphed: something hard and cynical; self-willed and resolute: it settled his passion and petrified his countenance. (175)

This sequence, following so hard on the heels of the story of betrayal, seems to suggest some relationship between Céline and the mystery of Thornfield: Is Céline locked away in the upper reaches of Thornfield Manor? Will Céline, like Mrs. Herbert in "Parson Clare," escape imprisonment, go beserk, and by mistake kill her own daughter? or, like the legitimate Lady Glenfallen, sneak into Jane's room to cut her throat? Or does her ghost inhabit the Hall? Though the narrator's voice is still doubled with young Jane's, there are other "voices in the word" of this situational topos; they are loud and clear, but not univocal, and though they lead us beyond Jane's vision, just where is uncertain.

Later, in bed, Jane's meditations emphasize the connection between Céline and the strange goings-on in the manor by reviewing Rochester's story, his brief suggestion that he is beginning to like Thornfield again after having hated it for so long, and his complex, intense, emotional glare at the Hall. Jane recalls the look and wonders what alienates him from Thornfield: "I hardly know whether I had slept or not after this musing; at any rate I started wide awake on hearing a vague murmur, peculiar and lugubrious, which sounded, I thought, just above me. I wished I had kept my candle burning; the night was drearily dark; my spirits were depressed" (182). Something brushes by her door. She has almost fallen asleep when she hears "a demoniac laugh—low, suppressed, and deep—uttered, as it seemed, at the very key-hole of my chamber-door. . . . I thought at first, the goblin-laugher stood at my bedside—or rather, crouched at my pillow" (182). Though some readers might now recall the blind wife in LeFanu's tale, with Jane in the situation of the bigamous usurper, Jane's suspicions are more mundane; she does not conjure up a demon or even an incarcerated wife or mistress but the ordinary if inexplicable Grace Poole. She does wonder, however, if Grace is "possessed with a devil" (183). She goes into the hall and finds that smoke is issuing from Rochester's room. He is unconscious, overcome by smoke, and his bed is on fire. Jane douses his bed and him.

With words and phrases like "demoniac," "goblin-laugher," "unnatural," "possessed with a devil," and emotional signals like "chilled with fear," "affrighted," "scared," "marrow-freezing," "a trembling hand," the Gothic has reentered the picture with a vengeance. Though Jane assumes the arsonist is Grace Poole, Rochester's history, his glare, and the juxtaposition of that and the fire suggest that Céline Varens (dead or alive), rather than the ghost of Rowland Rochester, may be the presence upstairs.

The power of the love story is in the process of obliterating all contrary signals. Indeed, with fires, the heroine in the hero's bedroom in the middle of the night, and veiled references to the possibility of dishabille, romantic love is verging on sexual love, a border closer to Godwin than Gothic, closer still to Richardson. When a fire in the middle of the night is put out and Lovelace goes to Clarissa to tell her the danger is over, she comes to the door with "nothing on but an under-petticoat, her lovely bosom half-open," as he describes the scene in his letter to John Belford (Letter 225, 723). He embraces her, carries her to the bed, and sits beside her, often referring in his letter to her near-nakedness. He kisses her; she is furious at his treachery; and, though she is induced to forgive him, she says she will not see him for at least a week.

There was, in fact, a much more immediately precedent "word" occupying this narrative space: in Mrs. Jewsbury's *Zoe* (1845), a fire

. . . . . .

scene precipitates a first approach to forbidden love. There the love is between the half-English, half-Greek (*cherchez l'étrangère*) Mrs. Zoe Gifford—mother of two sons, leader of fashion—and Everhard (*sic!*), a Catholic priest who has lost his faith. On the very night Everhard has decided that he loves Zoe and that, therefore, he must never see her again, there is a fire. The whole of Gifford Castle is aroused (so to speak). Knowing she would not leave unless her sons were safe, Everhard leads them out of the castle and returns for her. When he finds her and assures her her children are safe,

> she gasped, and fell an insensible weight in his arms.
>
> The surprise, the alarm, the possible danger, were forgotten, he only felt the warm, palpitating burden which lay upon his bosom; he was too much overpowered by sensations to move—they stupefied him—the intense enjoyment amounted to pain. He, who in his whole life had never touched a woman, now had a whole life of passion melted into that moment.
>
> He crushed her into his arms with ferocious love,—he pressed burning kisses upon her face, her lips, and her bosom; but kisses were too weak to express the passion that was within him. It was madness like hatred,—beads of sweat stood thick on his forehead, and his breath came in gasps. (80)

He carries her to the chapel, where the altar light reveals her state. She comes to. The passion is not one-sided, but though Zoe too yields to its power, she is the first to recover. There is a large shawl nearby which allows her to hide her shame, and Everhard, trained in self-control, manages to master himself.

> A light burned before the altar,—he bore her to the steps, and sprinkled her face and hands with water from a vessel that stood near. Zoe opened her eyes, and saw Everhard bending over her. The colour rushed over her face and neck. Everhard made an effort to turn away, but, almost unconsciously, he fell on his knees beside her; and the next moment, Zoe's burning arms were round his neck, and her long hair fell like a veil over him. Everhard's brain was in a whirl, and his veins ran fire, as he felt her warm breath upon him.
>
> Zoe was the first to recover from the delirium of the moment; she struggled to disengage herself from his arms, and seizing a large shawl

. . . .

which had fallen on the ground, attempted to cover herself with it, exclaiming,

"Oh, Everhard, what will you think of me? I have made you hate me—despise me. Forgive me for letting you betray yourself, it was the last thing you desired to do."

The sound of her voice in broken tones, recalled Everhard to his senses; the force of long years of the habit of self-control was not lost in this trying moment; with an effort almost superhuman he suffered Zoe to disengage herself, and retreated against a pillar at a little distance; he twisted his hands in each other, and stood crushing himself against the stone, whilst a spasm of sharp pain attested the energy of his efforts to master himself.

Zoe, meantime, lay crouched on the steps of the altar, she did not dare to raise her eyes towards Everhard. (80)

Kathleen Tillotson quotes from Jewsbury's letters to show how inflammatory this scene was considered at the time:

In 1845 Geraldine Jewsbury had to alter one scene of her first novel, *Zoe*, by arranging—in her own mocking words—"for a more liberal distribution of spotted muslin" [the "large shawl" in the passage?]. . . . She cannot have supplied enough of it, since *Zoe* was "put into a dark cupboard in the Manchester Library of that day—because . . . [it was] calculated to injure the morals of the *young men*." (60–61)

The link between Brontë and Jewsbury may be seen in the *Jerrold's* review of *The Half Sisters* alluded to earlier, for it praises Jewsbury in terms that might readily, and even more appropriately, apply to Brontë: "[It is] in the infinite variety of illustration of the feelings and emotions that she is superior to all other female writers we have met with." The review defends "her war . . . with convention, as far as it stands in opposition to the development of natural powers and feelings" (*Jerrold's* 7 [1848]: 371).

Surely Charlotte Brontë was not poking about in the dark cupboards of the Manchester Library while attending her father during his eye operation in Manchester and while beginning *Jane Eyre*, just a year after Jewsbury's novel was published? Brontë's heroine, who is the rescuer rather than rescued, is decorous from the beginning: Jane

. . . .

hurriedly puts on a "frock and shawl" (185) before venturing out of her room. Her hero, however, has no such opportunity but does so as soon as he can. When the fire is out, Jane offers to bring a candle, but he warns her, "at your peril you fetch a candle yet: wait two minutes till I get into some dry garments" (184). The fire is doused before the lovers can become inflamed, and Rochester is off to the third story to find out what happened. He returns, but before he answers Jane's questions he finds out what she knows and suspects, and he abruptly confirms that indeed it was, as Jane thought, Grace Poole. Few readers will have been convinced, though for most the scene in the bedroom is surely more absorbing than what might be going on up above, the mystery not having a ghost of a chance in the lurid glare of the dawn of sexual love.

That fire is not quite out. Rochester takes both Jane's hands in his, saying he could have tolerated no one else but her to have been his "cherished preserver" (187). There is "strange fire in his look." He will not let her go. Even Jane is beginning to suspect what the romantic reader has long been suspecting—that Rochester is strongly attracted to her. She extricates herself by (we assume) pretending to hear Mrs. Fairfax stirring.

Jane is less inflamed than the half-foreign Zoe, but her passion is no less real. Passion in these pages takes the form not of fire but of flood. Earlier in the chapter, Rochester has told her,

> "You think all existence lapses in as quiet a flow as that in which your youth has hitherto slid away. Floating on with closed eyes and muffled ears, you neither see the rocks bristling not far off in the bed of the flood, nor hear the breakers boil at their base. But I tell you . . . you will come some day to a craggy pass of a channel, where the whole of life's stream will be broken up into whirl and tumult, foam and noise; either you will be dashed to atoms on cragpoints, or lifted up and borne on by some master wave into a calmer current." (174–75)

And now, when Rochester finally releases her, Jane retires to her bed, but not to rest. She is tossed about by passion, joy, hope—and doubt:

> I regained my couch, but never thought of sleep. Till morning dawned I was tossed on a buoyant but unquiet sea, where billows of trouble rolled

· · · · · ·

under surges of joy. I thought sometimes I saw beyond its wild waters a shore, sweet as the hills of Beulah; and now and then a freshening gale, wakened by hope, bore my spirit triumphantly towards the bourne: but I could not reach it, even in fancy,—a counteracting breeze blew off the land, and continually drove me back. Sense would resist delirium: judgment would warn passion. Too feverish to rest, I rose as soon as day dawned. (187–88)

As the Clarendon edition explains (592–93), "Beulah" in Hebrew means "married." The editors cite Isaiah 62:4—"Thou shalt no more be termed Forsaken; neither shall thy land any more be termed Desolate"—and *The Pilgrim's Progress,* where the land of Beulah, lying beyond the shadow of death, is the scene where "the contract between the Bride and the Bridegroom will be renewed." So, after the fire, in Rochester's bed and in his eyes, comes the flood, over him and over his bed and over Jane's imagination. And Jane glimpses a joyous future in marriage, which, however, even in her imagination she could not as yet reach.

It is in this turbulent state that the first volume of *Jane Eyre* ends. Filling the foreground, despite the Gothic shadows that hover about the Hall, is the love story. The suspense, our expectations, center on the outcome of that story: will the freshening gale carry her toward marriage and bliss or will the offshore breeze keep her from that bourne? It is that question the reader must ask the text while putting down volume 1, reaching for and opening volume 2, and settling down for a good read.

This first major punctuated pause and the question mark compel a rapid mental review of the whole novel to this point. All the heteroglossic voices—the Godwinian, the Byronic, the Gothic; those of the foundling novel and the governess novel—now seem to be telling a dialogic love story. Because of the multiple refractions, the nature of that story and its outcome is in doubt: Is this the conventional romantic plot? Or is it to be the story of Godwinian or feminist rebellion precipitating the heroine into dire straits which she may or may not navigate successfully? Or is it a Gothic tale not only of mystery but

. . . .

of seduction? The voices are familiar but the cacophony is new; the old conventional parts in their very multiplicity have made an original and mystifying story, a new species of novel. Though not a "history of events," as Fonblanque would prefer, neither is *Jane Eyre* simply an analysis of a single mind.

. . . .

Strategies of the Text

T hough this study set out to read the text of *Jane Eyre* with rigorous sequentiality, it was immediately deflected from that "straight line" to the fictional context, the dialogue or discourse of the novel into which it was "speaking" and through which it was generating its ideational and affective significance. Though there will still be occasions when it must define itself and make its meaning in terms of the contemporary or traditional fictional context, the earlier portions of the text itself serve increasingly as its own context, much as an author's early novels serve as context for his or her later ones. Once again, therefore, the reader is deflected from the unilinear forward movement through the text, now not "beyond" the text but "backward" along the line of the text, in order to bring to the textual or reading moment or detail recollected past moments that seem relevant. The recollection acts almost like an "alien" text in refracting the present textual moment, and, more important for our purposes here, it renders synchronic, vertical, or spatialized what was diachronic, horizontal, temporal, and consecutive.[1] Connecting the past moment(s) to the present moment of reading is an act of com-prehension, making a pattern which then projects a tentative configuration of what is yet to come, a configuration of the novel as a whole. Like formal units, such spatialization may be seen as a function of the textual code or as an operation of the reading subject, and as we did in discussing segmentation of the text into units, we may invoke our dialogized quantum

. . . .

101

theory that accepts neither version as definitive but accepts both in a dialectical relationship. Looking for the moment from the vantage point of the critical reader, spatialization—the bringing together of elements from earlier portions of the text and projecting forward a configuration—though deviating from the unilinear progression from word-the-first to word-the-last of the text, is not a deviation from but is inherent in the act of reading.

The first section of this study concentrated on the linear and contextual dimensions. This second section, though it continues to read the text linearly and will not neglect the novelistic context when appropriate, will concentrate on the spatial or vertical dimension of the text. It will consider the directions for spatializing as strategies of the text but will often trace the realizing of the strategies through the reader's performance of the work.

To illustrate this recollective, projective, spatializing reading and the ambivalent roles of textual signals and the reader, we might depart for a moment from linear reading to look at a passage well into the third volume of *Jane Eyre:*

> I was almost as hard beset by him now as I had been once before, in a different way, by another. I was a fool both times. To have yielded then would have been an error of principle; to have yielded now would have been an error of judgment. So I think at this hour, when I look back to the crisis through the quiet medium of time: I was unconscious of folly at the instant. (534)

We see in this passage the three virtual dimensions of time in the fictional action of the novel that give the second, spatial dimension to the text: "now," despite the past tense of the narration ("I was almost . . ."), is the virtual present, the moment of the fictional action; "then" is the fictional past—in this case an event which has been dramatized earlier in the novel; "in this hour," which is the narrator's present, the moment in which she is writing this part of her autobiography, is, in terms of the fictional action, the future, for the reader does not as yet know of the events that intervene between the fictional present and the time of narration.

These signals guide the reader's active participation in the text.

. . . .

The virtual present is also the reader's actual present: the reader is at this moment taking in the information given in the text. The virtual past—"then"—is in the reader's actual past, the reader having read the scene referred to in the past, but the text here recalls it, and not other earlier scenes, into the reader's present, so that it is present only as memory is present. The narrator's present is, for the reader, present, past, and future: the thoughts being thought by the narrator "at this hour" are being read in the actual present, but the knowledge the narrator has of the fictional events between the fictional "now" and the narrator's writing about them is in the reader's future; yet, of course, the entire book has been written in the past, before the reader has read even the title and opening sentence. The time of the fictional action, then, is that of the reader who is taking in what is happening in the passage, recalling the earlier scene in which Jane was "beset" and comparing and distinguishing it from that of the present, unaware of what will happen between the time of this action and the time of the narration. The statement that Jane "was unconscious of folly at the instant" informs the reader that Jane at the time of the narrating knows that for Jane at the time of the fictional action, to have yielded would have been folly; it also heightens the suspense by informing the reader that Jane was then unconscious that it would be folly and so just might yield.

Except at the very beginning and ending of a novel, these three aspects of narrative time are continually present. We take in the information given in the text's present. We recollect what we have read and put it together with what we are at present reading in order to com-prehend the text, and we make a pattern of the as-yet-incomplete novel. This tentative configuration inevitably anticipates the narrative and thematic future of the text and is an image not only of "the whole story" but also of the "whole world" or worldview of the novel.

Other signals in the text can serve functions similar to such words as "then" and "now": repetitions of key words or images, for example, may invite the reader to recall in the reading present events from the reading or fictional past. Here, for example, the phrase "then . . . principle" would recollect for us that Jane had, in that earlier scene, based her refusal of Rochester on principles and the laws of God and man and had at the time identified violation of such laws not only as mere

. . . .

folly but also as something that has significantly figured in the novel already—insanity:

> "I will keep the law given by God; sanctioned by man. I will hold to the principles received by me when I was sane, and not mad—as I am now. Laws and principles are not for the times when there is no temptation: they are for such moments as this, when body and soul rise in mutiny against their rigour; stringent are they: inviolate they shall be." (404–5)

The word and concept of "principles" in connection with the later scene should act as a mnemonic trigger, especially since the reader has been reminded of it at least once before. When Jane has just become a teacher at Morton, she asks herself whether this rather desolate position is better than living in France as Rochester's beloved and indulged mistress. She answers, "Yes; I feel now that I was right when I adhered to principle and law, and scorned and crushed the insane promptings of a frenzied moment. God directed me to a correct choice: I thank his Providence for the guidance!" (459). Here again, to yield is identified not with folly—of which Jane is capable—but with insanity. It is difficult to believe that Jane, having already witnessed the example of Bertha, would allow herself to succumb to insanity—loss of rational or moral control. While we therefore expect her to resist, we also have a horrific vision of her future should she yield now to St. John.

If we can bring forward these passages with a certain degree of circumstantiality and verbal recall, this passage from the ninth chapter of volume 3 will not only educate our expectations and the projected configuration of the plot but will also weave the action together with the thematic patterns of passion and principles, uncontrolled passion and insanity, principle and Providence, into a deep and rich texture.

To say that the textual signals should recall the scene in which Jane was "beset" by Rochester and might well recall such thematic elements as principles, passion, insanity, and Providence is not to say that this is all they can or should recall. If all readers will recall Rochester's proposal, many the role of principle, some the intermediate reference to principle and insanity, each will respond to what he or she hears as other echoes—Jane's defiance of Brocklehurst, for example, who also "beset" her in his way and who, as a black pillar, may recall St. John

. . . .

Rivers, the man of marble. Neither do these signals definitively determine the reader's configuration and projection of the future shape or
development of the text. Nor does the richness of the reading and the
consequent configuration guarantee the projection of the right narrative or thematic outcome. At times, indeed, the rich reading only com-
plicates our expectations by multiplying the possibilities and therefore
inevitably involves "misreading." But good reading does not necessarily consist in guessing correctly what will happen or what the text
will show its world to be, but in being aware as much as possible of
what the novel suggests might be.

As with earlier chapters, the four chapters and afterword to follow
are not exclusively focused on what the theory-oriented titles and *Jane
Eyre*-specific subtitles denote. The strategies and subjects central to one
chapter are inevitably considered elsewhere as the sequential reading
of the text dictates. Thus we have already noticed in earlier chapters
that sometimes the narrator speaks in her own (mature) voice; sometimes monologically in that of the younger, experiencing Jane; and
often in a combination of the two that we refer to, following Bakhtin,
as hybridized. The modulation of the narrating voice is a significant
part of the narrative strategy and perhaps an even more significant
factor in the ontological strategy. Often these strategies coincide with
or complement each other. It is important for plot and suspense that
we do not know all that the narrator knows from the beginning but
are subject to the same doubts, errors, and discoveries in more or less
the same sequence as Jane; there are but few instances in which Jane's
ignorance or blindness or error is treated ironically. What Jane will
learn about the cosmos in the course of the novel is that Providence
and not she is in charge of her life; the reader who is reading here as
a member of what Rabinowitz calls the "authorial audience"—assuming and attempting to grasp an authorial intention—only gradually
learns the same lesson, and that is the apparent didactic lesson of the
novel, which would be rhetorically ineffective if it were prematurely
divulged to the reader over Jane's head. If Providence were Fate and
Jane's life predestined, both she and the reader could be apprised of
this at once. But Brontë's Providence merely guides and warns. It is the

. . . . . .

responsibility of the "pilgrim," who has free will, to notice these signs, read them aright, and follow the guidance. The reader, put in the same ontological state as young Jane, must also learn to look for and interpret signs. Both the suspense and the psychological and moral power of *Jane Eyre* rely heavily on the control of the hybridized and monologic voices. This is further complicated by the fact that Jane grows spiritually as well as physically during the course of the novel, so that Jane's voice in the early chapters is not necessarily the same as her voice in the middle or later chapters. There are, then, not two voices of Jane—narrator and actor—but three: narrator and younger and maturing Jane. Hybridization, along with the consequent spatialization, and the interrelation of plot and ontology are the major critical areas of exploration in the fifth chapter of this study.

The sixth chapter explores that portion of the novel in which the secret of Thornfield Manor is revealed and Jane leaves it and Rochester behind. These chapters offer a particularly dramatic instance of spatialization. In effect, the whole Thornfield half of the novel and even to some degree the Lowood chapters that preceded it are devastated. Jane's life and her life story retreat to the first pages of the novel. As Jane says, she is a cold, solitary girl again. This chapter examines the frequent repetitions, recollections, and revisitations of earlier scenes and details in this most recapitulative section.

One of the dramatic repetitions with variation involves the way the volumes are structured: the last words of the second volume echo the troubled-water imagery and Biblical allusions with which the first volume ended, but where the earlier was full of hope tinctured with anxiety, the later is full of despair. Here the strategy seems most indisputably to be the formal strategy of the text; the reader's only responsibility for realizing this powerful "reminder" is to notice.

The seventh chapter continues examining the roles of text and reader. St. John Rivers emerges as a virtual antagonist, at least for many readers. He offers Jane a new life as his wife and helpmate on a sacred venture, but for Jane (and the reader) this would mean giving up all thoughts of Rochester, of romantic love, of fulfillment of what she has to this point thought of as her own nature. Chapter 7 of this study argues that in order to realize both the affective impact and the nature of the ontological choice being made by the text, this possibility should be taken seriously and entertained as a potentially godly path. We should be in doubt about not only the outcome of the plot but even which outcome is the more desirable within the world and ideology of *Jane Eyre*. This is, in effect, to recommend reading at this point and at least for a time as a member of the "authorial audience." It is clear that the majority of readers then and now, and especially now, "see the text as it cannot see itself," and do not take the possibility of Jane's marrying St. John seriously and certainly do not think it desirable.

Here there is a dramatic instance of the ubiquitous but usually less-clearly visible dimension of the text that goes beyond the linear, spatial, and even the contextual dimensions: the reader's dimension or site (see n. 1). The reader, no matter how determined to be a loyal part of the authorial audience, can never fully "coincide with" the text or fully realize its or the author's "intention." The "words" of the text are always occupied for the reader by alien terms. In that sense, a sense that is constitutive of this study, *all* readings are therefore "misreadings."[2] Where there are significant historical or cultural shifts between the time of the text and of the reading, the entire ideological base of the text may seem alien or even invisible. Though to read a text only from our own cultural and ideological site is perhaps no more a misreading than that of the Victorian novel-reader, we forgo an advantage that we have over that reader: he or she cannot see the text from our historical-cultural-ideological position, but we can see it both from our own and, to some extent, from the recovered norms or conventions of 1847, which not only permits us to see the text as it cannot see itself—even as historical ignorance would—*but permits us to see thereby the contingency of our own ideological site.*

Perhaps part of the difficulty in comprehending St. John is "ideological" in a more purely literary sense: that is, he is the most truly original creation in this novel (at least, I have been unable to find a precedent for his character and role in the novels of the time). In a sense, then, he is not "narratable" and so cannot fulfill for the reader the dialogic role given him by the author or text.

The final chapter of this study also concentrates on St. John, but here in an attempt to explain why in terms of an authorial-audience

. . . . . .

107

reading he is the focus of the final, Biblically oriented words of Jane Eyre's autobiography. In doing so, the chapter explores historically and theoretically the nature of the largely period-specific genre of the fictional autobiography.

Chapter 8 suggests that *Jane Eyre* moves beyond Jane; the afterword suggests that it moves beyond Charlotte Brontë.

. . . . . .

5

Hybridization:
The Three Voices of Jane

Volume 1 ends with Jane rising from her sleepless bed at dawn, having tossed and turned with tantalizing visions of "Beulah." Volume 2 opens not long after. Jane goes downstairs that morning as tense and expectant of love as the reader is of a love story: "I both wished and feared to see Mr. Rochester" (191). Love, not fully or directly expressed, is foremost in her mind, and the love story foremost in the reader's. Both are teased by delay: Jane by events, the reader by the narrator's reticence. The house is abuzz with talk of the fire that Rochester is supposed to have quenched himself, but he is nowhere to be seen. Grace Poole, who, Rochester had confirmed, was the arsonist, is there, astonishingly cool. Jane wonders "why she had not been given into custody that morning; or at the very least dismissed from her master's service" (195). Jane's head and heart are filled with thoughts of love, so despite the contrary evidence of Grace's flat figure and coarse features, Jane can only make Grace part of a love story: perhaps when young, she was Rochester's mistress, and so now has a hold on him. . . .

The day passes—and so do several pages—and still no Rochester or word of him, until, at tea, Mrs. Fairfax mentions that Mr. Rochester has a fair night for his journey. He is off to the Eshtons, where among the house guests will be Miss Blanche Ingram. It is the first Jane and the reader have heard of her. Here is a much more likely and formidable rival than Grace or the faithless Céline; in the housekeeper's description, Blanche Ingram seems almost the beauty Jane had wished herself to be the night she arrived at Thornfield—"Tall, fine bust, sloping shoulders; long, graceful neck; olive complexion, dark and clear; noble features; eyes rather like Mr. Rochester's: large and black and brilliant as her jewels" (199)—and as accomplished as she is beautiful.

The love story now settles into the typical triangle. Jane must contend with the lovely and accomplished Blanche if she is to win what she now knows she desires, Rochester's love. What chance does plain Jane have? She feels there is none. She is ashamed at her vanity in misinterpreting Rochester's feelings:

> "It does good to no woman to be flattered by her superior, who cannot possibly intend to marry her; and it is madness in all women to let a secret love kindle within them, which, if unreturned and unknown, must devour the life that feeds it; and, if discovered and responded to, must lead, *ignis fatuus*-like into miry wilds whence there is no extrication." (201)

This is not merely Jane's personal, prudential code, but "occupied" territory; Margaret Russell, for example, in the fictional autobiography of 1846, has a similar experience and regret: "In an unguarded moment I had overstepped the native modesty of womanhood. . . . [I] loved— and without a return of love!" (68). In Harriet Martineau's *Deerbrook*, a governess novel of 1839, for a woman, unasked, to tell her love is "horrible and disgusting" (164). "A very important rule of behaviour [in popular fiction] was that a woman did not allow herself to love till she knew she was beloved. This was no doubt connected with the general belief in the spiritualized sexual organization of women, in contrast to the earthy passions of men" (Dalziel 97). This rule and its assumptions about female sexuality were not, however, universally accepted in the fiction of the period. We have already seen in Jewsbury that women's passions are acknowledged, even celebrated, in some contemporary fiction. Jewsbury, however, was notorious, and *Zoe* hidden from view at Mudie's, but even in *Fatherless Fanny*, the honorable Amelia proudly declares, "I was not as backward in declaring it [love], as some prudish things of my sex. I have no notion of women concealing their predilection till the last moment" ([Reeve] 441). The "consistency-building" reader (Iser 118–24) who has identified Jane with rebellion and feminism may find in this passage an "anticipatory caution"—Jane may be

. . . . . .

less radical than thought—or the reader may notice that this passage is in quotation marks. The impression that Rochester was growing to love Jane has come through dramatized action (the fire, for example), Rochester's words, and through Jane's interpretation, which appeared to be double-voiced and therefore to have the tacit blessing of the older Jane. The passage decrying secret love, however, is in quotation marks, and so is "unauthorized," neither underwritten nor contradicted by the older narrator. The reader's comprehension is still further ambiguated by the contradictory alien voices of contemporary fiction regarding proper female conduct. The suspense thus involves not only the outcome of the love story but the nature of the moral world of *Jane Eyre*.

The punishment Jane sentences herself to undergo seems related less to her offense in loving than to her foolishness in hoping to win Rochester's love. She must draw a harshly realistic self-portrait in chalk—"Portrait of a Governess, disconnected, poor, and plain"—and paint on ivory the most beautiful face she can imagine, "Blanche, an accomplished lady of rank" (201). Strong and determined as Jane is, as morally dangerous as she knows her love must be, as hopeless as she fears it is, warned as she has been of the destructive power of love and jealousy by Rochester himself, she still cannot uproot her feelings for him. As soon as he returns, three weeks later, her love is rekindled: "I had not intended to love him: the reader knows I had wrought hard to extirpate from my soul the germs of love detected there; and now, at the first renewed view of him, they spontaneously revived, green and strong! He made me love him without looking at me" (218–19). Jane has lost control over her passions, her self, her destiny. No matter whether he is Schedoni or Byron; no matter whether the third story is inhabited by the ghost of his murdered brother or a besotted mistress; she must believe in him and love him. Whether a Godwinian or governess heroine, she is in danger. Suspense is doubled: Is Rochester hero or villain? Will Jane win his love or not, and which would be better?

The rival is no longer Grace Poole but the haughty, buxom, beautiful, well-born Blanche. Jane still thinks Rochester is of her own kind, not like Blanche or her family and friends, but she cannot explain his strange conduct since the night of the fire or deny that, no matter how carelessly, he is courting Blanche. In an ugly scene, in which both

· · · · · ·

Rochester and Blanche know that Jane can hear what is being said, Rochester seems to egg on Blanche and her mother to further humiliate Jane:

> "You should hear mama on the subject of governesses; Mary and I have had, I should think, a dozen at least in our day; half of them detestable and the rest ridiculous, and all incubi—were they not, mama?"
>
> "My dearest, don't mention governesses: the word makes me nervous. I have suffered a martyrdom from their incompetency and caprice: I thank heaven I have now done with them!"
>
> Mrs. Dent here bent over the pious lady, and whispered something in her ear: I suppose from the answer elicited, it was a reminder that one of the anathematized race was present.
>
> "Tant pis!" said her ladyship. "I hope it may do her good!" (221)

In only a slightly lowered voice, she claims that she can see in Jane's face "all the faults of her class." Rochester, apparently determined to prolong Jane's mortification, insists she go on. Then Blanche and her brother recall how they used to torment their governesses, spilling tea, throwing books, even "blackmailing" a Miss Wilson who seemed to have had the audacity to fall in love with the tutor. Amy Ashton also recalls how she and her sister used to "quiz" their governess, "but she was such a good creature, she would bear anything." " 'I suppose now,' said Miss Ingram, curling her lip sarcastically, 'we shall have an abstract of all the memoirs of all the governesses extant' " (223).

In the governess novel of the day, such a scene is heavily occupied territory, the often-religious governess novel setting itself in moral and social opposition to the dominant fashionable, or silver-fork, novel. Mrs. Ryals, in Mrs. Hall's "The Governess, a Tale," for example, sounds as if she could join the Ingram party: "I will never again take a governess into my house to reside. . . . One was imprudent enough to wish to get married, and expected to come into the drawing-room when there was company of an evening. Another would have a bedroom to herself" (Hall 53).

The scene of social humiliation is a topos virtually constitutive of the genre, and it is through such scenes that Brontë's is refracted. In *Amy Herbert* (1844), for example, Emily Morton, the governess (whom we have seen attending the deathbed of a child), is thought of condescendingly as "remarkably" ladylike, yet is at first taken for a lady's maid (Sewell 43). When the pious and naive Amy tells her young friends the Harringtons that it is only their mother and not themselves who can discharge the governess, she is told, "What a simpleton you are! . . . There are hundreds of ways of getting rid of a person you don't like" (62). Later, the Harrington children have a visitor even ruder than they, who, like Blanche and her mother, speak of the governess as if she were not present:

> She [Emily] was not introduced to Miss Cunningham; . . . a whispered conversation followed between her [Miss Cunningham] and Margaret, quite loud enough to be heard. She was described as "the person who teaches us music and drawing," and her birth, parentage, and education were given. . . . all that showed she was aware of what was said was the momentary glistening of her eye as she caught the words—"Oh! she is an orphan, is she?" and then Margaret's reply—"Yes; she lost her father and mother both in one month." (103–4)

(Jane's parents too, we will recall, "died within a month of each other" [26]).[1]

Mrs. Sherwood's Caroline Mordaunt is treated as an inferior by Lady Euphrasia and abused by other employers. She, like Jane and Emily Morton, hears herself being insulted by implication as if she were not present during the conversation: after she becomes a lady's companion, two spinsters visit her mistress every evening to play cards and "to abuse domestics and companions of every description—which they did with little reference to the only person present of these denominations" (296).

The Countess Blessington's Clara Mordaunt, in *The Governess*, is not only harassed by the West Indian Hercules Marsden, but, when her eldest pupil discovers that Clara is in fact an heiress, the child insensitively remarks,

> "And so, Miss Mordaunt, you are a lady after all?" said Miss Williamson, looking at Clara, "Well, who'd have thought it; for though I told Betsey [the maid] that you were, it was only to vex her; I did not believe it. . . . This proves that mama is not always right, for she said that governesses were never ladies." (2:69–70)

. . . .

In Mrs. Ross's *The Governess; Or, Politics in Private Life*, the governess, Gertrude Walcot, is a lady by birth, but her mistress's mother, the Dowager Lady Lyster, claims, "There is nothing so intolerable as a well-born, and what people call a lady-like governess; a sort of schoolroom princess, who will do literally nothing she is desired to do" (Ross 79). In the same novel, Lady Hanway says, "the fact of her being a lady by birth [has nothing] to do with the matter:—she is a governess now, and as such her proper place is in the school-room. Do you know . . . the other morning . . . Mrs. Elphinstone came in, and she actually introduced her to us? Lady Lucy, I believe, did bow;—I took not the slightest notice" (78–79). Dr. Jameson, clearly speaking for the author in this didactic novel, protests against treating "a lady equal in birth to any one of us" as a "species of upper nursemaid" and advocates admitting the governess into the society of guests—to relieve her solitude, to keep her practiced in elegant society, and to show respect to her so that the children will respect her (166–67).

Mr. Johnson, in "Our Governess," however, resents the lengthy tradition of favorable (and therefore "unrealistic") treatment of governesses in literature: "Their woes have found imaginative record in novels and sentimental comedies for more than a century. In these productions they are invariably portrayed as females of high mental endowments, abandoned by the caprices of fortune to the indignities of vulgar mistresses and the tricks of wicked children" (Hall 79).

The scenic topos of the social humiliation of the governess does, indeed, go back, if not a century, at least as far as Jane Austen. The vulgar Mrs. Elton in *Emma* (1816), knowing that Emma's friend had been her governess, upon meeting her says she's "astonished to find her so lady-like! But she is really quite a gentlewoman" (250). The scene of Jane's humiliation is thus familiar in novels of a certain kind and carries with it the aura of the domestic and, more specifically, the governess novel.

Blanche sees herself and her apparently doting suitor acting out narratives of a kind quite different from those of governess novels, however. She would have him play both the singer-secretary-lover Rizzio and the "wild, fierce, bandit-hero" Bothwell to her Mary, Queen of Scots (224); she professes to "doat on Corsairs" (225); she thinks "an English hero of the road would be the next best thing to an Italian bandit; and that could only be surpassed by a Levantine pirate" (230). She professes a preference, in actuality as in fiction, for men of strength over those who possess "mere" beauty: "I grant an ugly woman is a blot on the fair face of creation; but as to the gentlemen, let them be solicitous to possess only strength and valour" (224).

Fiction, at least the kind of fiction Blanche prefers, is unrelated to reality. (When Frederika Bremer's heroine is advised not to judge the new neighbor, Bruno, by conventional standards because "deep passionate, Byronian natures require their own measure," she knows that such "knowledge of the age" is drawn "only from novels" [67].) Blanche reads novels passively, not to improve herself or to learn, but to pass the time: with a "haughty listlessness . . . [she] prepared to beguile, by the spell of fiction, the tedious hours" (236). Though she repeats "sounding phrases from books" and advocates "a high tone of sentiment," she herself is incapable of real sentiment (232). Blanche's preference for romantic, "culinary" (Jauss 19) fiction—the Byronic, the sentimental—is a moral measure of her falseness; she fictionalizes her reality. Her advocacy thus devalues the Byronic and romantic and thereby indirectly valorizes realistic, domestic, narrative, perhaps even governess novels.

Rochester, like Jane and the reader, seems to recognize Blanche's unworthiness. Jane sees that Blanche cannot charm him, does not know how to handle him, cannot love him, but she does not doubt that, after the custom of their class, they will marry anyway (231–32). Rochester is thus dissociated from the Byronic hero that Blanche would have him be, or would have him think she thought him to be. But with his dissolute past and with a look in his eye that may be "sinister or sorrowful," a look that suggests volcanoes and earthquakes and makes Jane not fearful but desiring "to dare—to divine it" (234–35), he does not sound like the hero of a governess novel.

There is, though, another sinful Edward, Edward Seymour in Rachel McCrindell's *The English Governess*. Once "the brother" of Clara Neville's "heart, the future partner of her life . . . with whom she might hope to spend, not only a life of holiness and usefulness on earth, but an eternity of bliss in the regions of never ending joy and praise" (30), he falls into bad company at Cambridge and becomes dissipated and

. . . .

irreligious. Clara breaks her engagement. Jane would be well-advised, perhaps, to drive thoughts of loving Rochester out of her mind, if he proves himself unreformed. Seymour is reported to have been killed in a steeplechase accident caused by his own recklessness. Later, with Clara's fortunes at a low ebb, while she attends her dying little nephew, Edward reappears. He is not merely alive but reborn: he has found God, resigned his army commission, and become a minister. . . . The Reverend Mr. Edward Rochester, then? Not likely, perhaps. But the pattern of a rake rejected, and by rejection and reversal reformed, is plausible—for a governess novel.

There is, however, the impediment of Blanche. While Rochester is in Millcote on business, a Mr. Mason from the West Indies arrives. Jane finds him weak-looking, sleek-looking, like a gander, and meek, like a sheep—altogether different from the falconlike Rochester. But Louisa Eshton and Mary Ingram "both called him 'a beautiful man.' Louisa said he was 'a love of a creature,' and she 'adored him;' and Mary instanced his 'pretty little mouth, and nice nose,' as her ideal of charming" (238). There is no word from Blanche. He does not suit her professed preference for a highwayman or pirate, but we know there is a discrepancy between what she says and what she truly feels. Those readers trying to project some honorable and credible escape for Rochester from what seems an inevitable but catastrophic marriage may find some hope in Mason: Blanche might throw over Rochester for his friend.

The contemporary reader had even more reason to hope for the man from the West Indies, for the romantic creole is occupied territory. At one point in *Fatherless Fanny* everyone is talking about "the interesting creole" ([Reeve] 179) newly arrived from Jamaica, but he turns out to be not Fanny's lover but her long-lost father. More often, the creole is either romantically attractive—both the Countess Blessington and Maria Edgeworth are "addicted" to "handsome creoles" (West 40)—or sexually threatening: the West Indian Hercules Marsden in the Countess Blessington's 1839 novel *The Governess* was, we remember, "characteristically" hot-blooded, and Oliver Twist's half brother Monks, whose mother responded to her unhappy marriage

· · · · · · ·

and separation by indulging in "continental frivolities" (333), settles on his own estate in the West Indies "to escape the consequences of vicious courses here" (335).

The possibility that Mason will take Blanche off Rochester's hands and the generic relation of *Jane Eyre* to the governess novel are reinforced by the appearance of an old hag, a gypsy fortune-teller, who does not seem to have told Blanche "anything to her advantage; and it seemed to me," Jane tells us, "from her prolonged fit of gloom and taciturnity, that she herself, notwithstanding her professed indifference, attached undue importance to whatever revelations had been made her" (242–43). When the others have finished, the gypsy insists that Jane, too, have her fortune told. The gypsy reinforces the possibility of Mason becoming a successful rival of Rochester's for Blanche: "I would advise her black-aviced suitor to look out: if another comes, with a longer or clearer rent-roll,—he's dished" (251). The scene is an echo of a scene from the classical progenitor of the governess novel, *Pamela:*

> One of the servants who wishes Pamela well and cannot get access to her, disguises himself as a gipsy, and, pretending to tell fortunes, brings her a letter warning her about the mock-marriage. In *Jane Eyre* Rochester disguises himself as a gipsy and, pretending to tell Jane's fortune, hints at the truth of his position. One tiny point is significant of the method. In *Pamela* the gipsy wishes to draw Pamela's attention to the fact that she is going to hide the letter in the grass, since she dare not give it to her then. She does it thus: "O! said she, I cannot tell your fortune: your hand is so white and fine, I cannot see the lines: but said she, and stooping, pulled up a little tuft of grass, I have a way for that: and so rubbed my hand with the mould part of the tuft: Now, said she, I can see the lines."
>
> In *Jane Eyre* Rochester disguised as a gipsy asks for Jane's hand, and then says, "It is too fine . . . I can make nothing of such a hand as that; almost without lines; besides what is in a palm? Destiny is not written there." (Spens 56–57)

When Jane discovers that the gypsy is Rochester, she is only half-surprised. She sensed from the beginning that this was no ordinary fortune-teller: "I had noted her feigned voice, her anxiety to conceal

. . . .

117

her features. But my mind had been running on Grace Poole—that living enigma, that mystery of mysteries, as I considered her: I had never thought of Mr. Rochester" (254).

It is unlikely that many readers, despite their familiarity with and sympathy for Jane, would have thought of Grace Poole. With the mention of Grace here, however, the deserted wing motif and the Gothic are recalled, and they are reinforced by Rochester's reaction to the news that a Mr. Mason has appeared at Thornfield:

> As I spoke, he gave my wrist a convulsive grip; the smile on his lips froze: apparently a spasm caught his breath.
>
> "Mason!—the West Indies!" he said, in the tone one might fancy a speaking automaton to enounce its single words; "Mason!—the West Indies!" he reiterated; and he went over the syllables three times, growing, in the intervals of speaking, whiter than ashes: he hardly seemed to know what he was doing. (255)

He sends Jane to fetch wine and report on Mason and the company. Rochester cannot believe all is normal: "They don't look grave and mysterious, as if they had heard something strange?" (256). No. "If all these people came in a body and spat at me, what would you do, Jane?" Rochester asks. This stranger, then, knows something mysterious or secret that would turn society against Rochester. The neighbor in Frederika Bremer's *The Neighbours* (translated by Mary Howitt in 1842 and again in 1844 by E. A. Friedlaender), himself a rather Byronic figure, is rumored to have "inherited . . . the property of an uncle in the West Indies" (55). The truth is, however, that he had actually earned his wealth there—in the slave trade. Is this the secret Mason knows and with which he threatens Rochester? Was this what Rochester's father and brother had forced upon him so that he might make sufficient money in the West Indies in order to preserve the whole Rochester estate for Rowland? (See Boumelha 62; and below, ch. 7.) Or is the secret more related to Grace Poole, the deserted wing, and the Gothic?

That very night, "in the dead of night," Jane is awakened by the full moon shining through her uncurtained window. As she reaches to draw the curtain, a savage shriek paralyzes her. Rochester soon comes for her and leads her upstairs, where behind some tapestry is the door to a room she had not known existed. "I heard thence a snarling, snatching sound, almost like a dog quarrelling" (262). Rochester tells her to wait, enters the room, and Jane hears "Grace Poole's own goblin ha! ha!" He bids Jane enter. She can still see only part of the room, but there is Mason, one sleeve and the side of his shirt "almost soaked in blood." Forbidding them to talk to each other, Rochester leaves Jane with the wounded man.

> Then my own thoughts worried me. What crime was this, that lived incarnate in this sequestered mansion, and could neither be expelled nor subdued by the owner?—What mystery, that broke out, now in fire and now in blood, at the deadest hours of night?—What creature was it, that, masked in an ordinary woman's face and shape, uttered the voice, now of a mocking demon, and anon of a carrion-seeking bird of prey? (264)

The scene is somewhat reminiscent of that in the red-room, but here Jane articulates her own and the reader's questions, summarizes, recapitulates (reminding us of the fire, for example), and does not, as she did in the red-room, speak in the voice of the narrator. Indeed, though these thoughts are not in quotation marks, they are not double-voiced and are marked by the interrogatives as indirect discourse, specifically and monologically Jane's. Jane, like the reader, is unsure what is going on and what is to happen next.

Both Mason and Rochester are solicitous for the creature's welfare. Before he leaves, Mason says, " 'Let her be taken care of; let her be treated as tenderly as may be: let her—' he stopped and burst into tears" (270). Rochester agrees to do so. Mason's care for a creature who has attacked him and, as he told Rochester, "sucked the blood: she said she'd drain my heart" (267) is puzzling. The creature must be a loved one, or a victim, or not responsible for her actions, or all three. Still, she is dangerous. Rochester assures Jane that he would not have left Jane alone without securely locking the door between her and the "wolf's den" (271).

A full moon;[2] violent incidents that occur only in the dead of night; a creature that has a woman's form, but snarls like a dog or wolf, sucks blood, and vows to drain her victim's heart! More than a hint of vampirism is in the air. Not only were vampires sometimes found in the

. . . . . .

119

shape of wolves, before Bram Stoker "stabilized" their nonhuman form as that of the bat, but here the sometimes-woman's voice is somewhat like that of "a carrion-seeking bird of prey," suggestive of, if not a biologically accurate description of, a bat.

Vampirism is a favorite subject early in the nineteenth century, and not merely as fantasy. In April 1847, while *Jane Eyre* was being written, the second in a series of articles called "Letters on the Truths Contained in Popular Superstitions" appeared in *Blackwood's*. The article, entitled "Vampirism," defined a vampire as "a dead body, which continues to live in the grave, which it leaves, however, by night, for the purpose of sucking the blood of the living, whereby it is nourished, and preserved in good condition" (61:432). The article reports authenticated testimony of epidemics of vampirism, exhumed bodies with blood in chest cavities, corpses with signs of life. It makes no reference to the vampire taking the form of bats, wolves, or dogs, but does refer to walking at night, stakes through the heart, and victims themselves turning into vampires—all part of the literary vampire repertoire.

Vampirism is very much part of the literary scene. The month before *Jane Eyre* appeared, the preface of *Varney, the Vampyre: or, The Feast of Blood* expresses gratitude for "the unprecedented success of the romance of 'Varney the Vampire'" and for its favorable reception by "the whole Metropolitan Press."[3] Louis James calls *Varney* "probably the best known of these [popular late-Gothic] penny-issue novels after *Sweeney Todd*" (99). Any allusion to the vampire in 1847 would surely recall that novel or its reputation. (And an added frisson may visit those readers of *Jane Eyre* who had read *Varney* in this edition, for the vampire leaves a manuscript which describes his earlier adventures with Charles II and . . . Rochester!) Mario Praz suggests that the first literary use made of the vampire legend was in Goethe's *Braut von Korinth* (1797), and that such tales were henceforth associated with Germany. In 1816 Byron read German ghost stories to a group of friends— the Shelleys, Dr. Polidori, Monk Lewis—and challenged them to write one themselves. One result was *Frankenstein;* another was *The Vampyre,* which was Polidori's elaboration of Byron's own *A Fragment* (1819) conflated with elements from Lady Caroline Lamb's *Glenarvon* (1816), in which Byron himself figured as the fatal lover, Ruthven Glenarvon.

The Vampyre, reprinted in 1840 in the cheap and popular Romancist and Novelist's Library (James 99), was originally published in the *New Monthly Magazine* as Byron's. Praz claims that it was Byron who was chiefly "responsible" for the vampire fashion, and that the vampire is connected with the Byronic hero or Fatal Man (Praz 76–78).[4] For many readers, then, Rochester's aura of Byronism would appear in a more sinister light, and the line between the Byronic and the Gothic would be erased. If Grace is a vampire, the projected configuration of *Jane Eyre* is radically changed. Goethe's female vampire says, "I am urged forth from the grave to seek the joy which was snatched from me, to love again the man I once lost and to suck his heart's blood. When he is ruined, I must pass on to others, and young men shall succumb to my fury" (qtd. in Praz 209). Polidori summarizes in his introduction another version of vampirism:

> In many parts of Greece it is considered as a sort of punishment after death, for some heinous crime committed whilst in existence, that the deceased is not only doomed to vampyrise, but compelled to confine his infernal visitations solely to those beings he loved most while upon earth— those to whom he was bound by ties of kindred and affection. (xxii)

Vampirism is in the novel more or less over the head of the young Jane and is there at the suggestion of the narrator or author herself. The reader, then, through this rubric sees young Jane and her perspective as other, and has questions that Jane at the time does not have. Was Mason, then, the lover Grace lost, as Goethe would have it, or is Grace forced to prey on Mason, her relative or one she loves, as punishment for some heinous crime she committed upon earth? What is Rochester's role? What is the creature or Grace Poole to him? Why is such a creature, one who tried to burn him in his bed, kept on at Thornfield (a question Jane asks herself)? Will he, though no longer a young gentleman, be Grace's next victim? Or was he, as Jane conjectured, once her lover? Or is he related to her? Is old kinship or affection the reason both men are so solicitous for the well-being of a creature so foul? Will Rochester soon be "vampyrised"? *Or has he been already?*

As was the case after the fire, after—and despite—this harrowing attack, the love story once more moves to the fore and partially

. . . .

eclipses the Gothic. Rochester tries to get Jane to agree that if one needs another in order to reform and live a better life, he would be "justified in overleaping an obstacle of custom," a custom he does not believe in anyway. Jane does not know how to answer and silently asks "for some good spirit to suggest a judicious and satisfactory response." A judicious response comes: " 'Sir,' I answered, 'a Wanderer's repose or a Sinner's reformation should never depend on a fellow-creature. . . . let him look higher than his equals for strength to amend, and solace to heal' " (274). It is a response that does indeed sound as if it is in quotation marks, that of a spirit other than Jane's; it strongly resembles Helen Burns's admonition that Jane thought too much of the love of human beings: God "has provided you with other resources than your feeble self, or than creatures feeble as you," Helen had told her (81). The spirit world, with vampire and guardian angels, seems circumambient.

Rochester meanwhile seems on the verge once more of professing his love for Jane, but he suddenly turns the conversation to Blanche and his impending marriage. This strange vacillation, with the vacillation of the narrative itself from love story to Gothic and seemingly back to love story, with the consequent ambiguating of Rochester's character and intentions, overdetermines expectation: there are too many possibilities, too many generic signals, too many possible ontological grounds.

Matters are not helped any by what seems like an arbitrary interruption and another ontological complication, though the spirit world is made even more, and more variegatedly, present. Jane is called away to the deathbed of her Aunt Reed, but she has been "warned" beforehand:

> Presentiments are strange things! and so are sympathies; and so are signs: and the three combined make one mystery to which humanity has not yet found the key. I never laughed at presentiments in my life; because I have had strange ones of my own. Sympathies I believe exist . . . whose workings baffle mortal comprehension. And signs, for aught we know, may be but the sympathies of Nature with man. (276)

We have already been made uncertain whether ghosts or vampires are native to this land; now we have another kind of supernatural

· · · · · · ·

or at least extraordinary aspect of reality to deal with. The present tense suggests that this is the monologic voice of the narrator, part of the "official" worldview, the reality of the novel. Though the passage is not fully double-voiced ("I never laughed at presentiments in my life"), what follows suggests that the narrator speaks for if not through young Jane: Jane has been dreaming of a child for a week, a sign, Bessie used to say, of trouble to oneself or one's kin; and, sure enough, Jane is called away to her aunt's deathbed. The ten-year-old Jane could be afraid that her uncle's ghost might appear; she could be flip about Scripture and uncertain what or where God is, and even less certain about heaven (96) and the spirit world. Eighteen-year-old Jane seemed easily convinced that the source of the demonic laugh was Grace Poole, yet she is able to say to Rochester that "The human and fallible should not arrogate a power with which the divine and perfect alone can be safely entrusted" (169). Presentiments, sympathies, and signs widen the field of Jane's trust in the more-than-phenomenal. The novel or narrator here endorses Jane's view but does not always do so. On the one hand, there may be ghosts and vampires—surely there's more to the third story than the mundane Grace—and it is likely that Helen's affirmation of God, heaven, and even a world of spirits will prove "true." The novel seems to be constructing an ontological force field with skepticism, superstition, and traditional Christianity as its vectors. At this point in the text, the nature of the world of the novel is as great a mystery as are the upper reaches of Thornfield Manor, the nature of Rochester, and the outcome of Jane's autobiography.

If Jane's dreams or presentiments make us search our memories of what has gone before for the proper ontological ground of the fictional world, Jane's physical return to Gateshead "spatializes" the text, making us think back over the fictional past, just as it makes Jane think back over her own past. Bessie and the breakfast room carry Jane and the reader backward toward the very first pages of the novel:

> There was every article of furniture looking just as it did on the morning I was first introduced to Mr. Brocklehurst: the very rug he had stood upon still covered the hearth. Glancing at the bookcases, I thought I could distinguish the two volumes of Bewick's British Birds occupying their old place on the third shelf, and Gulliver's Travels and the Arabian Nights

. . . . . .

123

ranged just above. The inanimate objects were not changed: but the living things had altered past recognition. (285–86)

The child Eliza has changed into a woman with a sallow and severe face; her intention, once her mother dies, is to enter a convent. She is a familiar figure in the fiction of the time (Clarendon 597). Eliza's sister, Georgiana, is out of, indeed the "author" of, a novel of another sort: in an afternoon and evening of confidential conversation with Jane, "a volume of a novel of fashionable life was that day improvised by her for my benefit" (293). Nor are the Catholic and the fashionable novel the only kinds foregrounded here. John Reed, the terror of Jane's childhood, we learn, has ruined himself and virtually ruined the family through gambling and has committed suicide. It was that which caused Mrs. Reed's apoplectic seizure. His life story could come out of almost any moral tale of the period. At Gateshead we seem virtually to be at Mudie's.

Jane Eyre is at this time defining itself as a religious or metaphysical novel, but as yet we are not quite certain of what sort. The religious nature of the episode is chiefly embodied in the two brief interviews Jane has with the dying Mrs. Reed (the unrepentant sinner's deathbed, like the child's, is a familiar scene in Victorian fiction):

> It is a happy thing that time quells the longings of vengeance, and hushes the promptings of rage and aversion: I had left this woman in bitterness and hate, and I came back to her now with no other emotion than a sort of ruth for her great sufferings, and a strong yearning to forget and forgive all injuries—to be reconciled, and clasp hands in amity. . . .
>
> I had once vowed that I would never call her aunt again: I thought it no sin to forget and break that vow, now. (288–89)

In the second interview she ponders the mystery of death and immortality and recalls Helen:

> "One lies there," I thought, "who will soon be beyond the war of earthly elements. Whither will that spirit—now struggling to quit its material tenement—flit when at length released?"
>
> In pondering the great mystery, I thought of Helen Burns: recalled

her dying words—her faith—her doctrine of the equality of disembodied souls. (297–98)

Jane now has a third voice. Her present, Thornfield voice has been "gradually and slowly wrought out of others' words that have been acknowledged and assimilated, and the boundaries between the two are at first scarcely perceptible" (Bakhtin, *Dialogic* 345n). The rebellious young Jane vowed not to call Mrs. Reed aunt; the words of Helen, perhaps of Miss Temple, and even her own response to the negative example of Rochester have made her change her mind and not regret having done so. This young woman is closer to the mature woman narrator than to the child Jane; if the anticipatory cautions of the early chapters have not been enough, now we ought to recognize that the young Jane, though she has an ineradicable voice in the world of the novel, does not always speak for the narrator, for the novel as a whole, but is in dialogue with the narrator. We are prepared to distance ourselves somewhat from Jane, to see or hear her change, to comprehend her narration while remaining alert to its double- or triple-voicedness. Those still in love with the rebellious, self-reliant child who confronted her elders may ignore or deplore the recantation, but to do so is to impose a monologic reading on a dialogic text. To silence that rebellious child entirely, however, is equally monologic. Jane at Thornfield has assimilated the voices of Helen and Miss Temple to her own earlier voice; the earlier Jane is still there, if now, even without the older narrator, hybridized. Jane has grown socially, psychologically, and morally, and is perhaps less uncertain about religious matters. As "authorial audience" the reader must keep pace, must qualify the positive primacy effect of the self-reliant, rebellious, secular Jane. Not all readers do.

Meanwhile the plot has not been standing still during this digression, this dialogic and ontological reconfiguration. Jane has been called to her aunt's bedside to be given at last a letter that Mrs. Reed had received three years earlier from Jane's uncle in Madeira. It reads:

"Madam,

"Will you have the goodness to send me the address of my niece, Jane Eyre, and tell me how she is: it is my intention to write shortly and

. . . .

desire her to come to me at Madeira. Providence has blessed my endeav-
ours to secure a competency; and as I am unmarried and childless, I wish
to adopt her during my life, and bequeath her at my death whatever I may
have to leave."

"I am, Madam, &c. &c.
"JOHN EYRE, Madeira." (299)

Mrs. Reed, out of hatred and spite, had written John Eyre to say that
Jane had died. She is now contrite and wishes to right the wrong before she dies. We have heard of Uncle John once before. When Jane
was leaving Lowood for Thornfield, she met Bessie, who told her that
some seven years earlier her father's brother had come seeking her at
Gateshead but had to leave for Madeira before he could follow her to
Lowood. Now there is the possibility of a bequest, and the plot topos
the *Spectator* complained about—the "convenient but not very novel
resource of an unknown uncle dying abroad [which] makes her independent" (Allott 75)—is in place.

Since Jane is now returning to Thornfield and Rochester, Uncle
John is abruptly shoved into the background. She finds Rochester, sitting on a stile. Stile-sitters sometimes are ghosts (see above, ch. 3).
Rochester is not, but he finds Jane somewhat amusingly ghostlike:
"just one of your tricks: . . . to steal into the vicinage of your home
along with twilight, just as if you were a dream or a shade" (306). He
asks her where she's been for a month.

"I have been with my aunt, sir, who is dead."
"A true Janian reply! Good angels be my guard! She comes from the
other world—from the abode of people who are dead; and tells me so
when she meets me alone here in the gloaming!" (306–7)

With our renewed uncertainty about Rochester's character, his intentions, and his very nature, and with flutterings of vampirism at
Thornfield, talk of the living dead is not a thoroughly funny or irrelevant joke.

But, it is summer; Rochester, like the weather, is all smiles; he
does not visit Blanche. "Never had he called me more frequently to
his presence; never been kinder to me when there—and alas! never
had I loved him so well" (310). The chapter ends, and though all is

sunshine and jocularity, that "alas!" and a thin veil of Gothic ever-so-slightly blur the happy rays, recalling the mysterious shadow of the upper reaches of Thornfield.

The days grow even sunnier, and one soft evening Rochester meets her in the garden. He plays upon her feelings mercilessly—teasing her about his upcoming marriage, his having found her a place as governess in Ireland—until she abandons her maidenly reserve and confesses her love. Only then does he tell her he is breaking off his match with Blanche. He proposes, Jane accepts and he begins to murmur about God sanctioning what he is about to do, and to hell with men's opinions.

"But what had befallen the night? . . . what ailed the chestnut tree? it writhed and groaned; while wind roared in the laurel walk, and came sweeping over us" (322). The interrogatives serve once again to put the passage "in quotation marks," distanced from the narrator who, from her position in the future, could, but at this point chooses not to, answer the questions. The reader is somewhat distanced from young Jane by the unanswered questions and looks over her head toward the future with more uncertainty than Jane exhibits. There is a fierce storm in the night, thunder and lightning. Jane is not afraid, but the reader may not be so indifferent: more than love is in the fictional foreground now, a kind of uneasy apprehension encircled by the whole repertoire of Gothic and other dire possibilities. The chapter ends ominously, all the more ominous since Jane seems so unaware. "Before I left my bed in the morning, little Adèle came running in to tell me that the great horse-chestnut at the bottom of the orchard had been struck by lightning in the night, and half of it split away" (323). They had been sitting beneath that tree when Rochester proposed, but there is no record of Jane's response to the news of the storm's destruction, despite her assimilation of at least some of Helen's awareness of a spirit world. Has human love, which Helen had warned her she made too central to her life, silenced Helen's voice? The mature narrator is still silent. Is this bolt from the blue just a bit of Victorian melodrama? stage business? heavy-handed symbolism? pathetic fallacy (passion = storm)? Clearly there must be trouble brewing, but what is the aesthetic or metaphysical signal here? The dramatic, almost theatrical

· · · · · · ·

placing of the news about the lightning-struck tree reveals the hand of the author/narrator, the last words of the chapter functioning as a sign without words, insisting that readers distance themselves somewhat from Jane and give to the event more thought than Jane does. It must signify in the configuration of the narrative. But how?

The significance of the event is refracted by analogues in the literary context. Lightning does not strike aimlessly in mid-nineteenth-century fiction. In Anne Marsh's *The Deformed* (1834, reissued 1844), the villainous Marchioness arranges the murder of the hunchback-hero to make way for her son, Lord Louis. Eighteen months later, she is celebrating Louis's coming of age, unrightful heir now to title and fortune, when the sky darkens and thunder is heard in the distance.

> One ray of sun shot between the dark clouds, and illuminated his face. The next moment—a crash of thunder—loud—terrible—rattled through the sky, and one bright flash penetrated, for a second, the horrible gloom. One flash—and a cry, a universal cry, rent the air—Lord Louis! Lord Louis! Lord Louis!—the thunder-bolt had fallen—and struck him dead at his mother's feet. (130)

The stricken Marchioness sees in the bolt the hand of God, and the author leaves no doubt that it is Providence that governs fate; she prefaces her short novel with an epigraph from Lamartine:

> Un Dieu descend toujours pour dénouer le drame,
> Toujours la Providence y veille et nous proclaime
> Cette justice occulte, et ce divin ressort
> Qui fait jouer le temps, et gouverne le sort.

Less spectacular but perhaps more germane is the oak tree that has been shattered by lightning in George Sand's *Consuelo* (1842, tr. 1847) which is described as "a supernatural omen of revenge" (Desner 97).

The early Victorian novel-reader, recalling these or similar fictional topoi, may suspect that there is a supernatural agency behind this event which Jane now dismisses so casually but which the narrator places so emphatically at the end of the chapter. At least for the time being, however, that suspicion is not reinforced, so it remains only one of many possible explanations. The narrator has been silent, not just here, but throughout these episodes—the attack on Mason, Jane's visit to her aunt, her return, the happy aftermath. That she could intervene at any moment and reveal what or who inhabits the upper story, is of course true, and part of the reticence can be attributed to the need for mystery and suspense. But there is a related, more significant reason. It is in these suspenseful pages that the nature of reality in the fictional world of *Jane Eyre* is most problematic—at least to this point. The ontological as well as the narrative suspense is here at its height. The strong suggestions of the Gothic, of vampirism, are followed by a double-voiced paragraph on presentiments, sympathies, and signs. That paragraph in turn is followed by the conventional deathbed scene of the sinner, Mrs. Reed, with Jane acting on the religious principles of Helen, invoking memories of Helen and her beliefs in the spirit world. The fairy world—and even the Gothic "return from the dead"—are treated lightly and all but melt in the sunshine of Rochester's love and proposal of marriage. Is there a spirit world interpolated in the sublunary? If so, is this world that of Gothic supernaturalism? that of fairy tales? that of traditional Judeo-Christian religion? or a combination of all of them? And what of presentiments, sympathies, signs, and dreams? Are signs—as Jane (the younger? the elder? both?) say(s)— "but the sympathies of Nature with man" (276)? How then to read the significance of the lightning-struck tree?

The generic signals do not answer those questions but simply reinforce their multiplicity. They offer the ontological possibilities of the worlds of the Gothic, of domestic realism (governess novels), of romance (love stories), of religious fiction. Are there vampires in this world? Is there a heaven? The narrator could say for sure who or what is up above—in heaven or the third story. The reader, unaided, however, must scan the horizon of possibilities. Suspense and significance are intensified by the search.

Such heavy thoughts are all but suspended during the lengthy days—and pages—spent preparing, materially and emotionally, for the wedding, and the "return" of Jane's earliest voice without the assimilated, dark spiritual tones of Helen almost lays to rest our fears. There is only the most oblique warning, in the shape of an "occupied" or alien space, perhaps a literary allusion. Just as Lovelace wants Clarissa to go up to London for a few days to buy clothes at his

. . . .

expense, Rochester wants to shower Jane with jewelry and rich clothes; but just as Clarissa says "[she] was not prepared to wear his livery yet" (Letter 123, 456), Jane, knowing her own limited claims to physical beauty, and refusing to be under obligation or to assume the role of a possession, resists. She refuses the compliment that she is preferable to "the grand Turk's whole seraglio": " 'I'll not stand you an inch in the stead of a seraglio,' I said; 'so don't consider me an equivalent for one: if you have a fancy for anything in that line, away with you, sir, to the bazaars of Stamboul without delay' " (339). We approve of Jane's independence and morality, but what does the echo of *Clarissa* portend?

Still, but less ominously, the Richardsonian heroine, Jane heeds Mrs. Fairfax's prudent—perhaps even prurient—advice to "keep Mr. Rochester at a distance: distrust yourself as well as him. Gentlemen in his station are not accustomed to marry their governesses" (334). Jane keeps him at bay with the "needle of repartee" (344). Though perhaps not wholly admirable to modern conceptions of frank and free behavior, Jane's prudence is consistent with her strong sense of independence, and her repartee is indeed delightful. It is also prudent in terms of Victorian mores and especially their representation in fiction. If no Hays or Jewsbury, Brontë somewhat more openly acknowledges sexuality than was the custom, and Jane is not quite so coy as the popular heroine, but she still keeps the distance thought proper, at least by Victorian popular novels:

> a declaration once made and an engagement entered upon, it [courtship] is still dealt with [in popular fiction] in [an] abstract and etherealized manner. No hint is given of the complexity of sexual love and the force of physical passion. . . . "They were affianced," says Mrs Yorick Smythies in *A Warning to Wives* [a novel of 1847, published by Newby, who was sitting on the novels of Anne and Emily Brontë all during that year], "and to Inez's delicate nature, that circumstance, instead of increasing her liberty of action, added to her coy and maidenly reserve." (Dalziel 111)

Jane's wit is largely based on what seems an essentially healthy self-regard, a refusal to submit her selfhood to sentimental notions of self-sacrifice—in the name of love or anything else. When Rochester sings "a sweet air . . . in mellow tones" (342), she seizes on a melodramatic passage in the final stanza—"My love has sworn . . . / With me to live—to die" (343)—to defend herself against his amorous advances: "Soft scene, daring demonstration, I would not have;—I whetted my tongue: as he reached me, I asked with asperity, 'whom he was going to marry now? . . . What did he mean by such a pagan idea? *I* had no intention of dying with him'" (343–44). In our delight in her deflating retort we are likely, with Jane, to ignore the more ominous and significant passages in his song. He sings, for example,

> . . . Might and Right, and Woe and Wrath,
>> Between our spirits stood.
> I dangers dared; I hindrance scorned;
>> I omens did defy. . . .

and, ominously,

> I care not in this moment sweet,
>> Though all I have rushed o'er
> Should come on pinion, strong and fleet,
>> Proclaiming vengeance sore:

> Though haughty Hate should strike me down,
>> Right, bar approach to me. (342–43)

If the song and Rochester's view of their relationship are taken seriously, something must be seriously wrong: Right stands between them; Rochester defies omens (Jane, remember, has always believed in signs and presentiments) and avenging Nemesis. It may be clever and in character for Jane to seize not on these intentional elements in the song but on the romantic hyperbole that offends her self-regard. The reader's uncertainty about the nature of the fictional world, however, calls attention to those darker details over Jane's head. Various voices, genres, ontologies—vampirism and superstition, Helen's spirit world and certainty of the soul's immortality, love and its sanctioned joys, lightning bolts and Providence—dialogically complicate our projections and configurations of the novel and its world.

Yet this is a happy, romantic interlude, with few disturbances and with bright possibilities. Jane, chafing under Rochester's largesse and the knowledge that she brings no fortune into this marriage, writes her uncle John in Madeira to tell him she is alive and about to be married. But at a point of strong narrative emphasis, the end of chapter 9 of volume 2 (chapter 24)—which, the manuscript reveals, was once intended as the end of the volume—the narrator's voice is at last heard, cautionary, almost ominous; she accuses her younger self of hubris:

> My future husband was becoming to me my whole world; and, more than the world: almost my hope of heaven. He stood between me and every thought of religion, as an eclipse intervenes between man and the broad sun. I could not, in those days, see God for his creature: of whom I had made an idol. (346)

To this would have been added a final sentence to end the volume: "The name Edward Fairfax Rochester was then my Alpha and Omega of existence" (Clarendon 346n)—a sentence that would have compounded the idolatry with blasphemy, clothing Rochester with God's own identity. (See Revelations 1:8—"I am Alpha and Omega, the beginning and the ending, saith the Lord. . . .")

This authorized warning also has reinforcement and refraction in the fictional context. Laura, the heroine of Mary Brunton's *Self-Control* (1811, reprinted in 1832), twice in her nightly examination of her thoughts and actions of the day, finds she is making an idol of the unworthy Colonel Hargrave: "She accused herself of having given up her love, her wishes, her hopes and fears, almost her worship to an idol" (111).

> The issue of her self-examination was the conviction that she had bestowed on a frail, fallible creature, a love disproportioned to the merits of any created thing; that she had obstinately clung to her idol after she had seen its baseness; and that now the broken reed whereon she had leaned was taken away, that she might restore her trust and her love where alone they were due. (256)

A reader may remember intratextually Helen's warning that Jane thought too much of "creatures feeble as you" (81).

Had the second volume of *Jane Eyre* ended as originally intended, there would have been a long pause for the retrospective and prospective reconfiguration of the novel. Poised on the eve of its climax, reaching the hills of Beulah, the love story would have had to share the foreground with a long-threatened "counteracting breeze" (187), the emphatic and ominous religious warning. The memorable chapter ending with the news of the thunderbolt, Jane's plea for "a good spirit to suggest a judicious and satisfactory response" to Rochester's question about the validity of "overleaping an obstacle of custom" (274), and innumerable other details in earlier portions of the text would cluster around the religious emphasis here. Such details would be reinforced by the religious aura of the governess novel occasionally hovering over *Jane Eyre* and the insistent questions about the nature of reality and the supernatural raised by the Gothic elements. Had volume 2 ended emphatically with Rochester eclipsing God in Jane's thoughts and vision, most readers, certainly most mid-nineteenth-century readers, would inevitably project strong moral and religious impediments to the marriage. These would be resolved, this volume-ending might well suggest, not as Godwin or George Sand might resolve them (in favor of passion and the self), but more conventionally, yet, somehow, not too unhappily. Somehow.

Even if such expectations or projections were to prove "correct," and this ending would prove an aesthetically justifiable foreshadowing, it would change the affective experience of the novel and its exploration of moral issues drastically. For to insist on a religious reading and configuration of the novel *at this point* would make the reader's understanding of the world of the novel outdistance Jane's. We would be "above" Jane, looking down on her struggle to come to an awareness of the reality we have already apprehended. The prevailing affective response would be irony, not sympathy. But now, despite the narrator's reminders by distancing utterance—"in those days"—and novelistic topoi and the consequent double-voicedness, the reader is not moved by the ending of the volume to the privileged position of the elder Jane but is once more, as the volume continues to the wedding day, almost monologically with the younger Jane, in the middest. And this at least partial blindness of the authorial reader, as well as of Jane, is essential for the narrative strategy and ontological grounding of the novel.

· · · · · · ·

6

Devastation and Revisitations:
A Cold, Solitary Girl Again

From the end of the ninth of the eleven chapters in volume 2 of *Jane Eyre* (chapter 24 in editions in which the chapters are numbered consecutively) to the new end of the volume, the sky grows darker and darker. At first, on the day before the wedding, only figuratively: "the pearl-coloured robe, the vapoury veil" Jane will wear the next day she shuts in her closet, "to conceal the strange, wraith-like apparel . . . which, at this evening hour . . . gave out a most ghostly shimmer" (347). The sky, however, becomes literally darker; the "Italian summer" is past. Rochester has been away, and the reader absent. During his—and our—absence, something disquieting and incomprehensible has happened, the details of which the narrator deliberately, ostentatiously, and awkwardly withholds: "Stay till he comes, reader; and, when I disclose my secret to him, you shall share the confidence" (348). This hybridizes the utterance as both young Jane's and the narrator's utterance and, moreover, it hybridizes or conflates the auditors, Rochester and the reader. Paradoxically, this fusing of action, narration, and reception does not mask but rather discovers the fictionality of the event.

As Jane awaits Rochester's return—on the day following the as yet undisclosed happening—the weather turns sympathetically turbulent. In the course of her troubled walk she comes upon the chestnut tree whose trunk had been split in half the night of Rochester's proposal of marriage. The halves are still joined at the base and root.

"You did right to hold fast to each other," I said: as if the monster-splinters were living things, and could hear me. ". . . you will never have green leaves more—never more see birds making nests and singing idyls in your boughs; the time of pleasure and love is over with you; but you are not desolate: each of you has a comrade to sympathize with him in his decay." (349)

The identification of a tree with lovers is somewhat refracted by its previous appearance in the fiction of the time, particularly the revisiting of a text earlier encountered in the repertoire: Frederika Bremer's *The Neighbours*. There, an oak tree, the site where the missing hero had proposed, carefully tended since with flowers planted around its base, is used as the emblem of the separated lovers. These lovers are happily reunited, as the tending and the emblematic flowers prophecy (207–8). The emblem here in *Jane Eyre* is more portentous. What Jane suggests is that she and Rochester, like the chestnut tree, will be split apart, will not marry (the time of love is over), and so will have no children (no green leaves); but they will—in their hearts, probably—somehow be together and so not entirely "desolate."

The gloomy emblem and the fictional context might further prefigure an unromantic outcome. If the omen is fulfilled, Jane will not marry Rochester, and we may be in for something like Mrs. Sherwood's *Caroline Mordaunt*, an antiromantic, religious, providentialist governess novel we have had occasion to refer to in every one of the preceding chapters: there the heroine makes a solemn but unpassionate match with a clergyman cousin. (We will have reason to remember this possibility in the third volume of *Jane Eyre*.) Or Jane may not marry at all—many governesses do not. Or the omen could be a false clue meant to mislead and mystify the reader.

The false lead is a recognized element in narrative strategy, but its function is usually assumed to be merely that of creating suspense. That it may function ontologically is largely unacknowledged and its praxis largely unexplored. The novel is narrationally dialogic: "oppositional" plots—narrative roads not taken—are often marked by the false clue, the ignis fatuus; even when the "right" choice is made and the "true" story unfolds, the other potential plots suggested by the false leads shadow the text. The novel is thematically dialogic

. . . .

135

or responsive as well, written "against" an opposition whose views and conventions are incorporated into the text. The opposing conventions are both ideological and narrational—thus the importance of the reader's alertness to and awareness of generic signals—and they are "rebutted" or rejected by the novel's narrative and thematic structure. The very notion of an opposition introduces into the text "voices" other than the monologic voice of the author or narrator, setting up a dialogue in which the presumptively intentional and oppositional views dialectically redefine each other. A worldview whose opposition is X and a similar worldview whose opposition is Y are therefore not the same, having been defined by their dialogic interaction with the oppositional utterance. The novel is dialogic thematically more than narrationally, since the fictional actions are definitive in the text (it is difficult to say that Rowland Rochester's ghost "in fact" haunts the third story of Thornfield if the novel says otherwise); but not only is the worldview often open to controversy but the authority of the narrator's or author's voice is more subject to dispute, more readily considered one voice among other, equally pertinent voices. Exclusively valorizing one voice, therefore, even that presumptively carrying the authorial intention as comprehended by the authorial audience, is a partial reading that in its omissions becomes, in effect, a misreading.

The false expectation or ignis fatuus created by Jane's musings about the lightning-struck tree is, however, rather different from and more subtle than the typical one, such as the Gothic false leads about who or what inhabits the third story, and it reveals a narrational strategy central to the effect and quality of *Jane Eyre*. That Rowland's ghost haunts Thornfield is never verbally suggested by the narrator, nor is it an interpretation or even suspicion of young Jane's. The narrator (or author: Bakhtin sees an author's hand most clearly in selection and juxtaposition) has merely juxtaposed passages about ghosts and the vaguely suggestive history of the Rochester family in the guise of sequential narration. The rest is the work of readers familiar with Gothic novels or shilling shockers. That Grace Poole is the cause of the disturbances is verbally in the text, however, as young Jane's hypothesis, reinforced by Rochester; but it, too, is unconfirmed by the narrator and unsubstantiated by the text. The action within the text—lightning

. . . .

striking the chestnut tree just as Rochester is proposing—seems to have authorized the tree as a sign of the future of Jane and Rochester; that young Jane takes no notice of it does not so much undercut the value of the sign as it underscores Jane's passion-induced blindness. The text, in a patently double-voiced passage, has authorized the validity of "signs" in the name of both the "pilgrim" Jane and the narrator. If signs—like presentiments—are authorized by the text/narrator, must we not therefore believe Jane's reading of the sign of the chestnut tree? Must we not believe that it prophesies correctly that Jane and Rochester will not "flourish," though they may still be "connected"? Must this not be a true rather than false harbinger of what is to follow? If not, is the text playing fair with the reader? How, given the clear authorization of signs by the text, can the love story of Jane and Rochester have anything other than, at best, a bittersweet ending?

Jane's reading of the significance of the tree is, however, in quotation marks. Thus, despite the authorization of signs, this interpretation of a sign is marked as only a monologic report of what she said to herself at the time and therefore not necessarily authorized by the narrator. The narrator is, then, "playing fair," and the reader best beware. Outside the quotation marks there are other cautionary words or phrases possibly separating the voice or vision of Jane at this narrative moment from that of the narrator. The moon is said to have "*seemed* to throw on me one bewildered, dreary glance" (349, emphasis added). Did it "seem" to Jane at the time that the moon glanced at her? Or is it the narrator who now recognizes that the moon "did" no such thing but only "seemed" to young Jane to do so? In other words, is this short passage double-voiced?

The subtlety in the handling of focus and voice here is reminiscent of the passage early in the novel in which young Jane, in the red-room, sees a moving light and thinks it heralds the appearance of a ghost: "I can *now conjecture* readily that this streak of light was, *in all likelihood*, a gleam from a lantern, carried by some one across the lawn" (15; emphasis added). Here, the ostensible purpose of the narrator's intervention—"now"—is to "unauthorize" young Jane's fear of an imminent ghost, but the contrary, the "fact" that it was not an apparition but a sublunary lantern light, is also not fully authorized—it is merely

. . . . . .

"conjectured," likely but not certain. The way is left open for all kinds of worlds—natural, supernatural, or spiritualistic.

The narrative agility in these scenes does more than create suspense or mood; it destabilizes the fictional and ontological repertoire. Is this the kind of fictional world in which nature, or God through nature, communicates with human beings, or is young Jane merely projecting upon nature her own fears? Such questioning of the ontology of the novel is as responsible for the affective quality, the excitement of the experience of reading *Jane Eyre*, as the somewhat conventional, not to say hoary, question of who or what inhabits the upstairs rooms at Thornfield Manor. Indeed, that these questions cannot be separated is the hallmark of Brontë's novel.

While the narrator has authorized signs but put the younger Jane's interpretation of the sign of the tree in quotation marks and so disclaimed responsibility, it is not just the subtlety or unobtrusiveness of this marking that allows us to be trapped into accepting young Jane's interpretation: it is the primacy of our sympathy for and belief in Jane—and thus in her reading of the world—from the very opening of the novel. That sympathy and trust is a measure of the reader's moral horizon, roughly that of the ten-year-old Jane,[1] and that which the novel is subtly challenging. The handling of focus, voice, and authorization is, then, more than narrative strategy; it is moral and ontological strategy as well. Those of us who are reading as members of the authorial audience are in the dark with young Jane and, like Jane, are being led toward the light.

Jane's account of the unsettling events of the night before are also placed literally "in quotation marks," narrated the following day by Jane to Rochester upon his return. These strange events are made to seem credible, or almost so, not only by our long-standing trust in Jane, but by her circumstantial narration of the events and her convincing responses to Rochester's questioning. They are also made to seem more "real" within the terms of the world of the text, paradoxically, by the wholesale problematizing of everyday reality in the text: an atmosphere of unreality has already been established by reference to the ghostliness of the bridal gown and veil, the unsettling wind, and the bewildered, blood-red moon; now Jane would reduce Rochester himself to the spectral. Jane tells him of her disorientation:

> "I cannot see my prospects clearly to-night, sir; and I hardly know what thoughts I have in my head. Everything in life seems unreal."
>
> "Except me: I am substantial enough:—touch me."
>
> "You, sir, are the most phantom-like of all: you are a mere dream."
>
> He held out his hand, laughing: "Is that a dream?" said he, placing it close to my eyes. He had a rounded, muscular, and vigorous hand, as well as a long, strong arm.
>
> "Yes; though I touch it, it is a dream," said I. (352)

The evidence of the senses, even the intimate sense of touch, is put in doubt. Everyday realism, Jane's ability to identify the real through her senses, the whole ontological grounding of the novel, is problematized. This is a very daring gambit. It risks the deconstruction of the referentiality of the fiction. It challenges the reader to say, "Of course, Rochester is a dream. The story I am reading is all a dream. Even Jane is a dream. All is fiction." But her account, even without this gambit, would strain the reader's credibility and change the register of referentiality of the text. While the tale is being told and until such time as it is satisfactorily explained in terms consistent with the rest of the story, the nature of the whole novel itself is in question.

She had disturbed dreams, she tells Rochester. In the first, he was leaving her, and, burdened by a little child, she could not reach him or make him hear her call. Disturbed dreams before a wedding were not unusual in brides, at least fictional brides, of the eighteenth and nineteenth centuries. Before her wedding to Sir Charles Grandison, Harriet Byron also has an anxious and confused dream in which there is a howling wind. She tries to hide but is "dragged out of a subterraneous cavern. . . . A dear little baby was put into my arms" (Richardson, *Grandison* 3:148; vol. 6, Letter 32). The wind at Thornfield is real and outside Jane's dream; Harriet tries to hide herself and escape, but Jane is abandoned; both brides are rejected; Harriet's baby is dear, Jane's a burden. Overall, Harriet's dream is anxious, Jane's foreboding. Even to dream of a baby, as Bessie told her and as Jane had confirmed before she was called to her aunt's deathbed, is a fatal omen.

. . . .

Both women wake and go back to sleep only to dream again, Harriet imagining Sir Charles Grandison a ghost, even as the awakened Jane finds Rochester—and all else—"unreal." Harriet dreams of Italy as "dreary, wild, covered with snow, and pinched with frost," England as "gilded with sun" (3:149). Jane's England was having an Italian summer as well. Jane's second dream is more continuous with her first than is Harriet's but also centers on the transformation of place: Thornfield Hall is in ruins, Jane is still carrying the child, Rochester is galloping away, "departing for many years"; she tries to get one last look at him, but as she bends forward, "the wall crumbled; I was shaken; the child rolled from my knee; I lost my balance, fell, and woke" (357).

But this is only the preface to the tale she has to tell. She awakens with light shining in her eyes, candlelight. She thinks it must be Sophie, her maid. But, "Mr. Rochester, this was not Sophie, it was not Leah, it was not Mrs. Fairfax: it was not—no, I was sure of it, and am still—it was not even that strange woman, Grace Poole" (357).

NOT GRACE POOLE. What to this point has been the most reasonable solution to the mystery of Thornfield; the most mundane and realistic possibility, and therefore the possibility most consistent with Jane's view of reality; the longest-lived hypothesis, present as part of the mystery from the moment after Jane first heard the goblin laugh, and that which testified to Jane's sanity and perspicacity—and thus to her reliability as a witness—has suddenly, definitively been erased. Grace Poole was Jane's sole candidate—if not the reader's, who has been looking over her shoulder at other possibilities throughout—for the source of the mystery. That the mysterious roomer is not Grace Poole not only heightens the suspense and sends the reader's (as well as Jane's) mind spinning through other possibilities, other configurations, but also suggests the limitation of Jane's vision: her hardheaded realism, her refusal to be spooked by the superstitious and the supernatural are now no longer unqualified virtues. It requires a total and instantaneous reconfiguration of the novel, its ontology, and its future course. If definitely and certainly not Grace Poole, who was it, then, who set the fire? Who bit Mason as if to suck his blood? Who was

snarling behind the curtain? What in the (fictional) world is there beyond Jane's mundane imagination?

This intruder, Jane insists, was a stranger. She can describe her
clearly enough to make her identity as someone other than Grace
entirely credible. She was a tall, large woman with thick, dark hair,
dressed in something white, a "gown, sheet, or shroud." Her features
were "fearful and ghastly":

> "—oh, sir, I never saw a face like it! It was a discoloured face—it was a
> savage face. I wish I could forget the roll of the red eyes and the fearful
> blackened inflation of the lineaments!"
>
> "Ghosts are usually pale, Jane."
>
> "This, sir, was purple: the lips were swelled and dark; the brow fur-
> rowed; the black eye-brows wildly raised over the bloodshot eyes. Shall I
> tell you of what it reminded me?"
>
> "You may."
>
> "Of the foul German spectre—the Vampyre." (358)

Young Jane thinks the midnight intruder looked like a vampire,
but the narrator makes no comment confirming that fearful supposi-
tion; it is the reader familiar with vampire tales, remembering that
Mason said his attacker sucked his blood and that something is snarling behind the curtain like a wolf or dog, who makes the inference.
Though the possibility of a Thornfield vampire had been hinted at
earlier, such a Gothic phenomenon seemed inconsistent with the ontology of the text and Jane's skeptical common sense. Even if a recent
article in *Blackwood's* attested to the reality of vampires, it did not to this
point seem likely that tough-minded Jane would believe in such "non-
sense." Now, however, for the first time, vampirism explicitly enters
the text, and on Jane's—or, at least, young Jane's—own testimony and
authority. We saw earlier that the vampire's face as it appeared at the
victim's window in *Varney the Vampire* was "perfectly white—perfectly
bloodless. The eyes look like polished tin" (2). This is quite unlike the
face Jane describes. But that description of the creature in *Varney* was
before his "hideous repast." Afterward, "That face . . . was hideously
flushed with colour—the colour of fresh blood; . . . the lips receded
much from the large canine teeth. . . . A strange howling noise came

. . . . . .

141

from the throat of this monstrous figure, and . . . then, as if some impulse had seized upon it, it uttered a wild and terrible shrieking kind of laugh . . ." (6). Purple or blood-red face;[2] canine teeth—not described in *Jane Eyre*, but Jane has mentioned canine snarling; a howl; and a shrieking laugh!

Rochester, of course, says Jane's experience was all a dream. The validity of dreams as signs and the existence of vampires are cleverly equated. Jane insists her experience was real. "And your previous dreams: were they real too? Is Thornfield Hall a ruin? Am I severed from you by insuperable obstacles . . . ?" he asks (359). Jane replies, with prudent ominousness, "Not yet." Whether we share Jane's inferred fear that what she knows was dream—ruin and separation—is a true sign of what is to come, we are soon convinced that the horrifying incursion was no dream. She had herself thought it might have been, but "there, on the carpet—I saw what gave the distinct lie to my hypothesis,—the [wedding] veil, torn from top to bottom in two halves!" (359).

This shakes Rochester (and, for a different reason, the reader who believes that Brontë's novel takes place in everyday reality). Rochester must acknowledge the fact of the intrusion, and he is concerned for Jane's safety; but he recovers his poise after a few moments, and "explains" what must have happened:

> "It was half dream, half reality: a woman did, I doubt not, enter your room; and that woman was—must have been—Grace Poole; . . . but feverish, almost delirious as you were, you ascribed to her a goblin appearance different from her own . . . ; the spiteful tearing of the veil was real; and it is like her. I see you would ask why I keep such a woman in my house: when we have been married a year and a day, I will tell you; but not now." (360)

Grace Poole as the only "possible" explanation of the mystery, seems to get something of a reprieve—depending on how we gloss "possible." Nonetheless Jane, like the reader, is not satisfied. Readers of earlier vampire novels may be even less reassured by Rochester's explanation, or by his promise to tell Jane the story of Grace Poole "when we have been married a year and a day." For in the vampire context that is an ominous stipulation.

. . . .

About this point in the narrative readers must review what they know of the mystery of Thornfield, and though all may not do so at precisely this time and in this way, it seems legitimate to revisit the vampire scenes and whatever other incidents and implications are drawn into its magnetic field. We know that the creature that attacked Mason was female, and we may presume it to have been Grace Poole. At the time we wondered why Mason and Rochester were so solicitous about this snarling, violent thing. Now, however, we know that unless Jane's eyes deceived her, this purple-faced specter was not Grace, was much larger than Grace. We may remember how Rochester received the news of Mason's arrival when he was dressed as a gypsy crone, and that Jane failed to penetrate the disguise because she thought it might be Grace Poole. Rochester dressed as a woman; Rochester and Grace!

Grace, then, probably attacked Mason as if she were a vampire. If it were someone we know, it had to be Grace, certainly not Rochester, for he was with Jane, tending Mason, and Mason referred to "her." Someone or something like a vampire was in Jane's room, but it was not Grace. Jane is sure of that. Rochester was away from home. Or was he? Wasn't he supposed to be away from home when he showed up as the gypsy woman? Was the large figure Rochester, again dressed as a woman? Is the mystery so deep because there are two vampires? Vampirism is, after all, "contagious"; victims often become vampires in their turn. Was Grace an earlier victim of Rochester's? And Blanche? It is difficult for the reader to rule out any of the possibilities, for not only was the state of knowledge such that *Blackwood's* could publish articles suggesting the reality of such apparent legends as vampires in the far reaches of Middle Europe, but the fictional genre of the Gothic in the 1840s was also problematic. Though from the beginning of the species there were those tales that explained away the apparently supernatural and those that affirmed it, in the 1840s more than ever the ontology of the genre was in doubt. For example, at one point Varney explains that he is spreading false rumors and arranging false incidents of vampirism to frighten the occupants of Bannerworth away so that he can search for hidden treasure, but later, when the treasure has been recovered, he discovers that he is in fact a vampire. James suggests that though some of the zigs and zags are in response to the success of

· · · · · · ·

the story and the publisher's wish that it be prolonged, Rymer is himself experimenting with types of characters, plot, and, we might add, ontological structures (100).

In Polidori's *The Vampyre*, a Greek girl, Ianthe, tells the English protagonist, Aubrey, "the tale of the living vampyre, who had passed years *amidst his friends, and dearest ties*, forced *every year*, by feeding upon the life of a *lovely female*, to prolong his existence for the ensuing months" (41–42, emphasis added). (Every year! Will a year and a day be one day too late? No, surely. Not Rochester.) Ianthe's description of the fiend sounds to Aubrey very much like Lord Ruthven, a profligate nobleman who leads young men to self-destruction through gambling. (John Reed, we remember, was ruined by gambling and committed suicide; when Jane told Rochester she had been called to her Aunt Reed's, he said he had heard of the family, including a son—"one of the veriest rascals on [*sic*] town" [280]. Was that ominously disingenuous? No, surely. Not Rochester.) Later, lost in a Greek forest, Aubrey hears "the dreadful shrieks of a woman mingling with the stifled, exultant mockery of a laugh" (46). He is thrown down by a superhumanly strong creature and nearly strangled. The attacker is shot. It is Ruthven, who has killed Ianthe and is himself dying. As we have seen, he asks that his corpse be "exposed to the first cold ray of the moon after his death" (56). Dying, he insists that Aubrey "swear by all your soul reveres, by all your nature fears, swear that *for a year and a day* you will not impart your knowledge of my crimes or death to any living being in any way, whatever may happen, or whatever you may see" (55, emphasis added). Later, back in London, Aubrey hears a voice reminding him of his oath. On the last day of the year of his oath, he learns that Ruthven is to marry the next day. His bride? Aubrey's sister! On the day of the wedding he escapes confinement (he has been thought insane) and manages to get into the apartment where the wedding is to take place. Ruthven blocks his way: "Remember your oath, and know, if not my bride to-day, your sister is dishonoured. Women are frail!" (71). There will be no interrupted wedding in this tale. By the time Aubrey can persuade anyone to believe him, "Lord Ruthven had disappeared, and Aubrey's sister had glutted the thirst of a VAMPYRE!" (72).

The dark shadow of the vampire and the threatened catastrophic

. . . .

interruption of the marriage ceremony and separation from Rochester hang over the morning of Jane's wedding day. Rochester had suggested that Jane sleep with Adèle for comfort and protection. She did not sleep. Adèle, however, "passionless" and innocent, is asleep when Jane gets out of bed. Jane is still seeing signs: to her Adèle "seemed the emblem of my past life; and he, I was now to array myself to meet, the dread, but adored, type of my unknown future day" (361). The chapter ends on that note of love and dread, precisely the elements, Praz contends, that are inherent in all tales of vampirism. In the specific instance Praz cites, *Melmoth the Wanderer* (1820), there are also the Byronic elements familiar to the reader of *Jane Eyre* and an element that is now threatening to manifest itself in Brontë's narrative, the interrupted wedding (76).

Choosing to believe Rochester not a dream and Jane's life not unreal, are we now being led to believe not only in the prophetic reliability of dreams but in vampires? The ripped wedding veil, whether it was ripped by a vampire or a vicious slattern, is a bad omen; we are prepared to be as apprehensive as Jane when she notices two strangers in the churchyard. She feels her "forehead dewy, and [her] cheeks and lips cold" (364). Not much later—for the reader, one page—in the middle of the marriage ceremony, one of the strangers steps forward and declares "the existence of an impediment" (365).

An interrupted-wedding scene is a topos not occupied only by Gothic tales of vampirism in the fiction of the period. Though *Melmoth* is Gothic melodrama, the slightly less Gothic but highly melodramatic "orphan" novel visited here before, *Fatherless Fanny,* offers another version. Amelia interrupts her own wedding by announcing that, to foil the marriage being forced upon her, she had that morning married Sir Everard, the man she loved. In Scott's *A Legend of Montrose* (1819), Annot Lyle's wedding is interrupted by the madman Allan M'Aulay (Dry 39), and in one of Chorley's *Sketches of a Seaport Town,* "The Furnivals," on the eve of her wedding Alice Furnival's groom, purportedly her cousin the Reverend Sydney Furnival, is unmasked as Mr. Barton, a cutlery salesman (65–66). Lady Georgiana Fullerton's *Ellen Middleton. A Tale,* published only three years before *Jane Eyre,* is, though also somewhat melodramatic, closer than Gothic or romances to what we

. . . .

145

think of as everyday reality; like Brontë's novel, it is told in the first person by the eponymous heroine and involves dreams and weddings. Ellen, like Jane, has a foreboding dream just before her wedding, but her dream, unlike Jane's, is, as she knows, the product of a guilty secret. She has covered up her involvement in a fatal accident and has thereby put herself in the clutches of the tempestuously moody and Byronic Henry, who, somewhat like Rochester, vacillates between keen remorse and lawless passion. He had witnessed the accident, but so had a Mrs. Tracy. It is she who appears to Ellen in her dream. And it is she who appears the next day at the wedding ceremony. She does not actually interrupt the wedding, but Ellen "felt that she had cursed me" as she leaves (285). The dream is realized, though the ceremony goes on, and Ellen is married. But, we learn in a long conclusion appended to the "confession," she dies of consumption and Henry goes mad; the outcome is not unlike that of *Melmoth*, though without the benefit of vampire or vampirelike intruder.

Ellen has a guilty conscience, Jane does not. If there is just cause for the interruption of Jane's wedding, it is more likely to be the fault of the groom, as it is in the interrupted wedding of another Jane, the half-orphan Jane Bruff in Theodore Hook's *Fathers and Sons*, also published in the 1840s. Jane Bruff is being pushed by her father to marry the roué George Grindle, though she loves his half brother, Francis. So she is not distraught when Miles Blackmore interrupts the ceremony with the news that the groom "has a wife living. I have necessary witnesses at hand to prove her right to that title" (3:349).

Jane's wedding is interrupted because of the same impediment: "It simply consists in the existence of a previous marriage: Mr. Rochester has a wife now living" (365). The speaker is the lawyer for Mason, who is brought forward to confirm that Rochester is married to Mason's sister, Bertha, and that she is alive . . . and living in Thornfield Hall! Rochester admits it is all true but adds details of his own:

> I have been married; and the woman to whom I was married lives! . . . I daresay you have many a time inclined your ear to gossip about the mysterious lunatic kept there [at Thornfield] under watch and ward. Some have whispered to you that she is my bastard half-sister; some, my cast-off mistress;—I now inform you that she is my wife, whom I married fif-

. . . . . .

teen years ago. . . . Bertha Mason is mad; and she came of a mad family:—idiots and maniacs through three generations! Her mother, the Creole, was both a mad woman and a drunkard!—as I found out after I had wed the daughter: for they were silent on family secrets before. Bertha, like a dutiful child, copied her parent in both points. (368–69)

He takes the company to the third story of Thornfield Hall and shows off his wife. "What it was, whether beast or human being, one could not, at first sight, tell," Jane tells us. When Bertha sees Rochester, "the clothed hyena rose up, and stood tall on its hind feet" (370). She attacks him, he pins her arms and has her tied up.

The mystery of Thornfield is solved. The "deserted wing" houses not a ghost but an incarcerated wife; the Gothic is resolved narrationally and ontologically in realistic, not fantastic, terms, more *Udolpho* than *Otranto*. Whole batteries of expectations have been realized, modified, reversed, or canceled out by the appearance of Bertha Mason Rochester on the scene, and new configurations of what is to come and of what kind of world this is must be assembled and projected.

Bertha is not a pure, innocent victim, locked away by her villainous husband, but a drunkard, a powerful, violent madwoman, "intemperate and unchaste," whose "excesses . . . prematurely developed the germs of [hereditary] insanity" (391). This female figure is "occupied" territory, and her image, role, and meaning are refracted by those of her predecessors, the chorus of mad wives, "intemperate and unchaste," in early nineteenth-century fiction. We have met some of them before: Mrs. Herbert, in *Sketches from a Sea Port Town*, who was stashed away for years and escapes only to kill her own daughter; like Bertha, she is large and violent, and her madness was largely engendered by lust and dissipation. There is no mock marriage, no bigamy or interrupted wedding in her story. In LeFanu's *The Purcell Papers*, the blind, first, real Lady Glenfallen raves, threatens violence, and her features "seemed to indicate the habitual prevalence and indulgence of evil passions, and a power of expressing mere animal rage" (Jack 461). Fanny Richardson, the first-person narrator of LeFanu's tale, was, as Jane nearly is, victim of a bigamous mock marriage. Glenfallen, less a hero than Rochester, goes mad and kills himself. Though we do not

. . . .

see his first, legitimate wife, the story of another Edward, Edward Leeford, the father of Oliver Twist, is recognizable in Rochester's story
of his marriage: two "Edwards" forced into marriage for family pride
and gain; wives who are "unchaste" and marriages broken (though the
Leeford marriage was broken before the wife indulged in "continental frivolities" [Dickens, *Oliver* xlix]); bigamous marriage—or intended
marriage—to an innocent girl. The character of Leeford's wife is only
briefly described but her evil nature is reflected in that of her son,
Monks, who has an estate in, of course, the West Indies, where he fled
to "escape the consequences of vicious courses" (xlix) in England.[3]

Bertha does not say a single word in the text and appears directly
on only a dozen or so pages and indirectly on another dozen (Lerner
280). Because she is "the other Mrs. Rochester," the solution to the
mystery of half the novel and the impediment to the happy ending for
much of the final quarter, she is nonetheless a major element in the plot
of the novel. Symbolically and thematically she is a major element as
well (Grudin 145). Not only is her image multitudinously occupied by
the mad wives and bigamous marriages in the contemporary fictional
context but for the past quarter-century, largely through the influence
of feminist criticism, Bertha has become the pivot upon which much
vigorous critical discussion and multiple interpretations of *Jane Eyre*
have turned. The contemporary fictional context and modern criticism
thus make Bertha's space doubly occupied and her role and meaning
multitudinously refracted. At this point it seems appropriate, then, to
pause in the sequential reading of the text of *Jane Eyre* to review this
modern "occupation."

Regardless of how they evaluate it or what they mean by it, most
critics see Bertha's intended role as "monitory": "Bertha does (to say
the least) provide the governess an example of how not to act, . . . a
lesson more salutary than any Miss Temple ever taught" (Gilbert and
Gubar 361). And most authorial readings see her as a warning to Jane
of the consequences of unbridled passion: "*Jane Eyre* is a didactic novel
which subordinates the values of passion to those of desire. . . . As a
figurative representation of something unspeakable and as a projection of Jane's own dark potential, Bertha is used to show why Jane

must act as she does" (Grudin 145); "[Jane's] past life suggests a . . . capacity for passionate excess," which Mrs. Reed described as " 'a compound of virulent passions, mean spirit, and dangerous duplicity'—a description which is eerily applicable to Bertha" (Nestor 60–61). The "excess," "the unspeakable," the "dark potential" link unchecked passion and madness: "Both Bertha's license and her insanity represent the tyranny of passion over intellect" (Grudin 148). The text links unrestrained passion and madness in Jane most explicitly after Bertha's existence has been revealed. Jane recognizes her temptation to yield to Rochester's proposition that she become his mistress to be a form of insanity: "I will hold to the principles received by me when I was *sane*, and not *mad*—as I am now. . . . They have a worth—so I have always believed; and if I cannot believe it now, it is because I am *insane*—quite *insane*" (104–5, emphasis added).[4]

Bertha's madness has been seen both as a warning against female sexuality and as a representation of Jane's repressed sexuality (e.g., Martin 103; Eagleton, *Myths* 32; Grudin 153–54). Gilbert and Gubar, however, see it as a covert representation of women's rage against the conditions of women in the Victorian patriarchal society. They contend that "the most successful [nineteenth-century] women writers often seem to have channeled their female concerns into secret or at least obscure corners. In effect, such women have created submerged meanings, meanings hidden within or behind the more accessible, 'public' content of their works" (72). Their reading of *Jane Eyre*, therefore, sought its submerged meaning or meanings, and, as the title of their seminal study—*The Madwoman in the Attic*—suggests, they found that meaning in Bertha. Bertha, they maintain, is "Jane's dark double," and each of her "manifestations" is a mad, enraged response to a thought or repressed response of Jane's: Bertha's setting fire to Rochester's bed, for example, follows his "apparently egalitarian sexual confidences"; Jane's "fears of her own alien 'robed and veiled' bridal image, are objectified by the image of Bertha in a 'white and straight' dress, 'whether gown, sheet, or shroud, I cannot tell' "; Jane's dream of Thornfield in ruins is an angry wish that Bertha fulfills; the baby that falls from Jane's knees in the dream is her own childhood self from whom she

· · · · · · ·

is released by Bertha's death in the conflagration (360, 362). The sub-versive feeling is Jane's—or Brontë's or women's—rage against patri-archy; her autobiography is the story of a journey toward wholeness, a female bildungsroman. Her "confrontation, not with Rochester but with Rochester's mad wife Bertha, is the book's central confrontation, an encounter . . . not with her own sexuality but with her own impris-oned 'hunger, rebellion, and rage,' a secret dialogue of self and soul on whose outcome . . . the novel's plot, Rochester's fate, and Jane's coming-of-age all depend" (339).

It is a shrewd and challenging reading that would be more for-midable if it did not implicitly (and unnecessarily) claim that it is a reading of Brontë's "intention." To make rebellion and rage, which are clearly in the text, central to the text, its real if submerged meaning, requires significant distortions or omissions which weaken the argu-ment. Jane's feeling about her "extraordinarily self-assertive act" of telling off Aunt Reed, for example, is, indeed, as Gilbert and Gubar point out, compared to "a ridge of lighted heath, alive, glancing, de-vouring," but they neglect to report what follows—"the same ridge, black and blasted after the flames are dead, would have represented as meetly my subsequent condition, when half an hour's silence and reflection had shewn me the *madness* of my conduct" (41, emphasis added)—or, indeed, what immediately precedes it—"A child cannot quarrel with its elders, as I had done . . . without experiencing after-wards the pang of remorse and the chill of reaction" (40). Had she not known that she would be rejected, Jane says, she would "willingly . . . have gone and asked Mrs. Reed's pardon" (41). Gilbert and Gubar might have acknowledged this framing of Jane's exultation at her self-assertion by guilt and regret, identifying it as part of the "accessible 'public' content" behind which nineteenth-century women authors hid their subversive content, but by omitting these "appeasing" passages, apparently in order to make the expression of rage more clearly inten-tional, they undermine their argument.

Another instance of their leaping to the subversive reading with-out at least pausing to deal with the "accessible content" concerns a passage following the revelation of Bertha's existence. Jane's voice

. . . .

within tells her she must tear herself away from Rochester, figuratively plucking out her own right eye, cutting off her own right hand. Gilbert and Gubar, again for the purposes of their theme of feminist rage, read this without qualification as a "terrifying prediction" of Rochester's fate arising from Jane's "disguised hostility" toward him (360). In context, however, this is literally a warning to Jane from within herself— "conscience . . . held passion by the throat"—to leave Thornfield and avoid committing adultery (which is what the passage in Matthew [5:27–30] is about). This Biblical passage had also been used before in contemporary fiction, in Mary Brunton's *Discipline* (1814), to represent the termination of a potentially sinful relationship.[5] Ironically, it has also appeared before in *Jane Eyre*—the girls at Lowood had been forced to learn this fifth chapter of Matthew by heart (69)—and it is perhaps from that exercise that the passage is in Jane's repertoire. Though Rochester, who has indeed committed adultery many times, will literally suffer such a fate—or nearly so, for it is his left hand he loses— it is difficult to translate this passage describing Jane's passionate love and tortured temptation to remain with him as "disguised hostility."

The critics' shift of Brontë's target from Jane to Rochester diverts attention from the increasing intensity of Jane's moral danger, the power of her temptation, the inadequacy of her unaided resources, and the increasingly religious emphasis of her life story, which a truly "authorial" reading would need to notice. Gilbert and Gubar's reading, refocused and redocumented, may serve to show the text as it cannot see itself, but is not convincingly that of the authorial audience.[6]

Later feminist critics also object to their predecessors' reducing one woman, Bertha, to the role of another woman's—Jane's—"dark double," making her ancillary, important only in relation to Jane's life and moral growth:

> contemporary feminist criticism must not, surely, reproduce the silences and occlusions of the nineteenth-century English culture in allowing the white, middle-class woman to stand as its own 'paradigmatic woman.' . . . it is possible to trace in the trajectory, in the very form of the novel [*Jane Eyre*], a complex configuration of the determinations of class, kind, gender and—what is nowhere spoken of but is omnipresent—race. . . . The

difficulty is to honour what can be honoured of its female heroism without suppressing a recognition of the social formation to which, along with her twenty thousand pounds, Jane is heir. (Boumelha 63–64)

Though Jean Rhys's 1966 novel, *The Wide Sargasso Sea*, told a version of Bertha's own story, it was not until the 1980s that feminist critics like Boumelha focused not only on Bertha but on the other non-English or non-middle-class women in Brontë's novel as potential subjects with their own lives and claims. One of the earliest (and angriest, and best), Jina Politi's "*Jane Eyre* Class-ified" (1982), looked at Bertha and *Jane Eyre* from the "outside," seeing Brontë's novel as it could not see itself, as a product and expression of English middle-class women's values. Following Politi, Gayatri Spivak's "Three Women's Tales and a Critique of Imperialism," and other critics of the mid-1980s, Boumelha finds that the early feminist view of *Jane Eyre* has changed and,

> another story emerges: "no social revolutionary," argues Lee R. Edwards, "Jane is rather a displaced spiritual aristocrat"; Politi analyses how "the narrative together with the girl-child will grow from revolted marginality to quiescent socialisation, reblending the marginality which it initially exposed, thus securing its survival through the convention of a 'happy ending'"; and [Judith] Weissman concludes that "the end of the book reveals the first half for what it is—not the rage of the Romantic radical who wants justice, but the rage of the outsider who just wants to get in." (60)

Cora Kaplan agrees that "Charlotte Brontë was no political radical" (173), supporting her position by challenging Virginia Woolf's gender-bound criticism of the "awkward break" of "continuity" between the "feminist" passage of Jane on the rooftop of Thornfield Hall in chapter 12 and the mad laugh of "Grace Poole" that interrupts it. She points out that in its inclusion of "men," "masses," "millions," and "human beings," Jane's meditation deals with "more than sexual difference," and that "its significant moment of incoherence" lies in the linking of "the subordination of women and the radical view of class oppression" which runs counter to "the class politics of the text" (172–73). The laughter that interrupts Jane's meditation, then, is a warning "quite literally that the association of feminism and class struggle leads to madness":

. . . .

[Bertha] and her noises become the condensed and displaced site of un-reason and anarchy as it is metonymically figured through dangerous femininity in all its class, race, and cultural projections. Bertha must be killed off, narratively speaking, so that a moral Protestant femininity, licensed sexuality and a qualified socialized feminism may survive. Yet the text cannot close off or recuperate that moment of radical association between political rebellion and gender rebellion. (174)

Boumelha confirms Brontë's "politics of class" by pointing out how she treats—or rather ignores—women of the lower class, the female servants, Bessie and Grace Poole (John Kucich ["*Jane Eyre* and Imperialism" 106] adds Hannah). She focuses, however, not on class but on the treatment of the issues of race and imperialism that surround Bertha, "the maddening burden of imperialism concealed in the heart of every English gentleman's house of the time." It is, she points out, from Bertha's blood relations and her native Jamaica that all the underlying wealth and the inheritances of the novel depend (60–61). "Race" and "racism" in the text may be difficult to define precisely for modern readers, perhaps, because of our almost exclusive construction of "race" in terms of "color" and the ambiguity of the term "creole." The OED says that in the West Indies "creole" means born in the West Indies rather than in Europe or Africa and is not related to color. Spivak insists Bertha is white, and Boumelha suggests that Bertha is "dark, but not black: while the word 'creole' marks a double displacement of origins, Bertha is fixed as white by her status as daughter of settler planters" (61). Nestor, however, points out Brontë's identification of character, behavior, perhaps capacity, and "blood": "Bertha's madness and licentiousness are inextricably linked to her Creole blood, whereas Jane's sound and chaste nature is the legacy of her English inheritance. Though Bertha is of mixed blood, the daughter of 'Jonas Mason, merchant, and of Antoinetta, his wife, a Creole,' her madness is . . . unequivocally linked to her foreign mother" (63).

Of course, unrestrained passion is, as Pumblechook would say, and Brontë seems to affirm, "not English": "There are references to a 'pleasure-villa' in Marseilles; the 'slime and mud of Paris' " and national/racial identification of Rochester's mistresses—French, Céline; Italian, Giacinta; and German, Clara—"which reads like a

. . . .

checklist of continental laxity" (Nestor 63).[7] As we will see later in the text, however, British superiority extends beyond sexual morality: "the British peasantry," Jane says, "are the best taught, best mannered, most self-respecting of any in Europe" (407), and, it surely goes without saying, any throughout the world. (See below, ch. 7.)

It does not seem likely that Brontë would deny such "patriotic" sentiments (though she may have been amazed that such an obvious truth as British superiority could be questioned). Recent analyses of the classist and racist/nationalist assumptions or ideology of the text do not, then, run counter to what is explicit or assumed in the text. They read the text from within the authorial audience's repertoire but also see the text from the "outside," interrogating that audience's unconscious preconceptions, thus seeing the text as it "is," but as it could not see itself.

After the revelation of the existence of Bertha Rochester, Jane, unlike some of her fictional predecessors, has to make a moral choice. Oliver's mother did not know there was already a Mrs. Leeford; she did not have to choose to stay with or leave her Edward. There was no second Mrs. Herbert in the Seaport Town. Fanny Richardson did not choose but was already involved in a bigamous or mock marriage, and when she learned the truth events unraveled so quickly it was not her choice that determined the outcome. Jane, however, must make a choice within social and literary conventions that will significantly influence the authorial audience's inferences of meaning in the world of the text. The Gothic topos has been preceded and infiltrated by so many other novel kinds—orphan or foundling novels, Byronic novels, bildungsromans, Godwinian "feminist" novels, religious novels—many with their own ideological presumptions, that the familiar literary and social norms have in *Jane Eyre* been defamiliarized. This is precisely the defamiliarization through multiple or newly juxtaposed conventions that, Wolfgang Iser suggests, generates the quest for meaning in the contemporary reader:

> literature takes on its function though the weaknesses of the prevailing system—either to break it down or shore it up. The contemporary reader will find himself confronted with familiar conventions in an unfamiliar

light, and, indeed, this is the situation that causes him to become involved in the process of building up the meaning of the work. (Iser 78)

Though it is the text that defamiliarizes, it is not necessarily the text that determines whether it thereby breaks down or shores up the prevailing system (as a reader-response critic should certainly know). Though most contemporary reviewers and readers were swayed by the defamiliarization of the literary conventions of genre and found the central "mystery of Thornfield" and the plot of *Jane Eyre* strange and original, a few, like fellow novelist Thackeray, thought it "hackneyed." Whether *Jane Eyre* sought to break down or shore up social and political conventions was even more dependent on the reader: Elizabeth Rigby in the Tory *Quarterly* and the reviewer in the *Christian Remembrancer*, concentrating doubtlessly on Jane's childhood revolt, the criticism of Brocklehurst, and the satiric treatment of Blanche Ingram and her aristocratic circle (as well as later things in the novel which we have yet to come to), thought *Jane Eyre* subversive of church and state, while the *Observer, Era*, and *People's Journal*, among other publications, saw it shoring up contemporary moral conventions and apparently detected no threat to the monarchy.[8]

The defamiliarization of social and cultural conventions does not, as Iser implies, lead automatically to a uniform "reassessment" of norms and therefore a single, occasion-specific evaluation or interpretation of the meaning of the text. It is the defamiliarization of the norms that "for the later reader . . . help to re-create that very social and cultural context that brought about the problems which the text itself is concerned with" (Iser 78). A text without "problems," without defamiliarized norms, can in later periods be viewed from the outside, seen as it could not see itself, but it cannot be entered into, its context recreated from the inside as well as seen from the outside, whether breaking down or shoring up conventions. The multifarious genres, manifold generic topoi, and social "incoherencies," signally implicated in Bertha and the mystery of Thornfield, keep *Jane Eyre* alive, relevant, meaningful, and unfinalizable. Modern readers, even when feminists all, can recreate and reinhabit its "social and cultural context" and the very "problems which the text itself is concerned with." Gilbert and

· · · · · · ·

Gubar can, like Elizabeth Rigby, find Jane revolutionary (though as a term of praise, not opprobrium), and an interesting group of the most recent feminist critics can, like most of the reviewers of the 1840s, though in somewhat different terms and with rather different evaluations, find Jane "a spiritual aristocrat," "a girl-child [who] will grow from revolted marginality to quiescent socialisation" (Boumelha 60).

So dramatic and traumatic is the revelation of Bertha and the solution of the mystery of Thornfield, so disruptive of the reader's expectations and Jane's, of her life and her life story, it is difficult to go on. Jane has remained calm, almost numb, throughout the scene and the disclosures. Now she retires to her room, to think.

> I was in my own room as usual—just myself, without obvious change: nothing had smitten me, or scathed me, or maimed me. And yet, where was the Jane Eyre of yesterday?—where was her life?—where were her prospects?
>
> Jane Eyre, who had been an ardent, expectant woman—almost a bride—was a cold, solitary girl again: her life was pale; her prospects were desolate. (373)

She is devastated, her life since Gateshead emptied of significance. Her memories of her recent past and the prospects then before her seem to mock her present state, but she cannot wholly exonerate herself from blame—"Oh, how blind had been my eyes! How weak my conduct" (374).

The novel too is laid waste. The love story as well as the Gothic mystery seems to be over, to have vanished. The reader too is bereft of recent prospects, expectations, generic indicators, and perhaps a bit ashamed of his or her "blindness" or conventional expectations. We are invited to retreat to the Jane of page 1: to concern ourselves with "a cold, solitary girl again."

Neither Jane nor the reader can (or would want to) retreat to Gateshead. Jane amid life's perils may have found or be about to find some "real knowledge" (100).

> . . . I seemed to have laid me down in the dried-up bed of a great river; I heard a flood loosened in remote mountains, and felt the torrent come: to rise I had no will, to flee I had no strength. I lay faint; longing to be

. . . .

dead. One idea only still throbbed life-like within me—a remembrance of God: it begot an unuttered prayer: these words went wandering up and down in my rayless mind, as something that should be whispered; but no energy was found to express them:—"Be not far from me, for trouble is near: there is none to help."

It was near: and as I had lifted no petition to heaven to avert it—as I had neither joined my hands, nor bent my knees, nor moved my lips— it came: in full, heavy swing the torrent poured over me. The whole consciousness of my life lorn, my love lost, my hope quenched, my faith death-struck, swayed full and mighty above me in one sullen mass. That bitter hour cannot be described: in truth, "the waters came into my soul; I sank in deep mire: I felt no standing; I came into deep waters; the floods overflowed me." (374)

It is at this point that the second volume ends, producing a powerful pause. The hectic forward movement of the love story and the mystery checked, the narrative comes to a close and curls back on itself. Thornfield, even Lowood, and the intervening years are as if erased. Her situation is now as it was—Jane is a cold, solitary girl again— but she has changed, as the reader's perspective of her must. She is not the girl who saucily told the Reverend Mr. Brocklehurst she did not like Psalms. She is a bereft young woman-child who, in her pain, finds in her "rayless mind," though she cannot utter them, the words of the eleventh verse of Psalm 22: "Be not far from me, for trouble is near: there is none to help." And the elder Jane, the narrator, can only describe that painful time in words adapted from another Psalm (69:1– 2): "That bitter hour cannot be described: in truth, 'the waters came into my soul; I sank in deep mire: I felt no standing; I came into deep waters; the floods overflowed me' " (375).[9]

" 'Psalms are not interesting,' " she had told Brocklehurst. He replied, " 'That proves you have a wicked heart; and you must pray to God to change it: to give you a new and lean one: to take away your heart of stone and give you a heart of flesh' " (35). Her saucy answer in retrospect seems ironic indeed: her heart is all too much of vulnerable "flesh." It is ironic, too, that that black marble pillar Brocklehurst seems in retrospect right—if no less repulsive—and spunky, lovable Jane wrong. We would seem to be driven at this point to review that

· · · · · · ·

past and dramatically adjust our judgments if not our feelings about Jane the rebellious child, and therefore our moral configuration of the world of the novel.

The passage at the end of volume 2 in its water imagery recalls the passage with similar imagery, and similarly placed, at the end of volume 1. Then, Jane, having rescued Rochester from fire, tossed and turned the rest of the night in a turbulent sea of trouble and joy, hope and doubt, glimpsing the shore of matrimony (Beulah), but, prophetically it turns out, being pushed away every time she nears it (187–88). The billows of trouble now overwhelm her, washing away that turbulent idyll of love that all but filled the second volume. Her dream of a parting from Rochester is about to be fulfilled but not quite in the way the dream "predicted." In the dream, Rochester rode away from her; now, in the wakened world, she must leave him—"from his presence I must go." The baby that rolled from her lap in the dream is now figuratively her love, which "shivered in [her] heart, like a suffering child in a cold cradle." The child/love is not dead, but "never more could it turn to him" (374). The prophecy of the cleft tree as well as that of the dream now seems justified: not only is there an impediment to their marriage but, she now feels, she could not give her love to him, no matter how precious and persistent it remains. A shadow darker than a vampire's wing is cast over the future of the novel, or at least over Jane's and Rochester's love.

All Jane has left at the end of the second volume is "a remembrance of God." So the volume ends as it would have ended with chapter 9, on a religious note. Had it ended earlier, as intended, the note would have been a warning—Jane was making an idol of Rochester and he was coming between her and God. The emphasis of such a volume-ending might well suggest there was trouble ahead, but probably would not jeopardize the reader's confidence in a happy ending. Now, however, the final note is more somber. If we can believe the experiencing-I—the mature narrator is strategically silent—Jane and Rochester are parted forever, even though some love may remain. If there will be passion ahead, it will be religious; if there is religion ahead, it will be religious passion, agony. This dark shadow over the future cannot wholly

. . . . . .

obliterate our hope that it will be otherwise, but it can (should) put it in doubt.

Modern readers may expect *Jane Eyre* to end happily because that, after all, is what Victorian novels almost invariably do, and that was what Victorian readers expected and demanded, we have been told over and over. It comes as a surprise to us, then, to discover that in October 1847—the very month in which *Jane Eyre* was published— a critic in the *Westminster Review,* reviewing Anne Marsh's *Norman's Bridge,* could complain that "it has of late been the fashion among novelists to avoid what is called 'poetical justice,' and to disappoint the reader with a catastrophe made as unhappy as possible, to harmonize with what is assumed to be the natural order of events" (48:132). Many of the domestic novels of the day and others that claimed in subtitles or text to be "stories of everyday life" distanced themselves from what they thought of as the romantic popular fashion, the happy ending. Thus Mrs. Hall, in "The Governess," published in *Chamber's* in 1842, says,

> And now, if my tale were to end, as made up stories do, with a report that the old man found his grandchild [Emily, a governess, suffering from consumption] much better than he had anticipated; that they lived for a short time happily together, and then the governess was married to a great lord, to the discomfiture of all gossip, I should substitute fiction for fact—which I cannot do. (92)

Cold, solitary Jane no longer seems a figure of romance but of a novel of domestic realism. There may be no happy ending, and if there is to be one, its means and nature now seem obscure. The final volume of *Jane Eyre* does not, despite the terminal nature of the ending of volume 2, open on a new scene,[10] nor does it promise relief from the despair at the end of the second volume or even a hint of a happy ending. Though Jane has already been reduced to a cold, solitary girl again, "erasing" Thornfield, Lowood, and even the moment of rebellion at Gateshead, more is yet to come. The very nature of reality in the world of *Jane Eyre* must be reassessed, and Jane's pride in the independence and power of her very self must be torn from her.

When the newly cold and solitary Jane asks herself what she is to

. . . .

do, "the answer my mind gave—'Leave Thornfield at once,'" comes immediately and insistently. She tries to squirm out of it, but "conscience, turned tyrant, held passion by the throat," and tells her that if she were to stay he would "thrust her down to unsounded depths of agony" (379). One Thornfield chapter, one long, wrenching farewell scene, one more devastating stripping away of a layer of selfhood remains.

That chapter opens with her coming to the surface of the flood, still questioning what she must do. It is then that the awful and relentless voice within tells her, "You shall tear yourself away; none shall help you: you shall, yourself, pluck out your right eye; yourself cut off your right hand: your heart shall be the victim" (379). When she emerges from her room, Rochester is waiting, full of love and violence, almost like Lovelace. He urges her passionately to enter a bigamous marriage, to fly with him to France. Jane confesses that she loves him but must leave him. To resist, she realizes, is cruel, "to yield was out of the question. I did what human beings do instinctively when they are driven to utter extremity—looked for aid to one higher than man: the words 'God help me!' burst involuntarily from my lips" (388). Again we revisit Lowood. Helen Burns had warned Jane that she cared too much for the love of human beings—as she cares for the love of Rochester now—and relied too much on her self and not on God and the world of spirits. Jane's agonized echoing of the Psalms, her recollection of the passage from Matthew, and now her involuntary prayer suggest a cataclysmic change in the moral world of the secular, self-reliant, and independent Jane. This is not the voice or world of the first, the rebellious and skeptical Jane, but a second, more knowledgeable Jane.

She will need all her new resources, for Rochester, telling her the story of his marriage and misery, pleads with her to come live with him and be his love. There are vague echoes of *Clarissa* again—Lovelace argues as does Rochester that he can be saved from returning to dissipation, perhaps debauchery, only through true, pure, self-sacrificial love; and Rochester at one point even conjectures about taking Jane by force (405). Lovelace has had in the intervening years numerous progeny in the English novel, however, and these sites the reader may revisit as well. Colonel Hargrave, in Mary Brunton's *Self-Control*, tells

Laura that "bound by your charms, allured by your example, my reformation would be certain, my virtue secure" (18), but when she resists,
he turns ugly: "Cold, pitiless, insensible woman—yes, I renounce you.
In the haunts of riot, in the roar of intemperance, . . . when I am lost
to fame, to health, to usefulness—my ruin be on your soul" (39). He
finally asks for, and receives, two years' "probation" to prove his resolve but fails again. In Bremer's *The Neighbours,* where we have seen
the tree emblematic of the lovers, the Byronic hero Bruno, whose past
sins are greater than those of Rochester, proposes to his childhood
sweetheart Serena and says he would change if he had a pure wife:
" 'She must become mine,' he says, 'if I am to find peace on earth' "
(193). Later, when they are to be married, he says he sought her in
order "to acquire an angel for my distempered soul" (373), but like
Jane she had not yielded while there was a moral impediment. When
Clara Neville, McCrindell's English Governess (visited in chapters 2,
3, and 5 above) discovers her fiancé is living loosely and has lost his
religion, she breaks the engagement, but he urges her not to treat him
so; even if he were worse, he insists, "she might very easily have re-
claimed him" (42). Later, he says she still has the power to reform
him if she would marry him. "Ah, Edward [yet another Edward]!" she
says, "you speak against your own convictions. I have no such power.
How can I hope to sway a heart which continually resists the stirrings
of the Spirit of grace?" (125). To those familiar with the fictional context, Rochester's threats and protestations sound hollow, and Jane's
response expected and applauded. Saving your lover's soul by sacri-
ficing your own moral values is not, in nineteenth-century fiction, a
laudatory, moral, or religious act.

Nor is this morality or definition of what is properly an act of love
limited to religious or domestic fiction. Such scenes appear not only
in the more modest and religious of eighteenth-century and contemporary novels but also in Gothic novels. In Radcliffe's *Udolpho,* Valan-
court, in his gentler way, tells Emily (who he thinks is casting him
off at another's behest), "Would you not otherwise be willing to hope
for my reformation—and could you bear, by estranging me from you,
to abandon me to misery—to myself! . . . if you still loved me, you
would find your happiness in saving mine" (515). There are as well

· · · · · · ·

comparable scenes in that very recent melodramatic, heated, notorious novel, Jewsbury's *Zoe,* which we had occasion to look at in relation to the fire-and-dishabille scene. The priest Everhard and Zoe part, and despite her attempt to live up to Everhard's image of her, Zoe is later tempted to "live the life of passion" by her strong feelings for the Byronic Comte de Mirabeau. Only the existence of a wife prevents her from doing so. Mirabeau must return to France, to a high post, and asks Zoe to accompany him, "to be my angel, my support, my councillor" (120). "If it is to become your wife, Gabriel, that you are asking me, I am willing to do so," she responds. Even though he is divorced he cannot marry again, he says, and when she refuses him he accuses her of being capable only of shallow love, of loving position and wealth like all ordinary women, and warns her that by her "selfish" refusal she will save her reputation but damn him: "When I am gone, what comfort will you find in the consciousness that you have saved yourself and lost me? for if you fail me now, all hope of good is over for me. You have the power to do with me what you will, make of me what you will" (121). Like Jane, she refuses; like Jane (and Clarissa), she says once she becomes his mistress, she will lose her power over him, and will be like the others.

Zoe is as staunch and moral in her refusal as Jane, and indeed rededicates her life in "Platonic constancy" to Everhard and is ennobled thereby—which may cast some shadow over what is to come in *Jane Eyre.* But Zoe is not your typical Victorian heroine. She is illegitimate, half-Greek, attains a "masculine" education, and hates domesticity. She is passionate (permissibly so because half-Greek, no doubt) and unconventional. As noted earlier, Jewsbury says, "Women gifted like Zoe often present instances of aberration from the standard of female rectitude" (41). They have too much energy and not enough channels for activity (42). Even when they have children, as Zoe does, they realize "the maternal instinct is only one passion amongst the many with which a woman is endowed" (104). Their feelings are so strong that maxims do not always guide them: "A strong, vivid sensation, a vehement temptation, has, when it comes, a vitality and reality that make the most firmly believed and most emphatic maxims seem very vague and ineffectual" (104).

. . . .

So Richardson and his progeny do not have the stage to them-selves, and the "generic static" makes the ultimate shape of Jane's story problematic. If Zoe is the prototype, the projected configuration of the last volume of *Jane Eyre* will assume the shape of the novel of Godwinian and feminist rebellion prefigured in the first volume: "vivid sensation" and "vehement temptation" may still deflect Jane from her "emphatic maxims"—and many readers have wished this to be the case.

Though Jane resists, and advises Rochester to "trust in God and yourself. Believe in heaven. Hope to meet again there"—a moral growth in Jane since Lowood, where she wondered if heaven existed— her struggle with her sense of right, with her "most firmly believed and most emphatic maxims," is terrible. When he pledges fidelity and asks her to pledge the same, she must play iconoclast. She experiences "an ordeal: a hand of fiery iron grasped my vitals. Terrible moment: full of struggle, blackness, burning! Not a human being that ever lived could wish to be loved better than I was loved; and him who thus loved me I absolutely worshipped: and I must renounce love and idol" (402–3). When he pits humanity, compassion, against mere law; when he argues that if she says no, he will be injured, but that if she says yes, since she has no family, no one will be hurt, Jane's "very Conscience and Reason turned traitors against [her]" (404). There is, however, a Self beyond feeling, conscience, and reason. "I care for myself. The more solitary, the more friendless, the more unsustained I am, the more I will respect myself."

But now as important as respect for the autonomous self are those "most firmly believed and most emphatic maxims" that Jewsbury finds weak in time of crisis, but Jane finds the only safe stars to steer by; we have quoted a portion of the passage before, but it is important enough to quote more fully here:

> "I will keep the law given by God; sanctioned by man. I will hold to the principles received by me when I was sane, and not mad—as I am now. Laws and principles are not for the times when there is no temptation: they are for such moments as this, when body and soul rise in mutiny against their rigour: stringent are they; inviolate they shall be. If at my individual convenience I might break them, what would be their worth?

They have a worth—so I have always believed; and if I cannot believe it now, it is because I am insane—quite insane: with my veins running fire, and my heart beating faster than I can count its throbs. Preconceived opinions, foregone determinations, are all I have at this hour to stand by: there I plant my foot." (404–5)

Even after this outburst, even when Rochester knows himself defeated, she cannot leave the room without turning back, kissing his cheek, smoothing his hair. " 'Farewell!' was the cry of my heart, as I left him. Despair added,—'Farewell for ever!' " (407). The temptation would not be so great, the struggle so titanic, if her love were not so powerful. Nor would other possible outcomes to the fictional events still be possible were it not for the din of generic voices, the generic overdetermination.

Jane gets help, though whether from within or without is uncertain. That night, having decided to leave Thornfield, she revisits her past at Gateshead in a dream; she believes that she is in

the red-room at Gateshead; that the night was dark, and my mind impressed with strange fears. The light that long ago had struck me into syncope, recalled in this vision, seemed glidingly to mount the wall, and tremblingly to pause at the centre of the obscured ceiling. I lifted up my head to look: the roof resolved to clouds, high and dim; the gleam was such as the moon imparts to vapours she is about to sever. I watched her come—watched with the strangest anticipation; as though some word of doom were to be written on her disk. She broke forth as never moon yet burst from cloud: a hand first penetrated the sable folds and waved them away; then, not a moon, but a white human form shone in the azure, inclining a glorious brow earthward. It gazed and gazed on me. It spoke, to my spirit: immeasurably distant was the tone, yet so near, it whispered in my heart—
    "My daughter, flee temptation!"
    "Mother, I will."
    So I answered after I had waked from the trance-like dream. (407)

This is an extraordinarily powerful though extraordinarily qualified episode. To start within the experience: Is the vision that of Jane's mother, Mrs. Eyre, emerging from the image of the moon, or is it the moon it-/herself that speaks to Jane and she to it/her?[11] This may be rendered moot, since the experience takes place within a dream and

· · · · · · ·

indeed communicates the montage-like experience of many dreams. But dreams have been authorized by the narrator for the accuracy of their predictive value earlier in the text (prior to the summons to her aunt's deathbed, prior to the invasion of her room by Bertha on the night before the wedding), and perhaps by their ontological relationship to presentiments, signs, and sympathies, which were explicitly endorsed by the narrator (276). This experience, too, may gain some credence in being described as a "trance-like dream." That the vision may be, indeed, that of Jane's mother, whose spirit is guarding her daughter, might be reinforced by the firm belief of Helen Burns that alongside this world is "an invisible world and a kingdom of spirits: that world is round us, for it is everywhere; and those spirits watch us, for they are commissioned to guard us" (81).

The substance of Jane's dream may seem qualified by its taking place "in the red-room at Gateshead" and by the fact that the vision of the moon/mother is preceded by a repetition of the experience of a gliding light. That earlier experience, we recall, had been explained away with the apparent, if qualified, authority of the narrator: "I can now *conjecture* readily that this streak of light was, *in all likelihood*, a gleam from a lantern, carried by some one across the lawn; but then . . . I thought the swift-darting beam was a herald of some coming vision from another world" (15, emphasis added). Should this episode, like the earlier, be "conjectured away," or should the red-room "herald of some coming vision" be retrospectively authenticated?[12]

There seems no easy way at this point to define with any certainty the ontology of *Jane Eyre*. Nor is there any easy resolution to the issue in the contemporary context. We have already seen that the secular and skeptical novelist Catherine Crowe had recently become convinced of the possible existence of ghosts. On the other hand, in an episode like that in *Jane Eyre* involving a dead mother, Fatherless Fanny (like Crowe and Jane, level-headed), is forced to face the possible reality of supernatural appearances by her own experience—only to have her experience explained away. Fanny, motherless as well as fatherless, is told of ghosts that haunt Bellafyn Castle and a rock where Lady Balla- fyn, Fanny's mother, walks in white. Fanny climbs the rock and prays, "Oh, would to Heaven that I might be permitted to behold it! . . .

· · · · · · ·

165

oh deign to show thyself"—even though under normal circumstances, Fanny's "better judgement [like Jane's] would reject the idea of the appearance of supernatural beings" ([Reeve] 323–24). A tall slender figure does appear, holding its arms out to sea, and praying. It is indeed Fanny's mother! It is only later that Fanny discovers that it is not her mother's ghost, but her living mother who has been hidden away in a "deserted wing."

We must not, then, jump to conclusions about the nature of reality in *Jane Eyre*. Or, rather, based on the previous details of the text and on the multivalent context, we should jump to many conclusions so long as we do not settle on one prematurely, for the experiential and even the interpretive function of this ontologically problematic passage at this point in Brontë's narrative does not lie in its meaning but precisely in its problematic nature, the fact that it puts in doubt just what is "real" in the fictional world of *Jane Eyre*. This reinforces the breakdown of the dominant generic structures—the Gothic, the governess-domestic, and all the others—at the end of the second and beginning of the third volumes of the text. The reader, like Jane, is in limbo.

Awake and asleep, however, Jane has decided to leave Thornfield, and at dawn she does so. She is tempted to go to Rochester, tell him she loves him and will live with him for the rest of her life. Her hand reaches for the knob of the door to his room, but she pulls it back, walks out of Thornfield and toward "a road that I had never travelled" (409). Even now she thinks of turning back, sickened by the thought of what her disappearance will do to Rochester. The dissolution of her former self, of her only self as she knows it, is all but complete. A few hours earlier, though Conscience and Reason and Feeling aligned themselves with Rochester, she could and would resist, she told him, because *"I care for myself. . . . I will respect myself"* (404); but that passage cannot be extracted from the context and be used to represent Jane's ultimate moral position or to define conclusively the reality of the world of the fiction. It is, in effect, one of Jane's voices, the voice of Jane at one stage of her moral growth, one of the many world-visions that speak through Jane. Like all other passages in this novel it must be treated *in sequence* and as occasion-specific, a tentative if momentarily convincing stage in the gradually evolving history of Jane's moral life,

. . . .

as if, that is, in quotation marks. For within a half-dozen pages her present moral solution or resolution will be itself devastated, her self no longer autonomous or in control, even her "frantic effort of principle" offering no sure guidance or goal:

> What was I? In the midst of my pain of heart, and frantic effort of principle, I abhorred myself. I had no solace from self-approbation: none even from self-respect. I had injured—wounded—left my master. I was hateful in my own eyes. Still I could not turn, nor retrace one step. God must have led me on. As to my own will or conscience, impassioned grief had trampled one and stifled the other. (410)

Jane is more devastated than when she thought of herself as a cold, solitary girl again. It is not her voice that now says God led her, but the qualified voice of the narrator: "God *must have* led me on." The experiencing-Jane, on the contrary, fears—or hopes—to die, prays in agony not for her own life but that she may not bring evil upon Rochester. She has neither self nor will. She boards a coach, intending (or being led? the narrator is silent) to go as far away from Thornfield as her money will take her.

The Thornfield center of the novel is left behind. Jane is not only a cold and solitary girl again, but a person whose world is not as she had imagined it to be at Gateshead and Lowood or during the months at Thornfield. Even her vaunted sense of "self" has been left behind, and she is dependent on forces or a force outside herself. Left behind are only shadows, and left behind for the reader all the generic landmarks: the Gothic, the Godwinian, the foundling, the governess, even the ontology of domestic realism. The reader is in the wasteland, the wilderness, and that seems to be where Jane is going.

. . . . . .

7

Ideology and the Act of Reading:
The Cold Cumbrous Column

Though the narrator says that God must have led her on as she left Thornfield, young Jane had not prayed for guidance, and the narrator's language describing Jane's journey neither indicates nor denies explicitly the presence of a directing force. Jane has not chosen her destination but has gone as far as the coachman will take her for twenty shillings. Stripped of her inner resources, she is now also at the end of her material resources—she has spent her last shilling and has left her belongings on the coach. She is destitute, lost, empty, and alone: "Not a tie holds me to human society. . . . I have no relative but the universal mother, Nature" (412). There is at this point no mention of a universal Father, no suggestion of an ordered or purposeful universe. There is no longer any hint of divine guidance, nor is the passage marked as monologic by quotation marks. It is, however, in the present tense and thereby deliberately separated from the authority of the retrospective narrator.

She is set down at Whitcross, "a stone pillar set up where four roads meet" (412). Jane does not find the name or crossing significant in any way. Despite her prayers of desperation, her theistically underwritten moral principles, her resorting to the once-rejected Psalms, she is still predominantly the down-to-earth secularist: the cross, she says to herself, "is white-washed, I suppose, to be more obvious at a distance and in darkness" (412). And still the narrator is silent, the passage monologic. The name of the destination, however, over Jane's head, takes its place in a suspiciously Bunyanesque series: Gates-head, Low-wood, Thorn-field . . . Whit(e)-cross. Has the narrator been giving the places of her past allegorical names? Has the editor/author Currer Bell done so? Are these names providential signs which Jane should be reading? What is problematized here is the narrative strategy, the relation of author to narrator, and narrator to her younger self and to the reader. What is suspended here, along with the plot and Jane's future, is the whole nature and authorial meaning of *Jane Eyre*.

Jane, meanwhile, entrusts herself not to God the father but to Nature, her mother, who, she is certain, will give her shelter for the night (413). Under the stars, however, she becomes aware of the Father, of God's "infinitude, His omnipotence, His omnipresence," but not as a source of guidance:

> Sure . . . of his efficiency to save what He had made; convinced I grew that neither earth should perish, nor one of the souls it treasured. I turned my prayer to thanksgiving: the Source of Life was also the Saviour of Spirits. Mr. Rochester was safe: he was God's, and by God would be guarded. (414)[1]

Jane goes to sleep comforted and for the reader the future looks bright, but we learn once again, however, how linear *Jane Eyre* is, how occasion-specific the local utterances, and how dangerous it is to project a total configuration of meaning or outcome based on a single passage. Though the next day is warm and beautiful, "Want came to me, pale and bare"; she wishes to die but feels it her responsibility to keep alive. She can find no work, no food, is reduced to offering her handkerchief or gloves for bread, but even then without success. The shift in mood may even problematize Jane's or our confidence that Rochester will be protected, which seemed so certain the night before in the bosom of Nature.

The narrator at last intervenes, not to authorize or interpret but to elide: "Reader, it is not pleasant to dwell on these details . . . : the moral degradation, blent with the physical suffering, form too distressing a recollection ever to be willingly dwelt on. . . . Let me condense now. I am sick of the subject" (419–20).

A few people help Jane a little, but not out of their human concern

. . . . . .

for her. A farmer gives her a slice of bread—not out of charity but because he thinks her "an eccentric sort of lady who had taken a fancy
to his brown loaf" (420). The next day, after a night of rain and fear of
"intruders," she is given some porridge because "T' pig doesn't want
it" (421). She can expect, and receives, but little help from her fellow
humans.[2] At nightfall it is still raining. Even her mother, Nature, no
longer seems willing or able to protect her. Her physical self is now as
devastated as her moral and psychic self was at Thornfield. She knows
if she sleeps again outdoors she will die:

> "And why cannot I reconcile myself to the prospect of death? . . . Because
> I know, or believe, Mr. Rochester is still living: and then, to die of want
> and cold, is a fate to which nature cannot submit passively. Oh, Provi-
> dence! sustain me a little longer! Aid—direct me!" (421)

Once more her choice is overdetermined: she will live because
she *knows—or believes*—Rochester lives; she will live because (human)
nature (life) will not give itself up—one does not willingly die of ex-
posure and starvation. Again, this is a "soliloquy," quotation marks
once more signaling that her present thoughts, including the belief that
Rochester lives, do not necessarily have the narrator's authorization.
The overdetermination and the unauthorized voice of experiencing-
Jane here as elsewhere leave the nature of the fictional world in doubt:
their function is at once to further the suspense about the outcome and
problematize the ontological grounding of the world of the fiction.

Immediately after her plea or prayer, Jane ascends a hill, seeking a
place to lie down and hide, "when, at one dim point, far in among the
marshes and the ridges, a light sprung up. 'That is an *ignis-fatuus*,' was
my first thought" (422). False lights, such as passion, have appeared
before in Jane's narrative, and false lights have proved potentially dangerous to other young women in the fiction of the time,[3] but this light
does not vanish: it burns on "quite steadily." Jane follows the light, discovers a house, peeks through a window, sees an elderly servant and
two young ladies. She knocks. The servant, though kindly, turns her
away. Jane resigns herself to death: " 'I can but die,' I said [aloud], 'and
I believe in God. Let me try to wait His will in silence' " (429). She is
overheard by the brother of the two ladies, a clergyman, who is just

now returning; she is taken in, fed, put to bed. "I thanked God—experienced amidst unutterable exhaustion a glow of grateful joy—and slept" (431).

The ambiguity of the interpolated phrase is typical of this entire episode—"grateful" to whom? To the clergyman and his sisters, to God, or to both? Or is the passage so thoroughly double-voiced that young Jane is grateful to the family and the narrator to God? The twenty pages of this chapter refer to God several times, but almost always double-voicedly, embedded in a factually descriptive, detached, understated prose, or in passages where choice and reasons are overdetermined, so that the grounding of the fictional world remains in doubt. It is not that the narrator does not intervene in this chapter, but when she does so it is not to clear up the nature of the cosmos. Some early Victorian readers may have seen these passages as unambiguously affirming God's presence in human lives; readers who identified *Jane Eyre* with the governess novel or domestic realism especially would be prepared for some revelation of a religious subtext or emergent theme. In subsequent years both the culture and its fiction became more and more secularized and the religious dimension of *Jane Eyre* more and more ignored. But the world of the 1840s in and out of fiction was itself in flux. There were many public and fictional voices enunciating literary, social, and moral norms that, when juxtaposed, mixed, or otherwise defamiliarized, cast the burden—or privilege—of interpretation on the reader.

The crucial segment of the episode in cosmological terms is probably that in which Jane asks herself why she struggles on and gives a typically overdetermined answer, then pleads, "Oh, Providence! sustain me a little longer! Aid—direct me!" (421). This is clearly more than an appeal to an ordinary Providence—"May it be that the world is so organized that I will survive"—but a prayer to an extraordinary Providence—"God, intercede directly on my behalf with help or at least guidance." As Paul Hunter points out, "Theologians usually distinguish between general (or ordinary) providences—in which God simply watched over developments he had willed through his natural laws—and special (or extraordinary) providences, in which a specific act of interposition was involved" (356). Jane is sustained, but is she

. . . .

aided and guided? A light does lead her to a house where she is taken in, but is the guiding light a response to her prayer, a coincidence, a bit of Victorian melodrama—or an ignis fatuus? Before she sees the light she chooses to walk out onto the moors. There is nothing in the prose of the three paragraphs—perhaps three-quarters of a page—to suggest that this choice is influenced from without. It is when Jane, turned away by Hannah, says aloud (ironically) that she will wait God's will in silence, that the listening clergyman responds. It seems likely, but neither he nor the narrator makes the point explicitly, that it is Jane's faith that convinces him to help her. Even when, as Jane prepares for sleep and the chapter ends, her prayer of thanksgiving and her "grateful joy" at her survival are joined in a single sentence, they are set apart by hyphens, just enough to sustain the ambiguity for those not predisposed to see a religious novel emerging.

Jane's appeal to Providence is refracted through the prevalence of Providence in all genres of fiction even as late as the middle of the nineteenth century, and Special Providence is virtually constitutive in religious governess novels. In *The English Governess,* Clara Neville, whom we have met several times before, sees from the beginning the hand of Providence in her life, follows where it leads, and is specially protected. There are moments of trial when she must struggle "to keep in mind that 'not a sparrow can fall to the ground' without the permission of our heavenly father" (216),[4] but that Providence directly intercedes in her life is ultimately made quite clear; her villainous stepfather catches up with her in Gibraltar on a ledge fifteen hundred feet above the Mediterranean and throws her over—but: "It was evident that her fall had been providentially arrested, first by some thorny shrubs which had entangled in her muslin dress, and then by a very large American aloe" (234). She hangs on until rescued. Her stepfather, however, stumbles and falls to his death, and that too is judged to be providential.

Though Providence is pervasive in the fiction of the time, those who read Mrs. Sherwood's *Caroline Mordaunt*—and they were legion, Sherwood being an extremely popular novelist—would have special insight into Brontë's strategy. We have already remarked in almost every chapter in this study details in *Caroline Mordaunt* that reappear

· · · · · ·

172

in *Jane Eyre:* disgusting porridge, coach rides to governess appointments, scenes of humiliation, and, as Vineta Colby has observed, the bringing of Caroline back to religion by a pious pupil who dies in her arms, just as the pious Helen Burns, a fellow pupil, dies in Jane's arms. *Caroline Mordaunt* thus has virtually become part of the repertoire of the novel and the reader. But unlike Brontë, Sherwood has from the first told the reader that this is the narrator's story of how Providence operated in her life; the very first words of the novel are:

> I am now arrived at that period of life, and, I thank God, to that state of mind, in which I can look back at the various adventures of my past years with no other feelings than those of gratitude to that Divine Providence which has rendered every apparent accident, and every difficulty which I have encountered in my passage down the stream of time, more or less subservient to my everlasting welfare. for I cannot doubt but that the peace I have enjoyed during some of the latter years of my life is no other than an earnest of that perfect rest in which I hope to enter, through the merits and death of my Divine Redeemer. (203)

The narrator-autobiographer of *Jane Eyre* could have begun in the same way, but Brontë's strategy has been to hybridize the narration, doubling the narrator's voice with that of the younger Jane's, masking her narrator's informed vision and revealing it only as it is discovered by the maturing Jane. The choice is a matter not only of narrative strategy but of rhetorical or moral strategy; or, rather, such narrative strategies are a function of worldview. Men and women in Brontë's moral universe must earn salvation. They must acknowledge their reliance on God, seek and choose to submit to providential guidance, read signs, and choose to heed warnings so as to find the path. So we must follow the young Jane, and for our own moral good learn to submit, read, follow, and avoid *along with her.* In Sherwood, our destiny, like Caroline's, has been predetermined; there is no reason to be kept in doubt, to search or interpret:

> . . . my heavenly Father predestined me, with thousands, and tens of thousands, and thousands of thousands of lost and undone creatures like myself, to glory, before the world began; and provided justification and sanctification for me in the death and merits of his Son, who is at once both God and man, before I entered into life; and, being entered, he

revealed his Son to my soul, and made me to be assured not only that I am justified, but also that I am sanctified: therefore I know that I am redeemed, and that I possess a life eternal, and that nothing can snatch me from my heavenly father's arms. (278)

But even in the final volume of *Jane Eyre*, we, like Jane, are not sure what choices she should or will make, how her story will end, just what she—and we—will discover. Providentialism is not necessarily predestinarian or fatalistic: God shows signs, but we may choose to notice and follow or not.

As Jane slowly recovers from her ordeal, she—and we—gradually learn about the house that gives her refuge and its occupants. The house is called Moor-House or Marsh-End (both names, but especially the latter, fit snugly enough into the Bunyanesque list of place names in the novel, and the two names—are we on the moor still or at the end of the marsh?—perpetuate the ambiguity of outcome and thus the suspense). The sisters, Mary and Diana Rivers, though not wealthy, are clearly ladies; their brother, St. John, a "parson." The governess strand, pulled forward once more by our learning that the Rivers sisters have been governesses, may suggest that St. John will be very important indeed in Jane's future: many fictional governesses, including Caroline Mordaunt, marry clergymen. That strand may in fact be made up of two filaments—a love story and a religious worldview—twisted into a single strand, so that to remain loyal to Rochester is to infer a secular, sublunary world; to choose the clergyman is to choose the religious worldview.

Though providential and governess novels underpin the narrative development and refract our comprehension and our tentative projections, at this late point in the novel projections may also be based on retrospection of all that has gone before in the novel *Jane Eyre* itself and our readerly need to make patterns from earlier details in the text as well as from context. Both sources raise the possibility of St. John's becoming a suitor: it is not only Jane Austen's Mrs. Bennett who may ask what other function a handsome and single gentleman can have in the life story of a young girl whose first love has been cruelly thwarted. And it is inevitable that if we think of St. John as suitor we must think

. . . . . .

of Rochester, and must, consciously or not, compare the two, for the history of Jane and Rochester is a palimpsest upon which the emerging story of Jane and St. John is inscribed. And the old lines or their mirror images abound. Jane helped Rochester up from his fall from his horse when they first meet; St. John lifts up Jane from his doorstep. Jane thought the dog that preceded Rochester might be a specter called the Gytrash (136), and Rochester later admitted that when he first came upon Jane he "thought unaccountably of fairy tales, and had half a mind to demand whether you had bewitched my horse" (149). When St. John responds to the words Jane utters aloud as she awaits her fate on the Rivers's doorstep, she is terrified. "Who or what speaks?" she asks; she becomes aware of him then as only a form: "—what form, the pitch-dark night and my enfeebled vision prevented me from distinguishing" (429). When she is taken in, the Rivers find Jane so thin and bloodless she seems a "mere spectre" (430). After their first meeting, Rochester did not seem anxious to see Jane again, sending for her only toward the end of his first full day home (though we later learn he was watching her without her knowledge [399]); and even thereafter, "for several subsequent days [she] saw little of Mr. Rochester" (157). St. John comes to see her only once during the three days she is recuperating. When, with Adèle and Mrs. Fairfax, Jane first entered the drawing-room, Rochester "appeared . . . not in the mood to notice us, for he never lifted his head as we approached" and even after Jane was seated "[he] neither spoke nor moved" (146–47). When Jane is left alone in the parlor with St. John, he keeps "his eyes fixed on the page he perused, and his lips mutely sealed" (440). Jane on both occasions has a chance to look at her new acquaintance carefully—and to describe him. She noted Rochester's

> broad and jetty eyebrows; his square forehead, made squarer by the horizontal sweep of his black hair . . . his decisive nose, more remarkable for character than beauty; his full nostrils, denoting, I thought, choler; his grim mouth, chin, and jaw. . . . His shape, now divested of cloak, I perceived harmonized in squareness with his physiognomy: I suppose it was a good figure in the athletic sense of the term—broad chested and thin flanked; though neither tall nor graceful. (146)

· · · · · · ·

St. John, she now notes, is

> young—perhaps from twenty-eight to thirty—tall, slender; his face riv-
> eted the eye: it was like a Greek face, very pure in outline; quite a straight,
> classic nose; quite an Athenian mouth and chin. . . . His eyes were large
> and blue, with brown lashes; his high forehead, colourless as ivory, was
> partially streaked over by careless locks of fair hair. (440)

The unhandsome, chunky, middle-aged roué whom she helped up
from his fall; the handsome, tall and slender, young, ascetic clergyman
who lifted her up from his doorstep—the contrast may well suggest a
choice in Jane's future.[5]

Though St. John is young and handsome, an upright clergyman
like many of the heroes of governess novels, and spends "a large pro-
portion of his time . . . visiting the sick and poor" (448), and though he
has saved Jane's life, he will have a difficult time replacing Rochester
in Jane's affections or the reader's. Rochester's love and Jane's love
for him, give him, among other things, the power of primacy. Though
Rochester himself was not initially presented with unqualified favor
and for a time seemed as likely to be Gothic villain as Byronic hero,
he has largely overcome our doubts. Rivers is presented with a similar "rhetoric of anticipatory caution," the characterization so qualified
from the beginning as to be ambiguous. That our uncertainty matches
Jane's is typical of this interpretive rhetorical strategy:

> [There is] a correspondence between the reader's and the protagonist's
> impression formation. The dynamics of response, hypothesis construc-
> tion, and chronological reconstruction, within the rhetorical framework
> consisting in the relationship between author and reader, has a con-
> currently sustained dramatic equivalent, within the fictive world itself.
> (Sternberg 130)

If, on the one hand, the governess genre and the implicit contrast
with Rochester, who has been "disqualified" as Jane's lover, make St.
John seem an "eligible" suitor, his early characterization does not seem
to promise romance. Jane calls him a "penetrating young judge" (442).
His kindness to her is not out of compassion but "evangelical charity,"
as Jane says and St. John acknowledges (444). He is not even an ideal
Christian, much less the perfect clergyman: "Zealous in his ministerial

. . . .

labours, blameless in his life and habits, he yet did not appear to enjoy that mental serenity, that inward content, which should be the reward of every sincere Christian" (448). His sermon is thrilling but bitter and seems to originate from his own disappointment and "insatiate yearnings and disquieting aspirations" (449). Both as potential lover and as religious model, St. John has a way to go. But if Rochester is the more compelling romantic hero, there are impediments to his love, and religiously and morally he is virtually beyond the pale. Jane may help St. John on his path to serenity, but it is difficult to see at this point how she can reform or rescue Rochester.

Most romantic and modern readers scarcely need the warmth of their feelings towards St. John restrained, regardless of governesses or Bertha Rochesters. Within the broad boundaries of "liberal humanism," St. John's "anti-life" austerity puts him ideologically beyond a different pale from that which obstructs Rochester. Such readers are only too eager to ignore or rush past the cautionary signs to reinforce Rochester's primacy, and their first impressions of St. John are of him not so much as a rival of Rochester's but as a younger counterpart of Brocklehurst. Q. D. Leavis, for example, sees him as only "a more subtle bully" than Brocklehurst:

> Just as Brocklehurst with his doctrine was seen by the child Jane as a "black pillar," so St. John Rivers is "a white stone," "cold as an iceberg" to her. . . . St. John is *apparently* a high-minded cleric representing an ideal in Victorian literature, the man who prides himself on subduing his impulses for the service of God. . . . Actually he is only a more subtle moral bully than Mr. Brocklehurst and his missionary vocation is an excuse for making others submit to *his* will and for forcing *them* to make sacrifices too. (22–23)

Even Eagleton, who sees St. John somewhat more sympathetically and compares him to Helen Burns rather than Brocklehurst, says that "like Helen Burns, he signifies a perspective which it is vital to acknowledge but perilous to take literally," and that he "presses the orthodox view that duty must conquer feeling to a parodic extreme" (Eagleton, *Myths* 23, 20). Others, like Gilbert and Gubar, grant that "unlike hypocritical Brocklehurst, he practices what he preaches," though "he is finally, as Brocklehurst was, a pillar of patriarchy" and "wants to

. . . .

177

imprison . . . her soul in the ultimate cell, 'the iron shroud' of principle" (365, 366). Though Gallagher also seems obligated to distinguish him from Brocklehurst—he is no hypocrite—she recognizes that he "seems to hold before Jane the possibility of spiritual change. His Evangelicalism is thus much more complex than the extreme represented by Brocklehurst" (Gallagher 66).

There are, indeed, signs or hints in the text that St. John, with a little guidance, might suit Jane. If he is cool, hard, restless, bitter, disappointed, we must remember Rochester's gruffness and apparent coolness, his restlessness and inexplicable mood swings, his Byronic/Gothic-villain ambivalence. Jane is not attracted to the soft and satisfied. Coolness does not necessarily indicate lack of passion, and "insatiate yearnings and disquieting aspirations" may be satisfied and calmed. Such a task has enmeshed more than one fictional— and, reportedly, real—heroine. Moreover, if St. John is not at peace, neither is Jane, as she herself acknowledges:

> I was sure St. John Rivers—pure-lived, conscientious, zealous as he was— had not yet found that peace of God which passeth all understanding: he had no more found it, I thought, than had I; with my concealed and racking regrets for my broken idol and lost elysium—regrets to which I have latterly avoided referring; but which possessed me and tyrannized over me ruthlessly. (449–50)

Their common restlessness and dissatisfaction may well serve as a bond of sorts. Jane has no peace because of regret, not for her actions, for leaving Thornfield, but for her loss of Rochester, a loss described here in terms—broken idol, lost elysium—that make that loss seem irrevocable, like a mourning for the dead, and, no matter how painful, morally necessary. We do not yet know the reason for St. John's lack of peace or the nature of his "yearnings" and "aspirations." St. John, too, recognizes a similarity in his and Jane's makeup: "[In her] nature is an alloy as detrimental to repose as that in mine; though of a different kind" (451); she is not, like him, ambitious, he says, but is "impassioned." He tells her,

> [you] cannot long be content to pass your leisure in solitude, and to devote your working hours to a monotonous labour wholly void of stimu-

lus; any more than I can be content . . . to live here buried in morass, pent in with mountain—my nature, that God gave me, contravened; my faculties, heaven-bestowed, paralyzed—made useless. (454)

If Jane cannot go back and if St. John's unhappiness is because of a goal or desire as yet unachieved, their restless paths may yet happily converge. St. John's obvious pleasure in Jane's accepting the humble position he offers her as mistress of a village school for poor girls, and the reinforcement of the governess theme in her new vocation (a schoolmistress was a "governess," and Jane thinks of the position as an alternative to "that of a governess in a rich house" [453]) further projects a possible future in which this governess, like other fictional governesses, may marry the clergyman rather than the gentleman.

While the rhetoric of anticipatory caution in the early depiction of St. John Rivers most obviously involves plot (suspense) and characterization, it also implicates doubts about the nature of the moral world of the novel. Though ideology may blind readers to one configuration or another, St. John is presented with a remarkable even-handedness that leaves open different possibilities. He seems to be described in two dissonant voices, or viewed in the context of two conventional but conflicting value systems, and is thus defamiliarized. Even his own loving sister Diana—who is so favorably presented that her words may be considered virtually "authorized"—testifies to the ambivalence:

"He will sacrifice all to his long-framed resolves," she said: "natural affection and feelings more potent still. St. John looks quiet, Jane, but he hides a fever in his vitals. You would think him gentle, yet in some things he is inexorable as death; and the worst of it is, my conscience will hardly permit me to dissuade him from his severe decision: certainly, I cannot for a moment blame him for it. It is right, noble, Christian: yet it breaks my heart." (455)

This short passage could almost be used as an example of primacy-recency response, the first five lines implicitly characterizing St. John as unnatural, repressed, and anti-life, the final four lines explicitly as "right, noble, Christian." But here the question is not merely whether the person described is one way or the other—there is no doubt about this, for the description is as precise as it is ambivalent—but whether

. . . .

179

his choices, his values are "good" or "bad," are to be approved or disapproved, whether he therefore will be suited to the role of hero and deserving of Jane. Secular, romantic, post-Freudian readers can scarcely be expected to approve the sacrifice of "natural affection"— much less the thinly veiled "feelings more potent still"—to an ambition, no matter how holy, and such readers are reinforced by the powerful primacy of Jane's love for Rochester. A devout reader can hardly blame a decision, no matter how severe, that is "right, noble, Christian." It is in the disharmony of these dialogic, *equally official* voices, the conflict of these conventional and current (perhaps in our culture, perennial) value systems (and the analogous and related generic conflict), that much of the originality and significance of *Jane Eyre* lies.

Conflicts of conventions or values on "the borderlines of existing systems," Iser tells us (72), enable a work to both operate within the literary and social conventions of its time and simultaneously call them into question, or at least hold them up for examination, even for contemporary readers. And, "for the later reader, the reassessed norms help to create that very social and cultural context that brought about the problems which the text itself is concerned with. In the first instance, the reader is affected as a participant, and in the second as an observer" (Iser 78). But in this portion of *Jane Eyre* there is a clear dialectical relationship between the phenomenology of reading and the ontological repertoire of the fictive world on the one hand, and the ideology of the reader on the other. Ideology is stronger than primacy: devout contemporary readers of religious fiction and of governess novels, particularly those novels with a religious cast, may well have inferred at this point in the novel that Jane, well rid of the immoral and irreligious Rochester and chastened by her experience, will remember Helen Burns's insistence on the superiority of divine to human love, of eternity to this brief life, and will marry St. John. Indeed, as Robert Colby says, "Probably a greater shock to Lady Eastlake's [i.e., Elizabeth Rigby's] generation than Jane Eyre's boldness in declaring her love to Rochester was her rejection of St. John Rivers, because the reward for the governess's trials, including [Anne Brontë's] Agnes Grey's, was generally marriage to a clergyman" (194). But perhaps a more secular,

· · · · · ·

humanist ideology raises an even higher barrier, blocking the reader's ability to permit the "reassessed norms . . . to create that very social and cultural context that brought about the problems which the text itself is concerned with." Such readers would have difficulty in engaging the text's struggle with those norms and apprehending the narrative and thematic strategies that govern it. It is here that the contemporary fictional context, not restricted to other masterworks, as a kind of third dimension of the text, can help in the recovery of such norms. Of service in such a recovery is that notable but not unique example of a governess novel, Mrs. Sherwood's *Caroline Mordaunt,* the novel we have already identified as so closely resembling *Jane Eyre* in its genre, plot, providentialism, and in many of its details, as to have virtually become part of the novel's and reader's repertoire. Caroline's cousin (and St. John will soon be revealed to be Jane's cousin) is a clergyman and her moral guide:

> My good cousin loved to enumerate these sundry perambulations [the trials she has undergone], and to trace the hand of God in all that had befallen me, showing how my various misadventures had been calculated to humble me, and bring me to a knowledge of myself . . . "blessed, therefore, are those who have been stripped of all self dependance, even although the process may not have been over agreeable to flesh and blood." (298)

Though Caroline does not love him as she understands love at the time, in order to serve as his helpmate (a request St. John will soon make of Jane), reader, she marries him, and now, at the end of the book, she is grateful for "the best of husbands," children, friends, peace, and happiness (305). *Caroline Mordaunt* offers a precedent that for readers then and now deeply problematizes the outcome of the narrative (specifically the love story) and the worldview of *Jane Eyre,* and offers us later readers the means by which we may observe how the norms of the social and cultural context "that brought about the problems which the text itself is concerned with" are being reassessed.

There are, for all the similarities between Sherwood's hero and St. John, significant differences. Caroline's clerical cousin, for example, is gentle, almost fatherly, not cold and ambitious. Though we may readily find governesses marrying clergymen and there are crowds of

. . . .

clerics in contemporary fiction, it is difficult to find a clergyman who resembles St. John. He is often identified with such Evangelical hypocrites as Mrs. Trollope's eponymous villain *The Vicar of Wrexhill* or Brontë's own Brocklehurst or such Calvinistic, Evangelical hard-liners as Dickens's Mr. Murdstone. These are not norms, or if norms, they do not raise the problems that Brontë's text is concerned with. St. John, however, is a norm and a problem, and, so far as I have been able to determine, is a clerical figure wholly new to the novel, one who, if found in life, had not yet been found narratable.

That such a clergyman may exist as a norm or ideal in the real world despite his absence in such a role to this point in the fictional world is suggested by the fact that the original of Rivers is generally thought to be not a fictional but an actual clergyman, the Reverend Henry Martyn (see, e.g., Gérin, *Brontë*; Winnifrith; Harrison). Martyn befriended Patrick Brontë in university—*St. John's* College, Cambridge—like Rivers had two sisters, and, early in the century, left his beloved in England, and went to India as a missionary. His letters and his friends frequently refer to his illnesses (chiefly tuberculosis), and in 1812 he died at the age of thirty-one in Persia. A Methodist saint, he translated the gospels into Hindi, Persian, and other Eastern languages, set up schools, and distributed tracts throughout the region. In 1807, while in the East,

> Such strong representations had been made by those whose judgment he highly valued, respecting the dreariness of a distant station in India, and the evils of solitude; that he had deemed it agreeable to the will of God to make an overture of marriage to her, for whom time had increased, rather than diminished, his affection. This overture, for reasons which afterwards commended themselves to Mr. Martyn's own judgment [Linda Greville was reluctant to leave her aged mother], was now declined; on which occasion, suffering sharply as a man, but most meekly as a Christian, he said, "The Lord sanctify this; and since this last desire of my heart is also withheld, may I turn for ever from the world, and henceforth live forgetful of all but God." (Sargent 261–62)

Such denial and dedication were not new to him, however. In 1803, before ordination, before leaving England, before being a rejected suitor, he wrote, "I desire. . . to be dead to the world, and longing for the

. . . .

coming of Christ" (Sargent 98), and this impatience—and struggle—
with this world and longing for the next pervades his letters and journals (e.g., from the journal entry of 13 September 1806: "It is an awful
and arduous thing . . . to root out every affection for earthly things,
so as to live for another world" [199]). Charlotte Brontë may have read
Sargent's *A Memoir of the Rev. Henry Martyn, B. D.* and found Martyn
a "narratable" character from the memoir or from her father's stories
of his old friend.[6] He was obviously admired in the household and revered by Evangelicals.

Martyn's piety and self-immolation were, in their fashion, a norm
of that bygone era we may recapture from biographies and letters,
but, before St. John, his ascetic Christianity was marginalized in early
capitalist England, and a life like his scarcely seemed "narratable."
The norms of spiritual sacrifice and the fulfillment of the secular self
were seldom presented as "problems" that involved complex exploration and reassessment, as opposed to either satire or pietistic affirmation, in the popular novels of the day. Even among popular religious novelists the conflict between religious self-denial and life in the
world was an uncomfortable topic, and, when raised, was usually resolved—again, especially in low church fiction—in a "common sense"
way that validated everyday, sublunary (and middle-class) life. Even
the very religious Elizabeth Sewell, for example, has her honorable
Mrs. Herbert say, "Certainly God does not require that we should all
live exactly the same lives as the [ascetic saints] . . .—He does not
command us all to leave our homes and go to the deserts" (327).[7]
Brontë's bringing asceticism from the borderline of the existing norms
into relation with the more dominant, "common sense," middle-class
Christianity recodifies, defamiliarizes, and reassesses the "social and
historical norms" (Iser 74, 78).

It is not so easy as Iser seems to assume for later readers to permit the literary text to enable them "to transcend the limitations of
their own real-life situation" (79), to read even initially as a member of the "authorial audience" while retaining the right and privilege
of subsequently seeing the text as it cannot see itself. Most modern
readers and critics valorize the passionate and rebellious young Jane,
and not only do not seriously consider St. John's emerging role as hero

. . . .

a possibility—unless Jane's life story is to be a tragedy of waste and patriarchal oppression, or of life-denying repression—but, as we have seen, have little good to say about St. John in any role, and that only grudgingly. A learned, sensitive, and open reader of *Jane Eyre,* Barry Qualls, may serve once more as an example of how one's unacknowledged or unrecognized ideology—here, roughly, "humanist"—can, in assuming an ideological norm a "natural" truth, distort the phenomenological processes of the act of reading. His resistance to the providentialist worldview, to seeing Jane "grow" from rebel to Victorian matron, and his jaundiced view of St. John are, as they almost always are by readers, connected. Earlier he has noted that Jane is now using the language of the Psalms, but rather than giving up his unqualified admiration of the Jane who confronted Brocklehurst and announced her dislike of the Psalms, rather than entertaining the possibility that Jane as a child was somehow immature or benighted and that her experience of suffering has taught her more humility, Qualls believes she is now confused: "That she chooses language from the Psalms rather than from the biblical histories she enjoyed as a child indicates her confusion and her want of a certain road to journey along" (60). Qualls sees in St. John, therefore, the "old religion," that which opposes and threatens her humanistic world: "Brontë concentrates her attack on the deadness of the old religion in the figure of St. John, whose otherworldliness affronts the present world of fellow-feeling which, Jane has learned, is essential to life" (63). By "life," Qualls, like most of us in the twentieth century, means earthly, not "eternal," life, but that is not necessarily what Jane or Brontë means without qualification by the term. And, as we have seen, "fellow-feeling" was not what Jane found from her fellow beings in her wanderings about the moors until Providence guided her to the home of her cousins. Qualls's distortion is not inherent in his values but in his misreading details of the text, implying that his reading approximates authorial intention. Without distortion or misreading, he might well read it from his ideological position, read the text "against the grain," show it as it cannot see itself, exploring the contradictions in the norms Brontë juxtaposes. That, indeed, is the reader's duty, for, as Iser says, what the text "does not do . . . is formulate alternative values . . . ; unlike philosophies and ideologies, literature does not make its selections and its decisions explicit. Instead, it questions or recodes the signals of external reality in such a way that the reader himself is to find the motives underlying the questions, and in doing so he participates in producing the meaning" (74).

The outcome of the plot may reward those who were never led to believe that Jane might marry St. John, but to ignore the possibility or not to take it seriously is to miss the affective force of this portion of the novel, the doubt and the suspense. Not to explore the "motives underlying the questions" Brontë raises in juxtaposing conflicting contemporary norms by prematurely imposing modern conventional views of that world is not only to miss the opportunity of recovering the "reassessed norms" of the 1840s but to misunderstand the nature of Jane's choice, the novel's evaluation of St. John, and, ultimately, the moral world of the novel as it sees itself.

Diana's characterization of her brother is soon validated for Jane. First, though, the Rivers learn that an uncle has died and that they are not to inherit even a small portion of his considerable fortune; the sisters leave "for distant B——"; St. John moves back to the parsonage, and Jane goes to Morton and her new position. The opening of chapter 31 (vol. 3, ch. 5) marks another geographical shift in Jane's life. She is in her cottage at Morton after her first day of teaching. Her feelings are described in the present tense and thus monologically, without the advantage of the narrator's hindsight. In her forthright way she admits that she feels desolate and degraded, but she is determined to make the best of her new lot: "Much enjoyment I do not expect in the life opening before me: yet it will, doubtless, if I regulate my mind, and exert my powers as I ought, yield me enough to live on from day to day" (458). She is convinced that she has progressed morally, for she knows her negative feelings are wrong and is convinced that, no matter what the emotional cost, she has made the right, the God-guided choice, avoiding the "silken snare" of living with Rochester in France: "Yes; I feel now that I was right when I adhered to principle and law, and scorned and crushed the *insane* promptings of a *frenzied* moment. God directed me to a correct choice: I thank His providence for the guidance!" (459, emphasis added).

The love and religious strands are thus even more tightly twisted

. . . .

185

together. For the first time Jane explicitly and unconditionally acknowledges that she has been guided, confirming her earlier feeling that "God must have led me on" (410) when, without will or conscience, she stumbled away from Thornfield. She does not yet affirm, however, that she had been led to Marsh-End in response to her plea for guidance from Providence. We are not yet quite certain that the world of *Jane Eyre* is governed by Providence, especially since the present tense withholds the narrator's authorization. But even the possibility that this might be so, clearly foregrounded for the moment, must influence the shape of the novel we project ahead or must problematize configurations that do not take Providence into account.

Jane's right choice, leaving Rochester, is not the painless choice, and she weeps. Her tears are interrupted by St. John. Once more he is juxtaposed to memories of Rochester (and, to make the parallel stronger, like Rochester long ago, he has been preceded by his dog). St. John notices her tears, infers that she has been thinking of her past, and, though he does not know that past, advises her not to look back and to control her desires: "It is hard work to control the workings of inclination, and turn the bent of nature: but that it may be done, I know from experience. God has given us, in a measure, the power to make our own fate" (461).

Like Mordaunt's hero, he is here Jane's moral guide, the more effective for instructing her not merely by exhortation and principle but by the example of his own life and struggles. He tells of his ambitions to be an artist, author, orator, soldier, or politician rather than clergyman, of his dark night of the soul, and of his recognition of a God-given vocation that would require all his skills and energies—that of missionary to the East. And he indicates that he has had to struggle with feelings and "human weakness" to persist in his course.

Jane soon sees the power of his temptation. A voice startles him "as if a thunderbolt had split a cloud over his head" (463); it is Rosamond Oliver, the heiress with "a face of perfect beauty." He is clearly in love with her—"I saw his solemn eye melt with sudden fire, and flicker with resistless emotion"—and she with him. Even physically they seem suited: "he looked nearly as beautiful for a man as she for a woman" (465). Jane watches his struggle, and affirms Diana's judgment: "This spectacle of another's suffering and sacrifice, rapt my thoughts from exclusive meditation on my own. Diana Rivers had designated her brother 'inexorable as death.' She had not exaggerated" (466).

The affirmation, the juxtaposition, and the emphatic position of this paragraph as the last in the chapter—giving the reader the oppor tunity to absorb, contemplate, and evaluate the character of St. John and of the moral world of the novel—if they are not designed to shatter the primacy effect of Rochester's love and of the negative view of St. John as "unnatural" or "antilife," certainly seemed designed to make it conceivable that Jane herself might, perhaps should, "overcome" her ill-fated love and find that her life will be joined to St. John's. Even at this late date, the conventional romantic ending—governess marries gentleman—is shadowed by anticipatory caution: can it be that this governess belongs to the other, the religious convention, and will marry a clergyman?

When Jane is convinced that Rosamond prefers St. John, that he loves Rosamond, and that, in her view, he can do more good in the world with Oliver's wealth than he can as a poor missionary, she tries a little matchmaking. Throughout the chapter, however, there are subtle reminders of the Thornfield experience. Jane sketches a portrait of Rosamond as she did of Blanche Ingram, for example, and, as different as the characters and the circumstances are, this detail puts Rosamond in the position of the beautiful rival of plain Jane. When we learn St. John has rejected Rosamond because one part of him knows that she will not make him a good wife—she could not sympathize with his aspirations, could not suffer and labor—just as, for other reasons, Blanche would not have made Rochester a good wife, it is difficult not to recognize that Jane *would* make him, as she would have made Rochester, a good wife (regardless of whether we believe St. John, or either man, would make Jane a good husband). St. John is clearly coming to think of Jane as a helpmate—"I watch your career with interest," he tells her, "because I consider you a specimen of a diligent, orderly, energetic woman" (479). They both describe giving all for love as madness: Jane refers to "the insane promptings of a frenzied moment" (459), St. John calls it "delirium and delusion" (476). Jane adhered to law and principle and thanks God for providential

. . . .

guidance in making a decision she knows is right; St. John is grateful that religion has pruned and trained his nature. If Jane regrets her lost love, St. John has resigned himself to rejecting the love that could be his, though acknowledging that religion cannot "eradicate" nature. Both seem to feel, then, they are right in their choices to sacrifice earthly love for moral and religious values. That St. John will not give up "one hope of the true, eternal Paradise" for "the elysium" of Rosamond's love (469) retroactively casts new light on Jane's "lost elysium," as she not long ago described her love for Rochester and his for her (450). Is the elysium of human love for her as for St. John, then, not the path to the true Paradise, not a legitimate goal in life? Was Helen correct in telling Jane years ago that Jane thought too much of human love? Was Caroline Mordaunt well-advised to marry her cousin and moral guide out of respect and admiration, anticipating, correctly, that love would be sure to come in due course?

We scarcely have time to consider how to project the future course of Jane's life and of the novel, when, before the end of the chapter, a new distraction is introduced. St. John is startled by something on a piece of Jane's drawing paper, looks hard at her face, and surreptitiously tears off an edge of the paper and takes it with him. When he leaves, Jane scrutinizes the paper. "I pondered the mystery a minute or two; but finding it insolvable, and being certain it could not be of much moment, I dismissed, and soon forgot it" (480). But these are the last words of the chapter, and we cannot dismiss the mystery quite so readily; does the paper have something to do with the converging paths of Jane and St. John? with Rochester?

This mystery, unlike that of Thornfield Hall, is soon solved, however. To elude Rochester, should he have searched for her, she had told the Rivers her name was Jane Elliott. But she had written "Jane Eyre" on the corner of paper he tore off. St. John therefore knows who she is and knows too that she is an heiress, for her uncle in Madeira has died and left her his fortune. (It was this "convenient but not very novel resource of an unknown uncle dying abroad mak[ing] her independent" that the *Spectator* reviewer did not like [Allott 75], and, indeed, it is not very novel even in governess fiction: Lady Blessington's governess heroine, Clara Mordaunt, is one of those who "[thanks to the

. . . .

timely death of a rich uncle] becomes the rich heiress again and marries a lord" [Ewbank 63].) To compound the romance-like nature of the plot—or is it the affirmation of a providential leading?—St. John and his sisters are now discovered to be Jane's cousins. Having found cousins, for Jane, "was wealth indeed!—wealth for the heart!" (491). The orphaned Jane who was unwelcome in her Aunt Reed's home and kept from their hearth because she did not suit them, and who went out into the world alone to experience life, now has a family, made up as she defines it of a brother and two sisters (as was the Reed family), a family that accepts her and that she loves. She insists on sharing her money with those whom her existence deprived of the full inheritance. Under those circumstances it would be "a legacy of life, hope, enjoyment," and, she tells St. John, much to the complication if not confounding of our projections and configurations, that she "will live at Moor-House . . . and I will attach myself for life to Diana and Mary. . . . I don't want to marry, and never shall marry" (493–94). There is some solace for attentive romantic readers, whether it is Rochester or St. John they prefer, however, for the promise is in quotation marks; it is the excited commitment of young Jane without the narrator's endorsement or authority. And there is another loophole: her reason for the pronouncement is, "No one would take me for love; and I will not be regarded in the light of a mere money-speculation. And I do not want a stranger—unsympathizing, alien, different from me; I want my kindred: those with whom I have full fellow-feeling" (495). Rochester and St. John are both, in different ways, enfranchised by this stipulation.

Early in volume 3, chapter 8, there is a rare intervention of the narrator and reference to events in the "future," the time between the narrative action and the narrating, that seem on the surface to be nothing more than a chauvinistic digression difficult to account for in terms of the frame of reference or world of the novel. Jane, preparing to move to Moor-House where she will live with Diana and Mary, is closing Morton-school, and the best of her peasant-scholars give her a sense of national (contemporaries would have called it "racial") pride: "The British peasantry are the best taught, best mannered, most self-respecting of any in Europe: since those days I have seen paysannes and Bäuerinnen; and the best of them seemed to me ignorant, coarse, and besotted, compared with my Morton girls" (497). The nationalistic utterance that seems so like a digression here proves to be peculiarly functional, though it may require some historical imagination to recapture several social norms and their relationships. It does not function as a very definitive clue to the future of the novel—an unmarried Jane as heiress or teacher may in the future visit the Continent; she may go there as Rochester's mistress or wife; or she may see "paysannes and Bäuerinnen" in Europe or in the East as St. John's wife or accomplice. The "digression" does serve, however, to reveal the clash of value systems, though their terms need to be "unpacked" (even if they cannot be justified) for modern readers.

Jane valorizes the domestic, in the sense of the home, and now, it appears, the domestic includes as well the homeland. Joined to the public values of patriotism are personal values not naturally associated with them—joy, the physical, and the sensual. Home and homeland, joy and sensuality, are subsumed by the larger category of the earthly, the here and now, and this sublunary life itself: all of these are under the sign of the domestic. St. John's "undomestic" values involve, on the other hand, the self-sacrificial, the heroic, the sacred, the transcendental, and the eternal, all of which in our secular century (and for many in the 1840s) are/were more likely to be associated with the life-denying. What must have created real doubt and suspense in Victorian readers is the possibility that St. John is identified with religious belief or the religious worldview and Rochester with the sensual and secular. How, then, as Robert Colby infers, could they have believed Jane will reject St. John, for to reject him seems virtually to reject God?

On the other hand, the exchange between Jane and St. John at this point in the text may seem somewhat confusing to modern readers who do not link, and to some degree oppose, the sensual and the domestic as defined by housework. Jane has been on a binge of cleaning and redecoration, activities most modern readers would not associate with her rebellious, adventurous, independent, and "better" self. Indeed, St. John insists that she look "a little higher than domestic endearments and household joys," though not in the sense we would do so. She counters, perhaps to us rather disappointingly if we do not understand the linkage in the term "domestic," that these things are

· · · · · ·

the best the world has to offer. St. John, for his part, links his advice
to look beyond housecleaning to his admonition that she not "cling so
tenaciously to ties of the flesh," for "this world is not the scene of frui-
tion"—clearly opposing the domestic to the transcendental. Opposed
too are the homey and the heroic, the hearth and the great world beyond England. Jane realizes that her domestic values—including those
of the senses—and St. John's cosmic ones are not compatible:

> The humanities and amenities of life had no attraction for him. . . . Lit-
> erally, he lived only to aspire—after what was good and great, certainly:
> but still he would never rest; nor approve of others resting round him. . . .
> I comprehended all at once that he would hardly make a good husband:
> that it would be trying to be his wife. I understood, as by inspiration,
> the nature of his love for Miss Oliver: I agreed with him that it was but
> a love of the senses. I comprehended how he should despise himself for
> the feverish influence it exercised over him; . . . I saw he was of the
> material from which nature hews her heroes—Christian and Pagan—her
> lawgivers, her statesmen, her conquerors: a steadfast bulwark for great
> interests to rest upon; but, at the fireside, too often a cold cumbrous col-
> umn, gloomy and out of place.
>   "This parlour is not his sphere," I reflected: "the Himalayan ridge,
> or Caffre bush, even the plague-cursed Guinea coast swamp, would suit
> him better. Well may he eschew the calm of domestic life; it is not his ele-
> ment. . . . He is right to choose a missionary's career—I see it now." (501–2)

The domestic—England, the earthly and earthy—is thus that which St.
John rejects and Jane values. The nationalistic digression, then, functions to further and more fundamentally define the dialogic clash of
values on the borderline of those "reassessed norms" we may now call
the domestic and the heroic.

St. John, who has pruned and trained his natural self, suppressed
the "fever of the flesh" (478), and turned himself into what Jane sees
as a "cold cumbrous column," is clearly not pleasing or attractive.
Whether he is nonetheless admirable will depend on how valid, how
heroic we consider the mission for which he has denatured himself.
His ambition as he defines it is to "spread my Master's kingdom; to
achieve victories for the standard of the cross" (479). He has, he says,
"hopes of being numbered in the band who have merged all ambitions

· · · · · ·

in the glorious one of bettering their race—of carrying knowledge into the realms of ignorance—of substituting peace for war—freedom for bondage—religion for superstition—the hope of heaven for the fear of hell" (477). His Christian asceticism is a prevailing norm. The text, through Jane, endorses his evaluation of his mission as "truly the most glorious man can adopt or God assign" (516).

For later readers like us, such a norm when juxtaposed to another of its period, like Jane's domesticity, can "help to create that very social and cultural context that brought about the problems which the text itself is concerned with" (Iser 78). From our postcolonialist site, however, we may, like John Kucich, see St. John's "missionary zeal serving as an apology for economic exploitation" (Kucich, "*Jane Eyre* and Imperialism" 105). Indeed, Gayatri Spivak says that though she is not "necessarily" accusing Brontë "of harboring imperialist sentiments" (257), "it should not be possible to read nineteenth-century British literature without remembering that imperialism, understood as England's social mission, was a crucial part of the cultural representation of England to the English" (243). Reading *Jane Eyre* "in the frame of imperialism" (257) will thus show us the text as it cannot see itself, "incite a degree of rage against the imperialist narrativization of history" (244), and be "politically useful" (257). Reading *Jane Eyre* in the context of imperialism, she suggests, will also ineluctably deconstruct the oppositional terms in St. John's mission—to bring European-Christian knowledge to Indian-pagan ignorance, religion to superstition, freedom to bondage (249)—and undermine his (and the text's) evaluation of his missionary project.

Jina Politi, in an earlier, more penetrating and inclusive postcolonial and Marxist-feminist reading of the text as it cannot see itself, "places" imperialism and St. John's religious zeal within the political framework of the whole novel, masterfully ringing changes on its use of the term *master*, a term first repressively insisted upon by John Reed but later voluntarily adopted by Jane in addressing Rochester.

> The political ideology behind the transformation of this term will be that people, i.e., races, nations, classes and women are happy in inequality and have no reason to revolt against the domination/subordination structure

. . . .

of their social existence so long as they are free to *choose* their masters and so long as this freedom of choice hides its exploitive purposes behind the humanitarian guise. (58–59)

The text will therefore "conceal the complicity of the Church and Imperialism and will present St. John as the disinterested missionary whose only purpose in life is to help the uncivilized Indians choose for themselves the true and only Master" (59). Politi sees the ideology of master/servant bound by love as more than authorial: "[it] writ[es] itself into *Jane Eyre* and, generally, into the text of Victorian fiction" (59). We are therefore seeing the text as Brontë could not see it and as it cannot see itself.

The text is also blind to the fact that the money that circulates in the novel is based upon colonial exploitation, including the vilest of all, slavery. As Penny Boumelha points out, there are "ten explicit references to slavery in *Jane Eyre*," all critical. "They allude to slavery in Ancient Rome and in the seraglio, to the slaveries of paid work as a governess and of dependence as a mistress. None of them[, however,] refers to the slave trade upon which the fortunes of all in the novel are based." It is, in fact, the inheritance from Jamaica that subsidizes St. John's mission, enabling him to "labour for his race" in India (62).

While reading from our postcolonial site illuminates unacknowledged ideological assumptions and consequent omissions and evasions in Brontë's novel, we must be attentive as well to our own cultural site and ideological assumptions. Just as Spivak warns us against essentializing "woman" and seeks to "situate feminist individualism in its historical determination rather than simply to canonize feminist individualism as such" (243), so we must not "anachronize" or essentialize imperialism but locate it too in its historical context.

First of all there is the history of the word itself. The first use of the term cited in the OED postdates the publication of *Jane Eyre* by some eleven years, for another decade refers only to Roman or French imperialism, and for thirty years is always used pejoratively.[8]

But "imperialism" by any other name would still stink. Well before the nineteenth century, colonies were "maintained for the sake of their trade with the Mother Country," a trade that was protected from outsiders by tariffs and in some cases outright prohibition (Somervell 176). This "old Tory" position, however, was challenged after the Napoleonic Wars by the Benthamite Liberals and other free traders, for, they claimed, free trade would make colonies useless and, as Cobden argued in 1842, would even eliminate the major cause of European wars:

> "The Colonial system, with all its dazzling appeals to the passions of the people, can never be got rid of except by the indirect process of Free Trade, which will gradually and imperceptibly loose the bands which unite our Colonies to us by a mistaken notion of self-interest. Yet the colonial policy of Europe has been the chief cause of wars for the last hundred and fifty years." (qtd. in Somervell 178)

Insofar as the term *imperialism* as we now use it implies "capitalist" exploitation, its use with reference to *Jane Eyre* may be somewhat anachronistic, for the opposition or indifference to colonialism in the first half of the nineteenth century was "mainly a middle-class creed" (Somervell 183). The triumph of British imperialism belongs to the last third of the century, as the history of the word implies, and, ironically, one of its contributing causes—along with the discovery of diamonds in Kimberley in 1869 and the frightening rise of Bismarck's Germany— was the Reform Act of 1867 enfranchising the working class, for the working class, along with Disraeli's Tories, were great supporters of imperialism (Somervell 183).

E. J. Hobsbawm—the title of whose volume *The Age of Capital, 1848–1875,* incidentally dates the beginning of the capitalist era as the year after the publication of *Jane Eyre*—also confirms the chronology implied in the history of the word *imperialism* by locating its rise during or following "the astonishing expansion of capitalism in the third quarter of the century" (130). No friend of imperialism, Hobsbawm nonetheless concedes that British rule in India, where St. John intends to begin his mission, at first brought an unusual stability and peace to a region seldom peaceful or "free." And, of specific relevance to the evaluation of that mission, Hobsbawm points out that in India as in South America "the imperialism of the capitalist world was to make no . . . systematic attempt to evangelize its victims (129).

. . . .

The mere existence of foreign rule in itself posed no major problem here [in India], for vast regions of the sub-continent had in the course of its history been conquered and reconquered by various kinds of foreigners (mostly from central Asia). . . . That the present rulers had marginally whiter skin than the Afghans . . . raised no special difficulties; that they did not seek conversions to their peculiar religion with any great zeal (to the sorrow of the missionaries), was a political asset. (133)

Not only, then, did neither Brontë nor St. John think of his mission as enabling the commercial exploitation of India, but historically—in 1847 or in the vague earlier time in which the novel was set—there would seem to have been no "complicity of the Church and Imperialism" that had to be "concealed" in order to "present St. John as the disinterested missionary whose only purpose in life is to help the uncivilized Indians choose for themselves the true and only Master" (Politi 59). That Christ was/is "the true and only Master" and that it would be to the best interests of the "pagan" Indians to know him and acknowledge his mastery, the text and Brontë would no more deny than they would the presumed superiority of the English culture. Indeed, they would scarcely expect to have to deny it, because they could not imagine its being questioned.

Except proleptically, the text of *Jane Eyre* could scarcely see St. John and his mission as complicit with imperialism. To see it thus would be more than seeing it as it does not see itself; it would be seeing it as it *could* not see itself. It would not be discovering its ideology but anachronistically imposing our own upon it. Whatever we may think of St. John, his creed, or his "courtship" of Jane, to appreciate the text as authorial audience, to appreciate its narrative and ontological strategies, "to re-create that very social and cultural context that brought about the problems which the text itself is concerned with," we must for the time being at least try to see that "cold, cumbrous column" as one of nature's heroes, even though his values may run counter to ours and lie across the "borderline" from and in conflict with Jane's own "domestic" values.

. . . .

Decentering the Narrator:
St. John's Way

That St. John does practice what he preaches, "Placing the same demands on his own life as he sets out for others" (Gallagher 66), is dramatized in an incident on the evening Jane and the Rivers are celebrating the return of Diana and Mary to the refurbished Moor-House. He does not join in the joyful spirit of the welcome-home festivities and is relieved to be called across the dark moors on a mission of mercy: "He did not return until midnight. Starved and tired enough he was: but he looked happier than when he set out. He had performed an act of duty; made an exertion; felt his own strength to do and deny, and was on better terms with himself" (504).

This sense of duty, this Christian goodness, this mercy, even this life of self-denial have their austere attractions even for Jane and, as we have seen, represent a prevailing contemporary norm, though one that even in the early capitalist England of the 1840s was a borderline or marginalized norm. It is not long before Jane falls under his "freezing spell" (508). Rosamond Oliver has married, and St. John is pleased his battle over self has been won. He watches Jane as she studies German, approves of her visits to Morton-school and admires her endurance of bad weather. Finally he asks her to abandon German and study "Hindostanee" with him. She agrees, though perhaps "obeys" is closer to her feelings. He was "a very patient, very forbearing, and yet an exacting master . . . By degrees, he acquired a certain influence over me that took away my liberty of mind. . . . I did not love my servitude"

(508). Those readers with long memories will recall that when she was anxious to leave Lowood, Jane prayed first for "liberty," but when that seemed denied, pled for "at least a new servitude!" (101). We may have felt the position of governess, so nearly servant-like, was the servitude granted. Now, however, this "new servitude" may be the true answer to that prayer (Gilbert and Gubar 365). On one occasion, at Diana's teasing insistence, St. John kisses Jane goodnight, and she "felt as if this kiss were a seal affixed to my fetters. . . . I daily wished more to please him: but to do so, I felt daily more and more that I must disown half my nature, . . . force myself to the adoption of pursuits for which I had no natural vocation" (509).

To disown half her nature cannot be good, surely, so it is a relief that at this point Jane as narrator intercedes again, in effect to apologize for having omitted telling us something central to her inner life: "Perhaps you think I had forgotten Mr. Rochester, reader." Not so, she says; the thought of him has been continually present. She had inquired about him, had even written Mrs. Fairfax twice asking his whereabouts, but surprisingly had got no answer. After six months she lost hope, "and then I felt dark indeed" (510). There is not much hope, then, for the disowned half—the romantic and sensual half—of Jane's nature.

Now that the hope of hearing from or about Rochester is dim, there is room once more for the projection of the possibility of Jane's lot joining her cousin's. There may be some justification for hoping so. That acceding to St. John's demands would mean disowning half her nature is qualified by "I felt" and is not therefore confirmed—or denied—by the voice of the narrator. It is possible, too, to conclude that "half" her nature may best be disowned if it is on the "wrong" side of a conflict between love of God and love of his creatures. Put this way, given nineteenth-century norms, the choice is not so easy as primacy, romance, and twentieth-century norms would suggest.

St. John says he finds her worthy and offers her "a place in the ranks of [God's] chosen" (513), which we may find arrogant, presumptuous, or otherwise ideologically antipathetic. But Jane—in the company, no doubt, of many Victorian readers—does not. She feels under a spell, but she asks whether the worthy would not be told of their role

. . . .

by their heart, for, though she is "struck and thrilled," her heart, she says, is "mute" (note: not negative, but mute). St. John offers to speak for her heart. There follows one of those passages, like the final paragraphs of the first two volumes, in which Jane—and to some degree the narration—is overwhelmed and confused. The first time this occurred was when the prospect of love and marriage loomed, the second time when that prospect was lost. This time, too, love and marriage are involved, but here the imagery is not of the sea or waters but of glens and hills, the allusion not to Psalms and the Old Testament but to the New Testament: "The glen and sky spun round: the hills heaved! It was as if I had heard a summons from Heaven—as if a visionary messenger, like him of Macedonia [who appeared to Paul, Acts 16:9], had enounced—'Come over and help us!' But I was no apostle,—I could not behold the herald,—I could not receive his call" (513–14).

The narrator neither authorizes the call from heaven nor justifies Jane's failure to respond if call it were. St. John issues his own call: "A missionary's wife you must—shall be. You shall be mine: I claim you—not for my pleasure, but for my Sovereign's service" (514). That she has had no "call," he declares, is only evidence of her humility—only Providence can make one worthy. And St. John has found her worthy: "docile, diligent, disinterested, faithful, constant, and courageous; very gentle, and very heroic," with "a soul that revelled in the flame and excitement of sacrifice" (515). Though she feels clasped in an "iron shroud," she is nearly persuaded that this is indeed her work and her way. The love story is subsumed, overwhelmed by the religious, by duty and service. She asks for a few minutes to compose herself before answering. She does not ruminate; her thoughts proceed logically but monologically toward a conclusion, *all the time narrationally qualified by quotation marks:* She is capable of the task, though she will likely die in India. With no news of Rochester, she has nothing to live for, certainly nothing to remain in England for. It is, indeed, a glorious vocation he offers her. If she goes, she will work wholeheartedly, will exceed St. John's expectations. But: "Can I receive from him the bridal ring, endure all the forms of love (which I doubt not he would scrupulously observe) and know that the spirit was quite absent? . . . No, such a martyrdom would be monstrous. I will never undergo it. As his sis-

. . . .

ter, I might accompany him—not as his wife" (517). Marriage, he says, is the only practical way they could serve together, and, though she now says she does not love him, enough love would follow. She scorns his notion of love (which we may recall, however, is not much different from Caroline Mordaunt's, and in her case love did follow; so Jane may be up against a borderline norm). St. John will not admit defeat; he gives her two weeks to think it over: "Refuse to be my wife, and you limit yourself for ever to a track of selfish ease and barren obscurity" (522). Though many modern readers quite understandably see St. John as the selfish one—his sense of "duty" masking the will to possession and sexual desire—his "threat" at this point in the novel has a certain weight. The rebellious Jane we applauded early on has been chastened, the self-reliant and self-guided Jane was left at Thornfield. Is the Jane who wants to fulfill her sense of life and love in earthly terms really the "selfish" one? St. John has, we recall, already urged her to look "higher than domestic endearments and household joys, . . . the selfish calm and sensual comfort of civilized affluence" (499).

Indeed it is she who in the next chapter makes the first move toward reconciliation, though she still insists she will not go to India as his wife. "He is a good and a great man," she tells Diana, "but he forgets, pitilessly, the feelings and claims of little people, in pursuing his own large views" (531). It is not because Jane is a "little person" that most readers applaud her disinclination to marry St. John, but it is imperative that we keep this evaluation in view—it reinforces the clash of contemporary ontological norms already brought to the surface: those of Jane's domestic and St. John's cosmic worlds. It raises the ante of anticipation, the suspense about the outcome of the plot, for more is put at risk than a conventional, romantic, happy ending.

The novel now approaches that which Jane will call her crisis and the point at which the narrative and ontological crux is defined. The passage is crucial as well in defining the relation of the linear and spatial dimensions of the act of reading. In the narrative the crisis is the necessity for Jane to choose once and for all to accept or reject St. John's proposal that she marry him and accompany him to India. The choice is also thematic and ontological: if Jane accepts, she knows it will probably mean her early death, and so will valorize the sacrifice of

. . . .

this life for the eternal, and the primacy of divine love over the human. In the event, however, this binary religious theme, which has surfaced periodically throughout the novel, is subsumed by a wider religious view that reveals itself as not merely constitutive but essential and pervasive in the novel. The crucial scene and situation also explicitly recall and thus "juxtapose" an earlier scene "spatializing" the text at this point. What follows the scene, however, suggests how rigorously sequential the "argument" of *Jane Eyre* is, how relentlessly the spatialized configurations are modified or contradicted by what follows.

Spatialization is doubly dangerous in *Jane Eyre* because of the subtlety of the first-person narration: some passages are double-voiced; some are overtly from the perspective of the elder Jane; others are monologically Jane-in-the-middest, sometimes, but not always, marked off by quotation marks, question marks, or the present tense. The subtlety, however, permits, even invites, deliberately or not, "misunderstanding"—that is, views that at the textual moment seem to legitimately fill gaps or project configurations of the novel and its world but turn out to be "wrong," not affirmed by later events. Moreover, the voices of the two Janes are not the only voices here: though St. John speaks in quotation marks and out of a worldview that is neither Jane's younger nor older view, his voice is not ultimately denied or discounted in the novel. These projected voices, like those of the contemporary fictional context, however, remain part of the reader's experience of the text no matter when or if they are countered or undermined by later events or elucidations (especially since, dialogically, the elder narrator/author is only one voice and not "the" voice or the one authoritative voice in the text).

On the evening Jane refused him and he had refused her refusal— giving her two weeks to reconsider—St. John reads from the twenty-first chapter of Revelations, and Jane thrills as he reads what is apparently directed at her:

> "He that overcometh shall inherit all things; and I will be his God, and he shall be my son. But," was slowly, distinctly read, "the fearful, the unbelieving, &c., shall have their part in the lake which burneth with fire and brimstone, which is the second death."
>
> Henceforth, I knew what fate St. John feared for me. (532)[1]

. . . . . .

Read monologically from a worldview emphasizing the autonomous (and sensual) self, St. John is threatening Jane with damnation in order to force his will and himself upon her. Jane—both Janes—does/do not read him so, nor does the authorial audience. She believes he has a voice and a belief system of his own and has her best interest, as he understands it, at heart. He truly believes he is saved and she, unless she accompanies him to India as his wife, is damned. Jane understands this at the moment and later, even as she narrates her story, for she gives his words in quotation marks, neither authorizing them nor denying their validity. He prays "for those whom the temptations of the world and the flesh were luring from the narrow path." We are likely to emphasize "the flesh," but "the world" and the rich man's loss of "his good things in life" (534) emphasize the earthly and not just the earthy. Nor does either of the two Janes even hint at the possibility that he was rationalizing his physical desires. Jane with both her mature voices acknowledges with awe how sincerely "he felt the greatness and goodness of his purpose" (533). His look "was not, indeed, that of a lover beholding his mistress; but it was that of a pastor recalling his wandering sheep." Just as she, on her principles, has renounced Rochester, so he, on his, has renounced Rosamond: "Like him, I had now put love out of the question, and thought only of duty" (535). If it is objected that this is only Jane's fallible reading of St. John, we must remember that though we may have three Jane voices they are all the voices of Jane. We have no way of going outside Jane's perspectives and into the mind of the other characters except in the narrative itself. If from outside Jane and the text we interpret St. John's motives as the text does not, this is not so much seeing the text as it cannot see itself as it is an "instance of ideological interference," where suppositions about human motivation differ (Rabinowitz 195).

The crisis is as much that of Jane's judgment and will as it is that of St. John's importunity. All sincere "men of talent," she says, "have their sublime moments: when they subdue and rule." Her "veneration" (cf. veneris and the conflation of divine and human love) for St. John, tempts her "to rush down the torrent of his will into the gulf of his existence, and there to lose my own" (534). Does "own" refer to "existence" or "will"? If the former, it refers only to Jane's certainty that she

. . . .

will die if she goes to India with St. John, but if the latter, it may legitimately reinforce the cause of the rebellious, self-reliant experiencing-Jane and isolate the issue as proud preservation of the self versus submergence to the "official" voice—to the patriarchy and its patriarchal God. Indeed, at this moment, St. John, for better or worse, does seem to represent the voice of religion, virtually of God: "Religion called—Angels beckoned—God commanded—. . . death's gates opening, shewed eternity beyond: it seemed, that for safety and bliss there, all here might be sacrificed in a second" (534). That life may be sacrificed for eternal bliss goes without saying for those who believe and believe that sacrifice is called for, and so it "seemed" (the reservation added by the narrator); yet it is perverse, destructive, downright evil for those for whom life ends at death. Jane is about to make the sacrifice. How close she comes, and how suspenseful the decision for the reader, can only be realized by imaginatively entertaining at least the possibility that St. John's cause is just.

Here the subtle interplay or double-voicedness may strongly influence response and interpretation. At the crucial moment *the narrating Jane* refers to Rochester and evokes an earlier scene and its moral register.

> I was almost as hard beset by him now as I had been once before, in a different way, by another. I was a fool both times. To have yielded then would have been an error of principle; to have yielded now would have been an error of judgment. *So I think at this hour, when I look back to the crisis through the quiet medium of time: I was unconscious of folly at the instant.* (534, emphasis added)

Jane at the moment is not recalling Rochester, and her choice is not determined, or, so far as we can tell, even influenced by her love for him. It is the narrator from the text's future ("at this hour, when I look back to the crisis") who evokes the text's past ("as I had been once before"), and "spatializes" the moment. (See above, introduction to pt. 2, for treatment of time element and spatialization in this passage.) As the scene approaches its climax, when there is physical contact between St. John and Jane, Rochester is evoked, but in a passage of delicate and precise ambiguity: "He surrounded me with his arm, *almost* as if he loved me (I say *almost*—I knew the difference—for I had felt what it was to be loved; but, like him, I had now put love out of the question, and thought only of duty)" (535).

How much consciousness is implied in "I knew"? in "had now put love out of the question"? Some, perhaps, but the narrator's voice seems to preempt the scene by calling attention to the fact that the very words and the punctuation of the text are her responsibility—"*almost* . . . (I say *almost* . . .)." For the authorial audience to grasp the text's full force and effectiveness here the reader must recognize that at the time of St. John's renewed and powerful proposal Jane did *not* consider her temptation foolish or impossible because of her love for Rochester. (Indeed, she says, "The Impossible—*i.e.*, my marriage with St. John— was fast becoming the possible" [534].) If it is necessary for the scene's effectiveness that the reader consider St. John acceptable and his offer perhaps even desirable, why should the narrator interject the name of Rochester and juxtapose the two proposals spatially? Would not this diminish the possibility that Jane would marry St. John? For whom?

Here it may be well to recall Bakhtin's insistence on the particularity of the utterance in time and place and the productive role of the auditor/reader. Perhaps Brontë is addressing *imagined* readers who would be only too likely to forget or to prefer to forget the morally flawed Rochester for the soldier of Christ. The narrative strategy seems aimed at the kind of reader Robert Colby had in mind when, in a passage quoted earlier, he says, "Probably a greater shock to Lady Eastlake's generation than Jane Eyre's boldness in declaring her love to Rochester was her rejection of St. John Rivers" (194). St. John, at least, is so sure he is fulfilling a divine plan that when Jane says, "[I] could decide if I were but certain, . . . were I but convinced that it is God's will I should marry you, I could vow to marry you here and now," he assumes she has acquiesced: " 'My prayers are heard,' ejaculated St. John."[2]

The conditionality of Jane's statement is intentional, but not because of memories of Rochester. However much her own will has been overwhelmed by St. John's, she is still not sure of God's will, and it is that she wishes to ascertain, and, having ascertained, to follow. She does not depart from the religious, certainly not the providentialist, tenets, and the novel does not force her to choose between religion

. . . . . .

and life or love. It brings to the surface more clearly than ever its (and Jane's now developed) religious grounding. She appeals directly to Providence for intercession and guidance: "I sincerely, deeply, fervently longed to do what was right; and only that. 'Shew me—shew me the path!' I entreated of Heaven. I was excited more than I had ever been; and whether what followed was the effect of excitement, the reader shall judge" (535).

What follows is the merging and modification of the religious and love themes through the famous or infamous incident of Jane's hearing at this moment Rochester's voice calling " 'Jane! Jane! Jane!' " (536), though he is a thirty-six-hour coach ride away. She believes her prayer has been answered and believes at this moment that her love for Rochester is now authorized by extraordinary but natural forces. The "shock to the reader of Lady Eastlake's generation" has been cushioned somewhat by the narrator's strategic introduction of Rochester into St. John's proposal scene. And the narrative device of the telepathic experience is authorized by precedent. Many of her readers then and now recall a similar incident in a well-known novel of the previous century: Moll Flanders's lover returns to her because he had heard her calling, not from quite so great a distance as Rochester's call, but at least from a somewhat preternatural twelve miles away:

> he told me he heard me very plain upon *Delamere Forest*, at a place about 12 miles off; I smil'd; Nay says he, *Do not think I am in Jest, for if ever I heard your Voice in my Life, I heard you call me aloud, and sometimes I thought I saw you running after me*; Why said I, what did I say? for I had not nam'd the Words to him, *you call'd aloud*, says he, and said, O Jemy! O Jemy! *come back, come back*. (Defoe 1:164)

These were in fact her words, and Moll is "amaz'd and surpriz'd, and indeed frighted." The Clarendon edition (607) cites Gaskell's testimony that Charlotte Brontë said such a call "really happened" and Fanny Ratchford's account of the appearance of Marian Hume to the Marquis of Duoro in Brontë's *The Legends of Angria*.[3] Dessner also instances George Sand, whose Consuelo hears distant calls from Albert even though she believes him dead (Dessner 97). Such telepathy often has the sanction of divine or human love; it was probably assumed to be actual and it was certainly assumed to be narratable. Not so for many modern readers. This "act of mental telepathy" is, for example, the climactic "silly feeble part" in Mark Schorer's catalogue of such parts in *Jane Eyre* (xi). Many readers and critics, embarrassed, perhaps, by this "melodramatic" event, have taken the license Jane seems to grant and have attributed the voice to Jane's excitement, and thus to unconscious desire. Others secularize the episode by suggesting that it is Jane on her own authority who "decides" (Leavis 25; Boumelha 27) or "resolve[s]" (Nestor 55).

Jane has given the reader the right to interpret the nature of the call, but judgment at this point must be tentative or suspended; the reader "*shall* judge" may seem to suggest that the judgment may be immediate, but it also may hint that the reader can judge appropriately only when Jane has told the rest of her story. We have already seen how occasion-specific the language is, and how subtly Brontë/Jane modulates the narration back and forth from the double-voiced to the monologic, and thus we have seen how cautious we must be about reifying any specific passage, claiming that *this* is what Jane and the novel "mean." In this very passage, for example, the experiencing-Jane—note the quotation marks—almost immediately attributes the call not to her excitement, as she has just proposed, but to "nature":

> "Down superstition!" I commented, as that spectre rose up black by the black yew at the gate. "This is not thy deception, nor thy witchcraft: it is the work of nature. She was roused, and did—no miracle—but her best." (536)

Nor is the case yet closed. Though the work of nature—She—the miracle of the call is also, it seems, the work of or at least has the authorization of God—He—for no sooner does Jane reach her room than she falls on her knees:

> [I] prayed in my way—a different way to St. John's, but effective in its own fashion. I seemed to penetrate very near a Mighty Spirit; and my soul rushed out in gratitude at His feet. I rose from the thanksgiving—took a resolve—and lay down, unscared, enlightened—eager but for daylight. (537)

· · · · · ·

The next morning, she entertains once more the possibility of "excitement," "a delusion," but prefers to think of it as "inspiration":

> it seemed in *me*—not in the external world. I asked, was it a mere nervous impression—a delusion? I could not conceive or believe it: it was more like an inspiration. The wondrous shock of feeling had come like the earthquake which shook the foundation of Paul and Silas's prison: it had opened the doors of the soul's cell, and loosed its bands—it had wakened it out of its sleep, whence it sprang trembling, listening, aghast; then vibrated thrice a cry on my startled ear, and in my quaking heart, and through my spirit; which neither feared nor shook, but exulted as if in joy over the success of one effort it had been privileged to make, independent of the cumbrous body. (539)

"Inspiration," out of context, might seem to authorize the psychological and secular reading of the experience that most twentieth-century readers would doubtless prefer—*if* we could suppress the reference to soul and the New Testament (a passage from the same biblical book, Acts 16, that, ironically, Jane had earlier cited as like the call St. John's importunate proposal had sounded in her [513]). But this is clearly described by Jane at this point as an out-of-body experience, an experience of the soul, and though "inspiration" may refract meanings having to do with inner experience, in the religious context, and *Jane Eyre* has become increasingly imbued with religious coloration, it refers specifically to the divine influence on human beings. Inspiration is an experience of the soul, then, not the body (nature); not a psychological experience, but one influenced by stimuli, probably divine, from without. But both passages contain the cautionary "seemed," and the second contains an "as if" and a question. We have not heard the last of the explanations or an authorized explanation yet.

Jane's trip back to Thornfield is full of excitement and suspense, both in general and in its specific details, details that, Florence Dry points out, are reminiscent of (and refracted by) Sir Walter Scott's *Waverley* (76–80): just as Edward (still another Edward) Waverley finds Tully-Veolon a fire-ravaged shell, Jane finds Thornfield Hall in ruins, destroyed months ago by fire, and there is anxious delay for both Edward Waverley and Jane before they find out the fate and the whereabouts of the inhabitants.[4] Jane hastens to the nearby inn and suffers with the reader through the innkeeper's lengthy recapitulation of the story of the mad wife and the governess. This serves not only to retard the outcome and so increase the suspense but also to pull the narrative carpet up from behind, as it were, the readers' retrospection done for them with all the pressures of the reading now projected forward.

Jane and the reader learn at last that Mrs. Rochester is dead and that Rochester, having lost a hand and an eye and having been blinded in the other in attempting to rescue his wife, is living at Ferndean. The lost hand and eye point to the passage in Matthew 5:27–32 that deals with adultery, advising those who are tempted to sin to pluck out their right eye and cut off their right hand rather than succumb. The Matthew passage has been alluded to earlier in *Jane Eyre*, as we have seen in the previous chapter, most recently in an emphatic position at the very beginning of volume 3 (379), when Jane's inner voice tells her to flee Thornfield after the revelation of Bertha's existence.[5]

As soon as she learns his whereabouts, of course, Jane is off to seek Rochester in his eyrie at Ferndean, and the chapter ends. The scene that many readers have long been waiting for, the reunion of Rochester and Jane, now quickly follows. Jane is at her sauciest, and most tender, teasing him with suspense and jealousy. At this point once more the love and religion themes interact and are at last harmonized. Rochester tells her of his own conversion: "Jane! you think me, I daresay, an irreligious dog: but my heart swells with gratitude to the beneficent God of this earth just now." He admits the justice of her having been snatched away from him and even of the lowering of his pride in his strength. "Of late, Jane—only of late—I began to see and acknowledge the hand of God in my doom. I began to experience remorse, repentance; the wish for reconcilement to my Maker. I began sometimes to pray" (571). His path has been in its way similar to that which Jane has trod, from rebellion to humility, from self-reliance to acknowledgement of Providence. Jane has gone through only metaphoric flood, Rochester through real and metaphoric fire. He then tells her that four nights ago, on Monday, near midnight, having long felt Jane must be dead, he prayed that if it were God's will, he might die.

· · · · · · ·

". . . I asked God, at once in anguish and humility, if I had not been
long enough desolate, afflicted, tormented; and might not soon taste bliss
and peace once more. That I merited all I endured, I acknowledged—that
I could scarcely endure more, I pleaded; and the alpha and omega[6] of
my heart's wishes broke involuntarily from my lips, in the words—'Jane!
Jane! Jane!'" (572)

She cross-examines him—did he speak aloud? the very words? Monday night near midnight? Yes. Yes. Yes. And he says he heard her reply, which he repeats. "Reader, it was Monday night—near midnight—that I too had received the mysterious summons: those were the very words by which I had replied to it." Jane is overwhelmed by the implication, for what this means is that the telepathy was not the work of nature, not intuition, if that implies only a secular inner voice, but that it was the work of Providence, of Divine Will:

The coincidence struck me as too awful and inexplicable to be communicated or discussed. If I told anything, my tale would be such as must necessarily make a profound impression on the mind of my hearer; and that mind, yet from its sufferings too prone to gloom, needed not the deeper shade of the supernatural. I kept these things, then, and pondered them in my heart. (573)

This is the final confirmation of the ontological world of *Jane Eyre*. It is, for the authorial audience, a world governed by Providence. Not Fate, if Fate implies predestination, but the intercession of God in warning and guiding the sinner, giving him or her every chance to follow the straight and narrow path, but giving that human being the choice, free will, to follow or not. If it has not already done so, this makes those of us reading as part of the authorial audience now read the novel backward, through "shew me the path" to "aid—direct me" to the chestnut tree and between and beyond on our way back to the very beginning of the novel. That retrospective spatializes the novel in a final configuration.

Rochester now knows it was not a mere vision and utters a prayer of thanksgiving and an entreaty that he be given "the strength to lead henceforth a purer life" (573). It is only now, when human love and divine are harmonized that Jane and Rochester can enter the wood and wend their way "homeward" — the last crucial word of the body of the autobiographical narrative that began with the protagonist exiled from family and hearth. Only then that we can turn to the "Conclusion," which brings the narrative up to the narrating present and begins with those plain but memorable words, "Reader I married him" (574).

The conclusion is in many ways conventional, typical of Victorian final chapters that bring the events of the narrative up to the time of the narration, if not to the first-readers' present. There is a brief description of the wedding day and an account of how Jane spread the news to those we know, including but not ending with St. John Rivers. Then there is a summary of the ten years since, their happiness, Rochester's recovery of his sight, their firstborn (a boy, of course), and then a return to the Rivers.

The last three paragraphs of the novel are devoted to St. John Rivers. He knows his death is imminent, he writes from the East. "My Master . . . has forewarned me. Daily he announces more distinctly, — 'Surely I come quickly;' and hourly I more eagerly respond, — 'Amen; even so come, Lord Jesus!' " These are the last lines of the novel, somewhat reminiscent of the call of Jane's "Master" and her response, but much more directly an echo of the penultimate line of the final book of the New Testament, the Revelation of St. John the Divine.

Why, in the autobiography of Jane Eyre, should St. John have the emphatic, sanctioned, if not sanctified, closing words that seem to echo, even encapsulate, her own narrative closure? The inadequacy of Jane to represent the human condition, Bakhtin would maintain, is typical, perhaps essential, in the novel (though once more we must in our minds adjust his gender-specific language):

> One of the basic internal themes of the novel is precisely the theme of the hero's inadequacy to his fate or his situation. The individual is either greater than his fate, or less than his condition as a man. He cannot become once and for all a clerk, a landowner, a merchant, a fiancé, a jealous lover, a father and so forth. If the hero of a novel actually becomes something of the sort, — that is, if he completely coincides with his situation and

· · · · · ·

209

his fate (as do generic, everyday heroes, the majority of secondary characters in the novel)—then the surplus inhering in the human condition is realized in the main protagonist. . . .

An individual cannot be completely incarnated into the flesh of existing sociohistorical categories. There is no mere form that would be able to incarnate once and forever all of his human possibilities and needs. (*Dialogic* 37)

That Providence leads Jane, when she asks for guidance, back to Rochester, away from St. John, does not mean in an authorial reading that St. John's way is wrong or antilife, as many modern readers would have it, but only that his way is not Jane's way. His path to salvation lies through self-denial, self-sacrifice, martyrdom. His is the life of *agape*. Jane's way to salvation—as the leadings and her experience and Rochester's indicate—lies through everyday, domestic life, the life of *eros* (Eyre-os?). St. John's way is wrong—for Jane; Jane's way, which for him would mean marriage to Rosamond Oliver, would be wrong—for him. This distinction has been increasingly recognized in the past decade or so. Politi, for example, spells the two ways out quite well, despite the ironic phrase "ordinary mortals" and her thinly disguised sneer at the "transcendental" (note also the lower-case "c" for "christian"); she is, after all, only obliged to see what is "there," not necessarily to like it or agree with it:

> [Jane] is meant for the "second" type of christian life which is accomplished in holy marriage, whereas St. John belongs to the first type, that of a higher calling which dictates a form of conduct that escapes the understanding of ordinary mortals. . . . this "difference" is only a mark of his transcendental calling, the path to christian heroism achieved only through the annihilation of the individual self. (59)

Gallagher emphasizes Jane's religious quest, contextualizes St. John's Evangelicalism as a "prevailing norm," and is more sympathetic:

> Faced with the dilemma of how best to serve God, Jane is tempted to follow the influence of St. John, but the answer that she receives to her prayer is a call to an earthly vocation: the sacrament of marriage. *Jane Eyre* suggests that Christian vocations encompass more than the mission field and that domestic life is a valuable avenue of service. This emphasis

is typical of nineteenth-century Evangelicalism, which saw "the family as a unit particularly favored by God" [Jay 142]. (68)

It is vital for the authorial audience's reading of the novel to see the two as different ways for different kinds of individuals, but each way as equally viable for the appropriate pilgrim. It is difficult, however, in a first-person novel to make the Other equal. The mode is almost by definition ego-centered. But the function of the fictional autobiography in the mid-nineteenth century, in the move between Romantic egoism and Victorian "duty" or socialization, is to exorcise that Romantic ego or transcend—not escape or ignore—egoism. Just as Jane must see that she is not in total control of her life (and Rochester that he is not in control of his) but that control of all is God's, so she as narrator, or Charlotte Brontë, must insist that there has to be more than just Jane's personal salvation at stake: there must be room for the Other. In a first-person narrative it is impossible to give St. John equal time or space, but he is given pride of place, the final words of the novel, a voice that powerfully echoes both Jane's at the climactic moment of her life and the language of scriptural closure, thus validating his "way," though it is Other. Though she is not "wrong," neither is Jane's way the only right way; her way and her life story, her narrating "I," are decentered, not just to make room for St. John but to reveal the real center, which, in the authorial world of Brontë's novel, is everywhere, God.

. . . .

Decentering the Author: Charlotte Brontë's Misreading of *Jane Eyre*

The novel that began with Jane ends with St. John; the novel that began with rebellion ends with martyrdom. Even the story of the proud, saucy, self-reliant orphan Jane Eyre ends with the chastened, religious, privileged, and satisfied wife and mother Jane Rochester.

Reading backward from the certainty of Rochester's conversion, the supernatural nature of his calling out across the vast distance to Jane, and her reception of that call after she has herself asked for a sign; back to the leading light in the Rivers's window when Jane asked Providence for guidance; further back to the twisting chestnut tree on the hitherto calm night of Rochester's proposal; through the still ambiguous instances of fairies dropping advice on Jane's pillow and the ambiguously discounted ghostly light in the red-room; we can at last see clearly and indisputably the nature of the universe according to the narrator, Jane Rochester, and wonder how we, like the younger Jane, could have missed the signs for so long.

The strategy of serial disclosure is superbly and significantly appropriate for the narrative, rhetoric, and ontology of *Jane Eyre*. It greatly enhances the suspense and justifies the very gradual release of the secrets of the plot and outcome as fitting and natural. The reader is surprised by sin, led to recognize that identifying with the proudly self-reliant young Jane has been not only a misperception but a moral lapse. The providentialist ontology is insinuated into the narrative and through the narrative cumulatively and precisely defines its own nature and further justifies the strategic reticence.

Mrs. Sherwood, as we have seen, uses an entirely different but appropriate narrative strategy for her predestinarian providentialism: *Caroline Mordaunt* begins with the first-person narrator's announcement that she has been providentially guided and, through no deeds of her own but "through the merits and death of my Divine Redeemer" (203), has been chosen to enter heaven. In Brontë's providentialism the individual has free will, is responsible for seeking and perceiving providential leadings and warnings, for choosing to follow such signs, and thus is responsible for his or her own salvation. Jane must acknowledge God's Providence, but she must learn to see and interpret events for herself, stand on her principles, use her reason, hearken to her conscience, and she must herself choose to follow the leadings and heed the warnings. Since her fate is undetermined, the narrative pattern is thus appropriately one of a journey toward enlightenment punctuated with crises and consequent choices. The reader, to participate experientially in her story (and to understand his or her own life in a providential, contingent cosmos), must therefore be kept in the dark just as Jane is.

Read as a self-consuming artifact—the authorial reader at the end of the novel now in the position of author, or at least mature narrator, looking back over the novel as a spatial, closed, and permanent structure, the misleadings and misunderstandings now dismissed— the world of *Jane Eyre* is revealed as patently providential. There is at last a sense of narrative and thematic unity and of significant and comforting closure. Even the apparently dissonant voice of St. John is subsumed within the providential vision, eros and agape representing two ways but one world. That vision even justifies the narrational mode and defines the novel's purpose: beneficiaries of providential deliverance are obligated to record their experiences to ensure their memory and to instruct and inspire others (Hunter 71). Like most novels, even dialogic novels, *Jane Eyre* has "a *conventionally literary, conventionally monologic ending*," an "*external completedness*" that is "compositional and thematic" and betrays the hand of the author (Bakhtin, *Dostoevsky* 39). As a finalized, spatial, and monologic construct re-viewed from the vantage point of the end, then, the authorial intention seems clear and ineluctable: *Jane Eyre* is a providential novel, and its structure and strategies are designed to that end.

The subtlety of the strategy of serial disclosure has its own risks, however. It underestimates the continuous experiential engagement of the reader with the text and the obliterative power of primacy. For a good many readers then and now, Jane Eyre is first and foremost the unloved, abused, but independent, self-assertive, and rebellious child at Gateshead and Lowood. Her restless adventurousness, her thirst for experience at eighteen when she chooses to leave Lowood; her passion and self-esteem at Thornfield, where she falls in love, is loved and betrayed; her refusal to sacrifice herself even to God's work in the East, and her defiant return to the man she loved and loves; only reinforce, elaborate, and deepen that image. Though there are brief and occasional "anticipatory cautions" about Jane's views and behavior, chiefly in the monologic and "intrusive" voice of the mature narrator, they are readily brushed aside by the hectic pace and forward thrust of the life story and the powerful early image of Jane. The brief and unrealized suggestions of a quite different Jane are easy to dismiss. She appears—or rather scarcely appears—in the eight skipped years at Lowood when, under the influence of Miss Temple, she had "more harmonious thoughts," "better regulated feelings," and "believed [she] was content" (99), a period covered summarily in two or three pages, chiefly as an introduction to her restless desire to seek "real knowledge" of life outside the schoolroom. The first ten years of her happy marriage are also virtually elided. The reader hardly knows the Jane Rochester who has narrated her life story: except as one register in the double-voicedness of the narration or as an occasional separate voice,[1] she is present only in the final few pages of the novel in largely expositional, undramatized narrative.

In Sternberg's account of the experiments involving the primacy effect, he reports not only that when contradictory blocks of information are presented, the "leading block established a perceptual set, serving as a frame of reference to which subsequent information was subordinated as far as possible" but, more surprisingly and significantly, that, "strange as it may at first appear, the overwhelming

. . . .

majority of subjects did not even notice the glaring incompatibility of the information contained in the two successive segments" (94). Brontë's strategy of serial disclosure and the power of primacy, then, enable readers not only to fail to anticipate (much less desire) the ultimately disclosed providentialism and its socializing, subduing consequences but to be "blind" to it. Though the "blindness" is excusable, if not justified, to overlook, ignore, or dismiss the providential ontology of *Jane Eyre* is a misreading of what seems demonstrable authorial intentions.

The "author" whose intentions are sought in an authorial reading is the implied or virtual author embodied in the text, not necessarily Charlotte Brontë in her proper person. Something of Charlotte Brontë's intentions, however, can be inferred from her complaints about how her novel was misread. It was not the "timorous or carping few" in the press and among early readers who most troubled her—she disposed of them in the preface to the second edition of her novel—but the "injudicious admirers" of her heroine, Jane's many friends, the well-intentioned readers. When she came to write *Villette*, therefore, she was determined that her new heroine-narrator, Lucy Snowe, "should not occupy the pedestal to which 'Jane Eyre' was raised by some injudicious admirers" (*Letters* 4: 52–53).[2] The Jane the "injudicious readers" too much admired is clearly the younger Jane, the Jane experienced in the temporal reading, buttressed by the primacy effect—and blinded by it. Brontë's image of Jane is that of a Jane off the pedestal, not the rebellious child or defiantly independent and wholly self-reliant young lady, but the mature Jane Rochester who writes the story of how she found God's plan and her place.

That the author's vision of Jane is essentially that of the matron at the end of the novel is reinforced by Mrs. Gaskell's report of Charlotte Brontë lamenting "that, when she read *The Neighbours*, she thought every one would fancy that she must have taken her conception of Jane Eyre's character from that of 'Francesca,' the narrator of Miss Bremer's story" (387). Gaskell is puzzled: "For my own part," she says, "I cannot see the slightest resemblance between the two characters, and so I told her; but she persisted in saying that Francesca was Jane Eyre married to a good-natured 'Bear' of a Swedish surgeon" (387).

. . . .

Bremer does *tell* us things about her heroine that resemble what we know of Jane Eyre: Francesca "is little, very little" (Bremer 9); poor; "had no beauty" (13); when sixteen, thought she "must have adventures, let it cost what it would" (43); and she says she thought herself in youth "unquiet and unreasonable" (51). Just as we see little of Jane Eyre when she is settled and mature, however, so we see little if anything of Francesca when she was young and adventurous. The young Francesca and the mature Jane are characters the reader has only more or less heard "about." The characters the readers of the two novels know from their reading experience do not substantially resemble each other, though they may be similar in the eyes or mind of the authors. The Jane Eyre Brontë does not see, the Jane who is injudiciously admired, and the Jane Brontë does see, who is only insubstantially there in the text, suggest that Brontë herself "misreads" Jane Eyre[3] and the work called *Jane Eyre*, the text presented to the reader but which must be performed into the work.

Like Charlotte Brontë herself, the author implied by the text misreads the text, as paradoxical as that may seem; for the experience of the novel being read and the shape of the novel after having been read are two different textual objects. The Author looks at the novel as a spatial configuration seen from the end with full disclosure, and sees one novel; the engaged Reader looks at the novel from the beginning and projects configurations sequentially and continuously, and experiences a quite different novel. Both are good readings and both are misreadings. *Jane Eyre* the novel as read and being read exists both as an *experience* of rebellion and as a meaningful *statement* of reconciliation to God and society. These two voices and ideologies are in dialogue: not in a dialogue with a reconcilable thesis and antithesis, nor as an antinomy, but interactively, as if the whole novel were a single utterance hybridized, "a mixture of two social languages within the limits of a single utterance, an encounter, within the arena of an utterance, between two different linguistic consciousnesses" (Bakhtin, *Dialogic* 358).

Such dialogic "misreadings"—the readers' or the (implied) author's—are virtually constitutive in long narratives, for they have both the experiential or horizontal dimension of the point-to-point reading and the global, spatial, or final configuration of the ending. While

· · · · · · ·

such dialogue is characteristic of the novel as a form, in *Jane Eyre* it is intensified, more dramatically constitutive, perhaps, because of the historical and cultural occasion of its utterance, that is, on the cusp of the Romantic and the Victorian; because of its psychological nego-tiation between passion and reason; and because of its intense real-ization of the powerful tension between individual desire and social restraint. A significant share of its greatness lies in dramatically and archetypically incarnating the tension of that dialogue of languages, of social forces "fused into a concrete unity that is contradictory, multi-speeched and heterogeneous" (Bakhtin, *Dialogic* 365).

The heterogeneity and contradictoriness of the dialogue suggest why all readings must be misreadings. A "reading" suggests a trans-lation of the text into a different language, one with its own—and different—frame of reference, and into a monologic "meaning." That "reading" or "meaning" seems convincing only when the frame of ref-erence into which the text is translated fits "collectively recognized values." The varying interpretations over time and even within the contemporary reception show clearly that these interpretations are not objective or definitive but "sophisticated subjectivity," culture- or group-specific (Iser 23). Our reading the text as it cannot see itself from a modern site in a way that seems "natural" or "self-evident" de-pends on the "sophisticated subjectivity" and "collectively recognized values" of the modern reader's culture or group and is once more a "misreading." Yet com-prehending the text means taking it some-how into our own frame of reference, for we cannot continuously "experience" the text without inwardly or outwardly articulating our responses, rendering it into our own language. Even the affective, ex-periential, aesthetic "meaning" for the reader reading the text "con-stantly threatens to transmute itself into discursive determinacy—. . . it is amphibolic: at one moment aesthetic and at the next discursive. . . . it is impossible for such a meaning to remain indefinitely as an aes-thetic effect" (Iser 22). We cannot, then, avoid mis/reading.

There is, however, another dimension of the reading of a novel text which is both aesthetic and discursive, formalist and historical, con-textual and dialogic, emphasizing, even celebrating, the multiplicity

. . . . . .

of "misreadings" (including its own) and the unfinalizable nature of the text. The dialogue of *Jane Eyre* is more "multi-speeched" even than outlined in the "misreadings" by author, real and implied, reader, and later critic. For each of the novel genres or species incorporated into *Jane Eyre* generates batteries of conventional expectations that are fulfilled or modified, and though the species operates within the fictive context of *Jane Eyre,* it retains its own voice, its own ethical, epistemological, and other ideological ideologemes—though, as is characteristic of literary works, "in an undeveloped, unsupported, intuitive form" (Medvedev/Bakhtin 17). Each of these generic voices joins the chorus of other voices in the novel. Fictional autobiography, for example, valorizes the individual's rights and freedoms—his *and hers*—and the mind's interiority, not as a mismaze but as the source of truth; it is ideologically radical (which in the nineteenth century includes the radicalism of laissez-faire). The orphan or foundling novel is often radical as well in its assumption of human innocence and innate virtue and of society's corrupting influence. The Gothic novel, while valorizing the imagination and both the role and limitations of rationalism, tends to support traditional, aristocratic, and patriarchal values; the governess novel valorizes the feminine and the genteel; domestic realism, the feminine, the traditional, and the bourgeois; and so on. These are oversimplifications, but they suggest the ideological, value-laden nature of the generic voices incorporated by the intertextuality of *Jane Eyre* and the ideologemes that were transforming the rebellious Romantic and aristocratic Regency world into the bourgeois Victorian world:

> Literature does not ordinarily take its ethical and epistemological content from ethical and epistemological systems, or from outmoded ideological systems . . . , but immediately from the very process of generation of ethics, epistemology, and other ideologies. . . . Literature is capable of penetrating into the social laboratory where these ideologemes are shaped and formed. The artist . . . sees [ideological problems] in *statu nascendi,* sometimes better than the more cautious "man of science," the philosopher, or the technician. The generation of ideas, the generation of esthetic desires and feelings, their wandering, their as yet unformed groping for reality, their restless seething in the depths of the so-called

. . . .

"social psyche"—the whole as yet undifferentiated flood of generating ideology—is reflected and refracted in the content of the literary work. (Medvedev/Bakhtin 17)

Jane Eyre is such a work.

Though *Jane Eyre,* like other horizon-changing novels, has a moral vision and social and psychological implications—ideologemes—it is also a specifically *novelistic* utterance at a specific time in the history of the proleptically Darwinian genre called the novel. Though it appears at a particular moment of social and political history, its position as a novel is on a different time curve: "The variety of events of one historical moment . . . are *de facto* moments of completely different time curves, determined by the laws of their special history, as becomes obvious in the different 'histories'—of art, of law, of economics, political history, etc." (Jauss 32). The varied voices of the novel species that carried ideologemes also carried *narrational* elements that severally and jointly were preserving and transforming the genre of the novel, elements that might be designated—in a word even uglier than its analogue—"narratigemes."

Charlotte Brontë was involved in the same project as her revered Thackeray. He, by deliberate parody of contemporary conventional narrative types, was trying to forge a new novel for the new, Victorian, bourgeois era; she was doing so by a different kind of parody, consciously, or not,[4] incorporating the different generic ways of telling a story in transgeneric narratigemes, holding up familiar, conventional "plots" or novel species for examination and evaluation by putting them in an "unfamiliar light" (Iser 78)—an intertextual, mutually altering dialogue. Such an activity, Bakhtin confirms, is of the utmost importance in the development of the novel: "Literary parody of dominant novel-types plays a large role in the history of the European novel. One could even say that the most important novelistic models and novel-types arose precisely during this parodic destruction of preceding novelistic worlds" (*Dialogic* 309). *Jane Eyre* is such a model.

The transgeneric familiar narrative scene or topos, the narratigeme, defamiliarizes, "parodies," and destroys the precedent novel conventions and creates a new dialogic form. It functions at the narrative level as heteroglossia does at the verbal. It could even be thought

. . . .

of as "heterogeneric": the novel species, types, or genres bringing their context and ideological implications to the topical scene, serving as the rough equivalent of the "languages" brought to the word or utterance via hybridization or heteroglossia. Indeed, since it operates on larger units and on narrative units, it may generally be a more appropriate and useful focus for dialogic analysis of long narrative forms like the novel than is heteroglossia.

Once the narratigemes in *Jane Eyre* are unpacked and their function in engendering and problematizing expectations of plot and ontology realized, how does one demonstrate their articulation? How can one evaluate whether they are successfully "fused into a concrete unity that is contradictory, multi-speeched and heterogeneous" (Bakhtin, *Dialogic* 365)? Unless it is sufficient merely to point to the "test of time" (e.g., the contemporary success of *Jane Eyre*, its host of imitators, and its subsequent canonization), the concrete demonstration of the dialogic, that "higher unity" which is not monologic, is, to me, one of the most daunting challenges of Bakhtinian criticism. Perhaps the narratigeme of the scenic topos may suggest a concrete way to demonstrate the multispeeched, multispecied *Jane Eyre*'s concrete unity. The narrative scene which, because it has appeared before in many different generic contexts and so brings with it "alien," refracting voices, serves to unify dialogic narrative at a higher level, just as Bakhtin claims Dostoevsky's seeing the event or "cross-section of a single moment" (*Dostoevsky* 28) does. The transgeneric narrative scene does so not as allusion, echo, or resolution, but by offering at once whole generic voices and signifiers: "We are not . . . talking here of antinomy or the juxtaposition of abstract ideas, but of the juxtaposition of whole personalities in concrete events" (Bakhtin, *Dostoevsky* 18; see also, e.g., 13, 21, 32). A narratigeme is, then, an intertextual event, the other texts representing the "personalities" or voices; the topos, the site of the interrelationships of those voices. We have seen how many species with their disparate ideologemes and narrative purposes and strategies pass through the topos of the rebellious child punished by confinement, for example. Each has a "voice" that neither stifles nor dominates the others; there is a dialogic nexus, a number of lines running through a single point. They are unified by the scene itself, but each retains its own ideologeme, its own

. . . .

221

perspective, which is not subsumed but can reappear later in another topical scene—the dying child scene, for example—with or without the others (Disraeli, for example, is not known for his pathetic scenes of dying children). Brontë simultaneously defamiliarizes these familiar scenes and dialogizes genres in these scenes in which the generic ideologemes and narratigemes interact but retain their own voice.

Jane Eyre is created intertextually out of the given species of the novel in midcentury and transforms what was given into one of the fountainheads of the novel of romantic realism in the Victorian period. By "this parodic destruction of preceding novelistic worlds," Brontë has created a horizon-changing novel, one of "the most important novelistic models and novel-types" of the nineteenth century (Bakhtin, *Dialogic* 309). Reading it temporally, spatially, intertextually, and from sites outside itself may serve as a paradigm for the reading of all such novels.

NOTES

Preliminaries: On Postformalism

1. By "misreading," as I trust will become clear, I mean all attempts to reduce the constitutive polysemy of a novel to a monologic or monosemic "meaning."

2. For some poststructuralists the granting of any authority to the text is mere formalism; to others any search for the kind of discursive meaning that Iser finds inevitable, any act of interpretation, is formalist. For Jane Tompkins, for example, critical concern with meaning and interpretation is formalist, or at best postformalist, so that even reader-response or "affective" criticism "owes . . . almost everything to the formalist doctrines it claims to have overturned" (202): "What has happened," she says, "is that the locus of meaning has simply been transferred from the text to the reader" (206), with the result that "virtually nothing has changed. . . . Professors and students alike practice criticism as usual: only the vocabulary with which they perform their analyses has altered" (225). Stanley Fish seems to have accepted that his is a less revolutionary role than he had earlier claimed; the introduction to *Is There a Text in This Class?* is entitled "Introduction, or How I Stopped Worrying and Learned to Love Interpretation."

3. Though this seems "natural," it is, of course, a procedure as implicated in theory and ideology and as radically contingent as any other, though since it seems "natural" to me, that specific ideology and contingency are more or less invisible. As Bakhtin says, in insisting on the necessity of dialogue, one cannot see the back of one's own head. See also Fish's "Commentary: The Young and the Restless" (303–16),

on the "dilemma" of antifoundationalism, that is, its necessity for itself operating from something very like a foundation.

PART I. Intertextualities

1. See the epigraph to this study from Leon S. Roudiez's introduction to Julia Kristeva, *Desire in Language,* which seems worth repeating here: "Kristeva's work reminds us that theory is inseparable from practice—that theory evolves out of practice and is modified by further practice" (12).

2. Kristeva adopts the term "ideologeme" from Medvedev/ Bakhtin and relates it specifically to genre and intertextuality:

> One of the problems for semiotics is to replace the former, rhetorical division of genres with a *typology of texts;* that is, to define the specificity of different textual arrangements by placing them within the general text (culture) of which they are a part and which is in turn, part of them. The ideologeme is the intersection of a given textual arrangement (a semiotic practice) with the utterances (sequences) that it either assimilates into its own space or to which it refers in the space of exterior texts (semiotic practices). The ideologeme is that intertextual function read as "materialized" at the different structural levels of each text, and which stretches along the entire length of its trajectory, giving it its historical and social coordinates. This is not an interpretive step coming after analysis in order to explain "as ideological" what was first "perceived" as "linguistic." (36–37)

Chapter 1. Species and Scenes

1. See Bakhtin, *Dialogic* 279, on the word or utterance that partakes of a social (or here, literary) dialogue: "The word is born in a dialogue as a living rejoinder within it; the word is shaped in dialogic interaction with an alien word that is already in the object. A word forms a concept of its own object in a dialogic way." Thus "edited by" is refracted by all its other appearances on the title pages of novels of various genres and "converses" or debates with them.

2. If Charlotte Brontë had read this novel, she would certainly have been moved by the episode in which Rose's mother has an operation for cataracts and Rose spends "a fortnight in town that she might be under the doctor's care" (160), for Charlotte accompanied her father to Manchester and stayed during his cataract operation, and it was in Manchester that she began writing *Jane Eyre.* (All citations to *Jane Eyre* are to the 1969 Clarendon edition, listed in the Bibliography.)

3. For this and subsequent information about the publication of

. . . .

Disraeli's novel, I am indebted to the generosity and expert knowledge of Robert O'Kell.

4. "Aquilius" is identified as Eagles in Allott (95). Some, like the *Weekly Chronicle* reviewer, thought Marsh might be the author of *Jane Eyre:* "We were tempted more than once to believe that Mrs. Marsh was veiling herself under an assumed editorship, for this autobiography partakes greatly of her simple, penetrating style, and, at times, of her love of nature; but a man's more vigorous hand is, we think, perceptible" (Clarendon 631).

5. This is a dramatic example of the echoing of character names in the fiction of early and mid-nineteenth-century fiction, especially within genres. Such repetition was rife in the governess novels discussed in chapter 2, and in different sets of names in other genres, e.g., the repeated names in women's religious novels. See Susan Rowland Tush, "George Eliot's Review of 'The Silly Novels by Lady Novelists' and Her Own Fictional Practice."

6. Lytton's novels were widely known and readily available. *Pelham, The Disowned,* and a number of his other works, for example, were available to the Brontës in the Keighley Mechanics' Institute library near their home (*Brontë Society Transactions* 11.5:355).

7. Brontë's Angrian tales had something of the Disraelian "Orientalism" in them, but she had, she thought, purged herself with the writing of a down-to-earth novel, *The Professor,* in which the hero would not spend a guinea he had not earned. The new edition of *Contarini* appeared while *The Professor* was still making its futile rounds of publishers, rejected, Brontë tells us, chiefly because the publishers "would have liked something more imaginative and poetical—something more consonant with a highly wrought fancy, with a taste for pathos, with sentiments more tender, elevated, unworldly" (4). It is tempting, then, to think of Brontë in *Jane Eyre* as deliberately playing off of Disraeli's "Angrian" autobiography, the perfect foil for pointing up and defining her own new vision of poetic reality.

8. According to Louis James, "it is very hard to define what a 'domestic story' is. . . . The term denotes not so much a particular subject as an approach to the subject. G. D. Pitt [*The Little Wife,* 1841] defined a domestic romance when he declared 'the events are brought home to the evidence of our senses, as consonant with scenes of real life' " (114). Stories of domestic romance, James says, "tell of people one can recognize. The reader can feel at home with it, place him (or more usually her) self in the picture. At the same time the realism is illusory" (134).

For "domestic" in the value system of *Jane Eyre* see below, the end of ch. 7.

9. I do not find it among the twenty-eight Hofland titles listed in "Where the Brontës Borrowed Books; The Keighley Mechanics' Institute" (*Brontë Society Transactions* 11.5:344–58). However, if the new edition of *Ellen* announced in the *Athenaeum* on 6 March 1847 is too late to serve as a "germ" for *Jane Eyre,* it does suggest that *Ellen* was still in the novel-readers' repertoire in 1847.

Chapter 2. Reality and Narratability

1. This rather uncommon name appeared, with a slight difference in spelling, in Geraldine Jewsbury's *Zoe,* a novel I will have occasion to mention several times later, wherein Peter Brocclehurst was a gossiping tailor; there is no apparent resemblance between the two characters. The "Brockenhurst thicket" appears in Scott's completion of Strutt's *Queenhoo-Hall,* published in the appendix to the 1829 edition of *Waverley.*

2. Rigby refers to Lowood as "a sort of Dothegirls Hall," and Chorley compares Brocklehurst to Squeers, as does the *Christian Remembrancer* reviewer (Allott 106, 71, 90).

3. Cf. the Reverend Mr. Drummer in G. W. M. Reynolds, *The Mysteries of London* (1846): "While he bolted huge mouthfuls of boiled beef, he favoured the company with an excellent moral dissertation upon abstemiousness and self-mortification" (2:30).

4. The prevalence of the ghostly was greater in the past century than it is now. In August 1848, the *North British Review* (8:213–26) reviewed a German, French, and British book of that year treating "Ghosts and Ghost-Seers" and reported that the German Seeress of Prevorst, Frederica Hauffe, had been introduced "a few years ago by an English gentlewoman, widely reputed for her novels of remorselessly real life, and at the time a thorough realist in philosophy, and a person whose goodness has never assumed the form . . . called piety at all." That woman was Catherine Crowe, author/compiler of *The Night Side of Nature,* the English volume under review and translator of the German volume. The reviewer thought dreams, presentiments, and sensuous illusions of various kinds might be the product of "nervous sympathy" and reported approvingly that Crowe thought the greatest of the seeress's revelations was "that the world of spirits is inter-diffused through the one we inhabit."

5. "The only making of sense that counts in a formalist reading is the last one, and I wanted to say that everything a reader does, even

. . . .

if he later undoes it, is a part of the 'meaning experience' and should not be discarded" (Fish, *Class* 3-4).

Chapter 3. Dialogic Genres

1. The first nine chapters have actually "recorded in detail" only some seven months—two and a half at Gateshead, four and a half at Lowood (Clarendon 611)—so the ratio of chapters to months is even more disproportionate than the apologetic narrator admits.

2. There seems no reason to doubt the English Catalogue date, 1835, though Block, the *Cambridge Bibliography of English Literature,* Thomson, and R. Colby suggest 1845.

3. Though this is one of the more obscure and critically unremarked novels referred to in this study, it may well have been known to the Brontës: it was published by Aylott in 1844; the Brontë poems, by Aylott and Jones early in 1846.

4. See the *Quarterly Review* for 1848 and Helen Shipton in the *Monthly Packet* for November 1896 (Tillotson, 149n).

5. The parallels between this part of *Jane Eyre* and Austen's *Northanger Abbey* are remarkable: the approach to the abbey and to Thornfield Hall (*JE* 105, *NA* 162-63); the modernity of Jane's room (117) and the disappointing modernity of the abbey (162-63); the "deserted wing" of the abbey where Catherine suspects General Tilney may have incarcerated his wife, "alleged" to have died nine years ago, and the death of Rowland Rochester nine years ago; the secret, which we know but Jane does not at this point, of what inhabits the third story of Thornfield Hall. Brontë's letters, however, show conclusively that in January 1848, months after *Jane Eyre* was published, she had not read any Austen, and in 1850 had read only *Pride and Prejudice,* which she found tepid (*Letters* 2:179, 3:79, in Wise and Symington). This is a remarkable demonstration of how the generic tradition can explain away what seems "clearly" to be "influence" or borrowing.

Relocating Gothic myth or mysticism in prosaic reality is not only a device of parodic travesty (Bakhtin, *Dialogic* 57), as in Austen, but an example in *Jane Eyre* of the kind of "serious" parody that Bakhtin finds constitutive of the novel as a genre.

6. There's another inhabitant in a "deserted wing," this time Fatherless Fanny herself in a variation of the "rightful heir" motif, which will be discussed later in the chapter. Her mother, in order to protect her from harm, entrusts her as a baby to Mrs. Bolton, the governess, who puts her in the "deserted wing" of Pemberton Abbey: "nor has it ever been supposed, since Mr. Hamilton's [her father's] absence,

. . . . . .

that any one inhabited that mansion, excepting the servant left to take care of it, whose superstitious fear of the wing I inhabit, which is reported to be haunted by a man dressed in complete armour, effectually secures me from any interruption from her" ([Reeve] 264).

7. The Clarendon editors, citing Winifred Gérin's *Branwell Brontë*, quote one of Branwell's unfinished stories in which he describes the folk belief in the Gytrash, " 'a spectre neither at all similar to the Ghosts of those who once were alive, nor to fairys nor to demons.' It usually appears in the form of some animal—'a black dog dragging a chain, a dusky calf' " (590).

8. Watt is introducing a "shocker" of 1818: *Lovel Castle, or the Rightful Heir Restored, a Gothic Tale; Narrating how a Young Man, the Supposed Son of a Peasant, by a Train of Unparalleled Circumstances, not only Discovers who were his Real Parents, but that they came to Untimely Deaths; with his Adventures in the Haunted Apartment, Discovery of the Fatal Closet, and Appearance of the Ghost of his Murdered Father; Relating, also, how the Murderer was Brought to Justice, with his Confession, and Restoration of the Injured Orphan to his Titles and Estates.*

9. Jauss, contending that "the way in which a literary work satisfies, surpasses, disappoints, or disproves the expectations of its first readers in the historical moment of its appearance obviously gives a criterion for the determination of its aesthetic value," and calling works that make no changes in the horizon of expectations " 'culinary' or light reading," must face the fact that after the "masterwork" changes the horizon, that horizon becomes familiar, and the masterwork or classic itself appears in "dangerous proximity with irresistible convincing and enjoyable 'culinary' art, and special effort is needed to read them 'against the grain' of accustomed experience so that their artistic nature becomes evident again" (18–19).

10. Mr. Hamilton, Fatherless Fanny's father, enters her room in Pemberton Abbey through a secret door behind a looking glass ([Reeve] 237).

Chapter 4. The Transgeneric Topic, Love

1. Jane reads and quotes selectively. Proverbs 15:18, which follows the Solomon statement—"A wrathful man stirreth up strife: but he that is slow to anger appeaseth strife"—might even at this point have served her well, and later it would have been well for her to recall 15:16: "Better is little with the fear of the Lord than great treasure and trouble therewith." Human and divine love are continuously related—joined or opposed—in interesting counterpoint in the novel.

. . . .

2. The master telling the governess about his mistress(es) is particularly offensive to Rigby. Somewhat later Leslie Stephen finds the scene like something "taken from the first novel at hand of the early Bulwer school, or a diluted recollection of Byron" (*Cornhill Magazine* [December 1877]: 723–29, qtd. in Allott 418).

PART II. Strategies of the Text

1. These geometric metaphors are useful but not rigorously consistent or universally agreed upon. I am using them roughly in the following way: my diagram of the sequential arrangement and reading of the text I am imagining as a straight, flat line from left to right, and I am referring to it by such terms as unilinear, horizontal, temporal, and (for its temporal dimension) diachronic. The recapitulative departure from this straight, forward-moving time-line, such as the supposed ghost of Thornfield calling up the supposed ghost of the red-room (whether this is conceived of as a function of the signal of the text or the action of the reader), I am imagining as disruptive of the straight line, of the diachrony, and I refer to it as synchronic (the "ghosts" lying side by side, occupying the same textual or reader-"moment") or vertical (the red-room ghost being brought up to and placed, as it were, "above" the Thornfield spot on the time-line) or spatial (i.e., "untemporal," violating or disrupting the unilinear, temporal movement forward of text and reader). This last, roughly approximate term is also useful to designate the configuration or the projected shape of the novel at any given moment in the text or the reading. Unlike horizontal and vertical, the spatial has shape, area, enclosure, which indicates a wholeness, completeness, or integrity of the text. The context (cultural as well as literary) I imagine as existing "beyond" the text, just as the reader in the real world, when he or she is not fully engaged in the act of reading, exists in a continuum and different context, operating from a different site that I imagine on "this" side of the textual/reading line; both of these contexts are in a third dimension, while the text and reading lines (spatial as well as temporal or unilinear) are on a plane surface. I try to keep these terms, rough as they are, consistent, which means I often have to use multiple terms—e.g., unilinear, temporal, horizontal—to reinforce or clarify my perceptions.

2. Rabinowitz uses "misreading . . . to refer not to readings that simply skirt the authorial audience [or readings such as Freudian readings that are "doing something else" (175)], but rather to readings that *attempt* to incorporate the strategies of the authorial audience but fail to do so" (42). The Freudian (or feminist or Marxist), I would contend,

. . . .

is not "doing something else," but, coming to a text with a more *systematic* ideological "conviction" than does the common reader, defines somewhat differently what constitutes an author's "intention" or the text's strategies. Rabinowitz calls the authorial reading "often incomplete" (and seems to mean something closer to "always incomplete"); he insists that we strive, in Eagleton's words, "to show the text as it cannot know itself" (43). I consider this one of the forms of "misreading."

Chapter 5. Hybridization

1. Governess heroines are even more frequently orphans than the run-of-the-mill Victorian heroes and heroines. Besides those already mentioned, for example, Margaret Russell's mother dies when the heroine is twelve; Elizabeth Mathews's Ellinor in *Ellinor; or, The Young Governess* (1809) is at her mother's deathbed when the novel opens.

2. The moon that awakened Jane plays a sinister role in vampire narratives—and the blood-sucking raises that specter. Early in Polidori's tale, the vampire Ruthven is shot to death by robbers. Before he dies he gives orders that his corpse be "exposed to the first cold ray of the moon that rose after his death" (56). The corpse disappears. Ruthven, very much alive, or seemingly so, reappears later in the tale. Was it the moon that awakened the vampire on the third story of Thornfield Manor?

3. Block gives its date of publication as 1844 and convincingly identifies the author as James Malcolm Rymer, not Thomas Preskett Prest, as claimed by Sir Devendra P. Varma and Margaret L. Carter in the 1970 reprint of the 1847 edition. The title page of Rymer's 1846 novel, *Jane Shore*, identifies it as "by the Author of 'The Black Monk,' 'Varney the Vampire,' &c.," confirming the earlier, pre-*Jane Eyre* date of its first publication.

4. Thorslev points out that the Byron fragment had nothing to do with vampirism before Polidori got hold of it and maintains that Praz exaggerates the "fatal" aspects of Byronism, mixing the man and his poetry (9). But readers then and now associate Byron—man and work —no matter how inaccurately, with the darker elements, the "Satanic" school.

Chapter 6. Devastation and Revisitations

1. In the previous chapter of this study a distinction was made between the voice of the child Jane and that of the young adult, who seems to have incorporated some of the lessons of Helen Burns and

Miss Temple, but is not yet as fully mature and fully knowledgeable as the narrator. Here the distinction between the two younger Janes is not relevant, however, since there is no issue of morality or religion involved.

2. The *Blackwood's* "Letter" cites the "authentic" case in which "Stanjorka, the wife of Heyduke, twenty years old[,] had died after an illness of three days, and had been buried eighteen days. The countenance was florid, and of a high colour. There was blood in the chest and in the heart. The viscera were perfectly sound. The skin was remarkably fresh" (61:432).

3. Florence Dry sees Rochester's story like "George Staunton's, but combined with the elder Staunton's": " 'The father of George Staunton . . . during service in the West Indies had married the heiress of a wealthy planter . . . his own fortune was that of a younger brother.' This quotation is from [Sir Walter Scott's] *The Heart of Midlothian* [ch. 34], but it might have come from *Jane Eyre*" (40). It is not his mother, the West Indian heiress, however, who goes mad, but George's lover, Madge Wildfire, whose "mind became totally alienated" (Dry 40), though not through debauchery.

4. Unbridled passion is indeed associated with insanity in the nineteenth century (see Grudin 147, on the "scientific theory" of "moral madness"), but it is not gender-specific. In males as well as females, lust and insanity—defined, indeed, as the loss of rational control, the submission of reason to the emotions—were often related. The interpolated tale in the eleventh chapter of *Pickwick Papers*, "A Madman's Manuscript," for example, reads almost like a mirror image of Rochester's story, told by "a male Bertha." He marries a poor girl whose father and brothers force her to the altar, though she loves another. Because he fears passing on insanity to a child, he decides to kill his wife, perhaps by setting his house on fire, but instead drives her mad (leaning over her bed, a razor in hand, just as Lady Glenfallen did in the LeFanu tale) and kills one of her brothers. Now, from the madhouse, he adds to the manuscript,

> The unhappy man whose ravings are recorded above, was a melancholy instance of the baneful results of energies misdirected in early life, and excesses prolonged until their consequences could never be repaired. The thoughtless riot, dissipation, and debauchery of his younger days, produced fever and, delirium. The first effects of the latter was the strange delusion . . . that an hereditary madness existed in his family. (Dickens, *Pickwick* 166)

. . . .

That Bertha's insanity was hereditary was not a delusion, though it was also brought on "prematurely" by acts "intemperate and unchaste."

5. The upright hero, determined to leave the willful, irreligious heroine, says, "Since I must 'cut off the right hand' better the stroke were past" (Brunton, *Discipline* 219).

6. Lerner also challenges Gilbert and Gubar's reading, though on other grounds, suggesting that the claim that Bertha expresses what Jane feels or wishes is simply asserted and that "if Bertha represents the very opposite to Jane . . . if her presence in the attic symbolizes all that Jane does *not* feel, if she tears the bridal veil when Jane with her whole being wishes to wear it, if she tries to burn Rochester and this horrifies Jane because she feels *no* hostility to him, even unconsciously, then *the parallels would be just as strong*" (291, emphasis added).

7. Nestor is rather unorthodox in finding in Jane a "fear at the threatening aspect of sexuality . . . compounded by a certain disgust at its expression," arguing that what appears to be "simple racism" is but Brontë's tendency to "define libidinal drive as Other, or foreign to the self" (59).

8. Viewing *Jane Eyre* as subversive is not exclusively determined by the conservative religious or political ideology; as suggested earlier, the Radical *Examiner* seemed to want to co-opt this popular new novel for Godwinism and the left (see above, ch. 1).

9. "Save me, O God; for the waters are come into my soul. / I sink in deep mire, where there is no standing; I am come into deep waters, where the floods overflow me." The prayerful opening phrase of Psalm 69 is suppressed: young Jane is still apparently unable to pray. In Rachel McCrindell's *The English Governess*, Clara Neville's fiancé becomes dissipated and irreligious at Cambridge. The epigraph to chapter 3, in which this comes to light, is from Psalms 43:7, which contains some of the same imagery: "Deep calleth unto deep at the noise of thy waterspouts: all thy waves and thy billows are gone over me."

10. The changes of scene, which are also moral stages or stages of growth, in Bakhtin's terms, "chronotopes," are indeed structural elements here but are quite separate from the volume structure: not only are Gateshead and Lowood both in the first volume, but there are no internal or sectional markings within the volume. The eight-year gap between chapters 9 and 10 is not structurally marked, and the move out into "life," to Thornfield and her arrival and first months there, even the advent of Rochester, all take place within that volume. Thornfield takes up half the novel, figuring in all three volumes. Nonetheless

. . . .

232

the volume breaks are also structural and are so marked, as the water imagery and its accompanying hope-to-despair movement suggest. This structural counterpoint—the chronotope of romance versus the religious/realist suggestions of the volume-structure—coincides well with the affectively perceived mixed nature of *Jane Eyre* as romance and novel.

11. See Robert Heilman, "Charlotte Brontë, Reason, and the Moon," on the role of the moon in Brontë's fictional world.

12. Gilbert and Gubar, 341 and passim, rightly stress the importance of the red-room experience and the repeated references to it at crucial points in the text, though I believe their reading of it as paradigmatic of the "plot of enclosure and escape" ignores the religious element in the novel, largely by "Freudianizing" it.

Chapter 7. Ideology and the Act of Reading

1. This is another example of later passages qualifying or, as in this instance, responding to earlier ones. This testimony to God's presence and the immortality of the soul answers the doubting questions Jane had asked herself when speaking with Helen:

> "Where is God? What is God?"
>
> "My Maker and yours; who will never destroy what he created. I rely implicitly on his power, and confide wholly in his goodness: I count the hours till that eventful one arrives which shall restore me to him, reveal him to me."
>
> "You are sure, then, Helen, that there is such a place as heaven; and that our souls can get to it when we die?"
>
> "I am sure there is a future state; I believe God is good: I can resign my immortal part to him without any misgiving. God is my father; God is my friend; I love him; I believe he loves me."
>
> "And shall I see you again, Helen, when I die?"
>
> "You will come to the same region of happiness: be received by the same mighty, universal Parent, no doubt, dear Jane."
>
> Again I questioned; but this time only in thought. "Where is that region? does it exist?" (80)

2. Quoting the passage "Human life and human labour were near. I must struggle on; strive to live and bend to toil like the rest" (416), Barry Qualls, his humanist ideology showing, says, "Brontë insists that human aid and communication are vital to Jane's salvation" (62; see also Gates 86: "Jane . . . [learns] of the interconnectedness of

· · · · · ·

human life and of the need for dependence and compassion as well as for independence"). Qualls ignores the rejection by her fellowmen that almost immediately follows this passage. Her "salvation" (Brontë surely would not use that term to mean earthly survival) follows her plea to Providence for guidance.

3. Though this is literally the phosphorescent marsh light called by this name, the false light is also metaphorically a misleading, in providentialist terms. The believer must distinguish true leadings from such false ones. Ignis fatuus is elsewhere in *Jane Eyre* used to suggest the false guidance given us by our passions. Rochester tells Jane that after he put Bertha in Thornfield, "I transformed myself into a Will-o'-the wisp. . . . I pursued wanderings as wild as those of the Marsh-spirit. I sought the Continent . . . to seek and find a good and intelligent woman" (395). Jane believes "it is madness in all women to let a secret love kindle within them, which, if responded to, must lead, *ignis fatuus*-like into miry wilds whence there is no extrication" (201). Mary Hays asks whether women's "capacity [is] only an ignis fatuus since it doesn't lead to fulfilment" (1:172). Clarissa is in fact bedevilled by false lights: "But I, presumptuous creature! must rely so much upon my own knowledge of the right path!—little apprehending that an *ignis fatuus* with its false fire . . . would arise to mislead me! And now, in the midst of fens and quagmires, it plays around and around me, throwing me back again, whenever I think myself in the right track" (Richardson, *Clarissa* Letter 173, 566).

4. In early capitalist Britain, the conception of a Special Providence was useful for the rich and unscrupulous to sanctify their material prosperity. Thus does Dickens's Mr. Pecksniff implicitly make use of the concern of Providence for the sparrow:

> "It [to offer a four-thousand-pound dowry for his daughter] would sadly pinch and cramp me, my dear friend," repeated Mr Pecksniff, "but Providence, perhaps I may be permitted to say a special Providence, has blessed my endeavours, and I could guarantee to make the sacrifice."
>
> A question of philosophy arises here, whether Mr Pecksniff had or had not good reason to say, that he was specially patronised and encouraged in his undertakings. All his life long he had been walking up and down the narrow ways and by-places, with a hook in one hand and a crook in the other, scraping all sorts of valuable odds and ends into his pouch. Now, there being a special Providence in the fall of the sparrow, it follows (so Mr Pecksniff would have reasoned), that there must also be a special Providence in the alighting of the stone, stick, or other substance which is aimed at the sparrow. And Mr Pecksniff's hook, or crook, having invariably knocked the sparrow on the head and brought him down, that

gentleman may have been led to consider himself as specially licensed to bag sparrows, and as being specially seized and possessed of all the birds he had got together. That many undertakings, national as well as individual—but especially the former—are held to be specially brought to a glorious and successful issue, which never could be so regarded on any other process of reasoning, must be clear to all men. (*Martin Chuzzlewit* 393–94)

Dickens felt compelled to add a footnote to this 1844 passage: "The most credulous reader will scarcely believe that Mr Pecksniff's reasoning was once set upon as the Author's."

5. There is another implicit contrast, that between the Rivers and Reed households, each with two sisters and a brother named John, the one so conflicted, cruel, and profane or religiously perverse, the other so harmonious, loving, and devout.

6. Vineta Colby (159) refers to Mrs. Sherwood's "semi-fictional biography of a real-life missionary, *The Life of Henry Martyn* (which Janet Dempster of George Eliot's 'Janet's Repentance' read with deep interest)," but I have been unable to find a record of such a work, though Mrs. Sherwood did write *The History of John Marten, a sequel to the Life of Henry Milner* (1844), which may have been confused with Sargent's *Memoir* but has no relation that I can see to Martyn. In "Janet's Repentance," the title is given as Colby indicates, but no author is named (nor does David Lodge name an author in his note to the text in the Penguin edition, identifying only Martyn). On the other hand, Mrs. Sherwood spent years in India and knew Martyn in Cawnpore, and her impressions of him are given in the *Memoirs*, though Sargent cites no published or manuscript sources (288, 302). Valentine Cunningham (*Everywhere Spoken Against*) identifies the memoir Janet Dempster is reading as Sargent's (xx).

7. Susan VanZanten Gallagher, citing Elisabeth Jay's *The Religion of the Heart: Anglican Evangelicalism and the Nineteenth-Century Novel*, points out that nineteenth-century Evangelicalism considered celibacy "somewhat perverse," a view she finds echoed in "Brontë's negative depiction of St. John's rejection of Rosamond and of Eliza Reed's retirement to a convent" (68). Jane initially thinks St. John's action "wrong," or at least unfortunate, but later she "understood, as by inspiration, the nature of his love for Miss Oliver: I agreed with him that it was but a love of the senses . . . ; how he should mistrust its ever conducing permanently to his happiness, or hers" (501–2).

8. *Imperialist* from 1600 to 1800 refers to adherents of German Empire and later to Napoleon. Its third definition in the *OED*, "an

· · · · · ·

advocate of 'imperialism' in British or American politics," dates only from 1899—and all four citations thereafter are favorable! Though *colony* is, of course, an older term, *colonialism* as a system or principle first appears in 1886. India was never, strictly speaking, a colony (that is, a territory or country settled by the English) but was instead a "dependency," under the control of Britain (though in Brontë's day only indirectly, through the East India Company).

Chapter 8. Decentering the Narrator

1. St. John's "&c" replaces these words from the Biblical text: "and the abominable, and murderers, and whoremongers, and sorcerers, and idolaters, and all liars"; in context not all these words need have been elided. The preceding line, Revelations 21:6, also includes "I am Alpha and Omega, the beginning and the end. I will give unto him that is athirst of the fountain of the water of life freely." Rochester as the "Alpha and Omega" was deleted from the initial ending of volume 2, as we have noted, so "idolaters" would have been appropriate from the narrator's perspective and might have reinforced the novel's characterization of Jane's love, and the water of life reinforced its imagery; but the passage is marked dialogically and appropriately as St. John's utterance, and he would not have access to Jane's earlier thoughts.

2. Wayne Burns, 307–11, has a hilarious and unsettling Freudian reading of this entire scene.

3. The Clarendon note also cites, I believe mistakenly, a passage in Marsh's *The Deformed:* the midnight scream in *The Deformed* that, Mrs. Gaskell reports, Brontë feared might lead readers to think she had plagiarized from Marsh is not the "Lord Louis! Lord Louis! Lord Louis!" quoted above (see ch. 5), which occurs during the day and involves retribution by lightning. There is another literal "midnight scream" that occurs when the hero, the deformed, is found dead. Brontë seemed to think the "Good God!" exclamation that follows similar to the exclamations of the guests at Thornfield when Mason is bitten and screams.

4. John Reed—the critic, not Jane's cousin—cites another Scott precedent: "The insane Bertha Mason's death in the blazing destruction of Thornfield Hall . . . had as its model a similar death of a maniac in a burning tower in Scott's *Ivanhoe*" (201).

5. This, too, is territory "occupied" by contemporary fiction; one such instance has also some intriguing verbal resonance. In "The Manor and the Eyrie," in Harriet Martineau's *Forest and Game-Law Tales* (1845–46), the family house having burned down, one of the servants having been blinded and having lost a hand in the fire, the father now

. . . . . .

searches for an "eyrie": "There you shall have a bed of *ferns* this night as soft as the doe can find for his fawn. Then we will seek some *eyrie* which God has sheltered for us" (1:91, emphasis added). Besides the echo of Eyre-eyrie and fern-Ferndean, Rochester is frequently referred to as an eagle (most recently on 570). Katherine King called my attention to this passage. Martineau recounts in her *Autobiography* that she had been "taxed with the authorship" of *Jane Eyre*, and she herself had believed that it must have been by a friend who knew of her childhood, while Brontë told her, she says, that reading Martineau's "Household Education" was "like meeting her own fetch—so precisely were the fears and miseries there described the same as her own" (qtd. in Gérin, *Brontë* 411).

An article entitled "Novel Writing Made Easy" in *Chamber's Edinburgh Journal* for 29 August 1846 makes it clear that the wounded hero is not private property and even suggests why, despite the biblical passage, it is his left hand that Rochester loses: while, it says, a hero may be wounded in the arm or leg, "No vital organ must be endangered. Taking a left arm in extreme cases is perhaps allowable; the legs must be kept intact" (129).

6. See above, n. 1.

Afterword: Decentering the Author

1. Of course all the words of the text are that narrator's, but this study has shown on many occasions how reticent the narrator has been to judge or even clarify young Jane's views; such reticence is constitutive of Brontë's providentialist strategy.

2. We may gain further insight into Charlotte Brontë's view of Jane Eyre and *Jane Eyre*, in fact, by seeing in *Villette* a response or corrective to the reception of Jane Eyre, if not to the novel itself:

> Jane thirsts for experience, Lucy shirks it. Jane is chastened for her excessive restlessness and self-reliance; Lucy is spurred to action despite her desire to hide. *Villette* makes untenable the narrow and simplistic understanding of Providentialism that might be inferred from reading *Jane Eyre* in isolation. The role of Brontë's Providence [*Villette* makes clear] is not purely patriarchal, nor does it necessarily reward passivity and social conformity with earthly happiness. Its function is not merely to chasten rebelliousness, to domesticate, as it does for Jane; it also energizes, engages, and socializes, as it does for Lucy, making her more adventurous, making her face reality and the outside world, involving her in life and love—and loss. (Beaty, "Afterword" 480–81)

. . . .

3. Gaskell's report does not make clear whether Brontë supposes Rochester to be good-natured and grumpy like Francesca's husband. It is clear elsewhere—in Brontë's letter of 14 August 1848 to her publisher's man, W. W. Williams—that she believes Rochester's "nature is like wine of good vintage, time cannot sour but only mellow him. Such at least was the character I meant to portray" (*Letters* 2:245). She resents comparisons with Anne's Huntingdon in *The Tenant of Wildfell Hall*, who, she says, is "naturally selfish, sensual, [and] superficial" (2:244); and with Heathcliff, who is "naturally perverse, vindictive, [and] inexorable" (2:245)—and made worse by hard usage. That many readers see the three as resembling each other shows clearly the influence of the conventions of the Gothic hero/villain. The strategy of serial revelation also means the reader's first impressions of Rochester are not entirely favorable, and "good-natured" is scarcely the first quality that leaps to mind when we think of Charlotte Brontë's hero.

4. She was hurt when she heard that her idol, Thackeray, thought the plot of *Jane Eyre* unoriginal: "The plot of 'Jane Eyre' may be a hackneyed one. Mr. Thackeray remarks that it is familiar to him. But having read comparatively few novels I never chanced to meet with it, and I thought it original" (*Letters* 2:150). As this study has demonstrated, Thackeray was of course right; this seems another instance of Brontë's "misreading."

. . . . . .

BIBLIOGRAPHY

I. Eighteenth and Nineteenth Century: Novels, Manuals

Austen, Jane. *Emma: A Novel.* 1816. London: Oxford University Press, 1971.

————. *Northanger Abbey.* 1818. Oxford: Clarendon Press, 1933.

The Autobiography of Rose Allen. London: Longman, Brown, Green, and Longman, 1847.

Blessington, Marguerite, Countess of. *The Confessions of an Elderly Gentleman.* 1836. London: Longman, Orme, Brown, Green, and Longmans, 1838.

————. *The Governess.* 2 vols. London: Longman, Orme, Brown, Green, and Longmans, 1839.

Bremer, Frederika. *The Neighbours. A Story of Every-day Life.* 1842 [first English translation]. Translated by Mary Howitt. London: C. Bell & Sons, 1910.

Brontë, Charlotte. *Jane Eyre.* 1847. Edited by Jane Jack and Margaret Smith. Oxford: Clarendon Press, 1969.

————. *The Professor.* 1857. Edited by Margaret Smith and Herbert Rosegarten. Oxford: Clarendon Press, 1987.

Brooke, Henry. *The Fool of Quality; or, The History of Henry Earl of Moreland.* 1770. 5 vols. London: Edward Johnston, 1792.

Brunton, Mary. *Discipline: A Novel.* 1814. London: Bentley, 1832.

———. *Self-Control.* 1811. London: Colburn and Bentley, 1832.

Carlyle, Thomas. *Sartor Resartus: The Life and Opinions of Herr Teufelsdröckh.* 1834. Edited by Charles F. Harold. New York: Odyssey Press, 1937.

Chorley, Henry F. *Sketches Of a Sea Port Town.* 1834. 2 vols. Philadelphia: E. L. Carey and A. Hart, 1836.

Defoe, Daniel. *Moll Flanders.* 1722. Vol. 1. Shakespeare Head Edition of the Novels and Selected Writings of Daniel Defoe, vol. 8. Oxford: Basil Blackwell, 1927.

Dickens, Charles. *Dombey and Son.* 1848. Edited by Peter Fairclough. Harmondsworth: Penguin, 1977.

———. *The Life and Adventures of Nicholas Nickleby.* 1839. 2 vols. London: Oxford University Press, 1950.

———. *Martin Chuzzlewit.* 1843–44. Edited by P. N. Firbank. Harmondsworth: Penguin, 1975.

———. *Oliver Twist; or, the Parish Boy's Progress.* 1838. Edited by Kathleen Tillotson. Oxford: Clarendon Press, 1966.

———. *Pickwick Papers.* 1837. Edited by James Kinsley. Oxford: Clarendon Press, 1986.

Disraeli, Benjamin. *Coningsby; or, The New Generation.* 1844. New York: Capricorn Books, 1961.

———. *Contarini Fleming.* 1832. Vol. 4, The Bradenham Edition of the Novels and Tales of Benjamin Disraeli, First Earl of Beaconsfield. London: Peter Davies, 1927.

Ferdinand Franck; an Auto-Biographical Sketch of the Youthful Days of a Musical Student. London: R. Ackermann, 1825.

Fielding, Sarah. *The Governess; or, Little Female Academy.* 1749. London: Oxford University Press, 1968.

Fullerton, Lady Georgiana. *Ellen Middleton. A Tale.* London: Edward Moxon, 1844.

The Gallant Glazier; or, the Mystery of Ridley Hall. In *Douglas Jerrold's Shilling Magazine,* 6 (December 1847): 517–34.

. . . .

Galt, John. *The Annals of the Parish; or, The Chronicle of Dalmailing; During the Ministry of the Rev. Micah Balwhidder.* Edinburgh: William Blackwood, 1821.

———. *The Member: An Autobiography.* London: James Fraser, 1832.

———. *The Radical: An Autobiography.* London: James Fraser, 1832.

Gaskell, Elizabeth. *The Life of Charlotte Brontë.* 1857. London: Dent, 1971.

Godwin, William. *Caleb Williams.* 1794/1831. New York: W. W. Norton, 1977.

Hall, Anna Maria [Mrs. Samuel Carter]. *Stories of the Governess.* London: J. Nisbet and Co., 1852. First published in 1842 in *Chamber's Edinburgh Journal.* Includes "The Old Governess," "The Governess, a Tale," "The Daily Governess," and, on 23 March 1844, "Our Governess," a first-person story by "Mr. Johnson." Title page includes statement "Printed for the Benefit of the Governess' Benevolent Institution."

Hays, Mary. *Memoirs of Emma Courtney.* 2 vols. London: G. G. & J. Robinson, 1796. Reprint. New York: Garland, 1974.

Hofland, Barbara. *Ellen the Teacher: A Tale for Youth.* 1814. Boston: Chase and Nichols, 1863.

Hook, Theodore. *Fathers and Sons.* 3 vols. London: Henry Colburn, 1842.

Inchbald, Elizabeth. *A Simple Story.* 1791. London: Oxford University Press, 1967.

Jewsbury, Geraldine Endsor. *Zoe: The History of Two Lives.* New York: Harper and Brothers, 1845.

LeFanu, J. Sheridan. *The Purcell Papers.* 3 vols. London: Richard Bentley & Sons, 1880. Includes in vol. 3 *A chapter in the History of a Tyrone Family, being a tenth extract from the Legacy of the Late Francis Purcell, P. P. of Drumcoolagh,* first published in *Dublin Magazine* for October 1839.

Lytton, Edward Bulwer. *Devereux.* 1829. Boston: Estes and Lauriat, 1891.

———. *Pelham; or, Adventures of a Gentleman.* 1828. London: Richard Edward King, n.d.

McCrindell, Rachel. *The English Governess. A Tale of Real Life.* Philadelphia: Herman Hooker, 1844.

Malet, Lady. *Violet; or, The Danseuse: A Portraiture of Human Passions and Character.* 2 vols. London: Henry Colburn, 1836.

. . . .

Margaret Russell: An Autobiography. London: Longman, Brown, Green, and Longmans, 1846.

Marsh, Anne. *The Deformed.* In *Two Old Men's Tales.* London: Richard Bentley, 1844.

———. *Mount Sorel; or, The Heiress of the De Veres.* 2 vols. London: Chapman and Hall, 1845.

Martineau, Harriet. *Deerbrook.* 2 vols. New York: Harper and Bros., 1839. Reprint, Garden City, N.Y.: Dial Press, 1984.

———. *Forest and Game-Law Tales.* 3 vols. London: Edward Moxon, 1845.

Martyn, Henry. *Journals and Letters of the Reverend Henry Martyn.* 1837. Edited by the Reverend [Samuel] Wilberforce. New York: M. W. Dodd, 1851.

Mathews, Elizabeth Kirkham. *Ellinor; or The Young Governess. A Moral Tale.* 1806. York: Thomas Wilson and Son, 1809.

Maurice, F. Denison. *Eustace Conway; or, The Brother and Sister. A Novel.* 3 vols. London: Richard Bentley, 1834.

Napier, Elizabeth. *The Nursery Governess.* London: T. & W. Boone, 1834.

Peacock, Thomas Love. *Nightmare Abbey.* 1818. Reprint. London: Humphrey Milford, 1923.

Polidori, John. *The Vampyre. A Tale.* London: Sherwood, Neely, and Jones, 1819.

Radcliffe, Ann. *The Mysteries of Udolpho, A Romance.* 1794. London: Oxford University Press, 1966.

[Reeve, Clara]. *Fatherless Fanny; or, A Young Lady's First Entrance into Life, being the Memoirs of a Little Mendicant, and Her Benefactors.* London: J. Tallis, 1819. Robert Colby says "ca. 1818" and does not indicate author. Andrew Block lists it under Prest, but he was born about 1810. Title page says, as Block himself notes, "By the author of *The Old English Baron* [i.e., Clara Reeve?]," though there seems no reason for the query.

Reynolds, G. W. M. *The Mysteries of London.* 4 vols. London: G. Vickers, 1845–48.

Richardson, Samuel. *Clarissa; or, The History of a Young Lady.* 1747–48. Harmondsworth, Middlesex: Penguin Books, 1985.

. . . .

————. *The History of Sir Charles Grandison in a Series of Letters Published from the Originals by the Editor of Pamela and Clarissa.* 1754. 6 vols. Oxford: Shakespeare Head Press, 1931.

————. *Pamela; or, Virtue Rewarded.* 1740. New York: W. W. Norton, 1958.

Ross, Miss [name on title page; Block says Mrs.] *The Governess; Or, Politics in Private Life.* 1836. London: Smith, Elder, 1843. This is running title and title as it appears in Block, but 1843 title is *The Politics of Private Life.*

Rymer, James Malcolm. *Varney the Vampire.* 1847. 3 vols. New York: Arno Press, [c 1970]. (Sometimes attributed to Prest, but see Block.)

Sargent, the Rev. John. *A Memoir of the Rev. Henry Martyn, B. D.* 1820. Boston: Perkins and Marvin, 1831.

Scott, Sir Walter. *Waverley; or, 'Tis Sixty Years Since.* 1814. London: Dent and Dutton, 1906.

Sewell, Elizabeth Missing. *Amy Herbert.* 1844. London: Longmans, Green & Co., 1886.

Sherwood, Mrs. Mary Martha. *Caroline Mordaunt; or, The Governess.* 1835. Vol. 13, *The Works of Mrs. Sherwood.* Boston: Harpers, 1834–58.

————. *The History of John Marten.* London: J. Hatchard and Son, 1844.

The Shilling Shockers: Stories of Terror from the Gothic Bluebooks. Edited by Peter Haining. New York: St. Martin's Press, 1979.

Thackeray, William Makepeace. *The Luck of Barry Lyndon.* 1844/1856. Edited by Martin J. Anisman. New York: New York University Press, 1970.

Torrens, Henry Whitelock. *Madame de Malguet; A Tale of 1820.* 3 vols. London: Longman, Brown, Green, and Longmans, 1848.

Weeton, Miss [Ellen]. *Journal of a Governess, 1807–1811.* Edited by Edward Hall. London: Oxford University Press, 1936.

Trollope, Frances. *The Vicar of Wrexhill.* 1837. 3 vols. London: Richard Bentley, 1840.

[Whateley, Mrs. Elizabeth]. *English Life, Social and Domestic in the Middle of the Nineteenth Century, Considered in Reference to Our Position as a Community of Professing Christians.* 2nd ed., rev. London: John W. Parker and Son, 1851.

. . . .

Wise, T. J., and J. A. Symington, eds. *The Brontës: Their Lives, Friendships and Correspondence.* 4 vols. Oxford: Basil Blackwell, 1932.

II. Nineteenth Century: Reviews, Criticism

[Chorley, H. F.] "Our Library Table." *"Jane Eyre. An Autobiography."* *Athenaeum* 1043 (23 October 1847): 1100–1101.

[Eagle, John]. "Letter to Eusebius." *Blackwood's Edinburgh Magazine* 59 (1846): 408–19.

"Ghosts and Ghost-seers. 1. *Die Scheron von Prevorst, etc.* Mitgetheilt von Justinus Kerner. 3te Auflage. Stuttgart und Tübingen, 1838. 2. *Arcanes de la Vie Future dévoilés, etc.* Par M. Alph. Cahagnet. Paris, 1848. 3. *The Night Side of Nature.* By Catherine Crowe. In 2 vols. London, 1848." *North British Review* 8 (August 1848): 213–26.

"Mrs. Hofland, *Ellen the Teacher,* new edition." In "New Books." *Athenaeum* 1010 (6 March 1847): 251.

"Letters on the Truths Concerned in Popular Superstitions: Vampirism." *Blackwood's Edinburgh Magazine* 61 (1847): 432–40.

Leyland, Francis A. *The Brontë Family: with Special Reference to Patrick Branwell Brontë.* London: Hurst and Blockett, 1886.

"Anne Marsh, *Norman's Bridge."* *Westminster Review* 48 (October 1847): 132.

"Harriet Martineau's *The Billow and the Rock."* *Edinburgh Review* 85 (April 1847): 247.

"Rachel McCrindell, *The English Governess,* new ed." Reviewed in "New Books." *Athenaeum* 1016 (17 April 1847): 412.

"Novel Writing Made Easy." *Chamber's Edinburgh Journal,* n.s., 5 (29 August 1846): 129–31.

Review of *The Half Sisters,* by Geraldine Jewsbury. *Jerrold's* 7 (1848): 367–76.

Review of *Margaret Percival,* by Elizabeth Sewell. *Athenaeum* 1001 (2 January 1847): 42.

Review of *The Protégé,* by Mrs. Catherine Ponsonby. *Athenaeum* 1029 (17 July 1847): 756.

[Rigby, Elizabeth]. "Article V. 1. Vanity Fair; a Novel without a Hero, by William Makepeace Thackeray. London: 1848. 2. Jane Eyre; an Autobiography. Edited by Currer Bell. 3. Governesses' Benevolent Institution—Report for 1847." *Quarterly Review* 84 (December 1848): 153–85.

"Sherwood, (Mrs.) [Mary Martha], *History of the Fairchild Family, Pt. III."* Reviewed in "New Books." *Athenaeum* 1026 (26 June 1847): 668.

III. Twentieth Century

Allott, Miriam, ed. *The Brontës: The Critical Heritage.* London: Routledge and Kegan Paul, 1974.

Bakhtin, M. M. *The Dialogic Imagination.* Translated by Caryl Emerson and Michael Holquist. Austin: University of Texas Press, 1981.

———. *Problems of Dostoevsky's Poetics.* 1963. Translated by Caryl Emerson. Minneapolis: University of Minnesota Press, 1984.

———. *Speech Genres and Other Late Essays.* Translated by Vern W. McGee. Austin: University of Texas Press, 1986.

Beaty, Jerome. Afterword to *Villette,* by Charlotte Brontë. New York: New American Library, 1987.

———. "*Jane Eyre* and Genre." *Genre* 10 (Winter 1977): 619–54.

———. "Jane Eyre at Gateshead: Mixed Signals in the Text and Context." In *Victorian Literature and Society: Essays Presented to Richard D. Altick,* edited by James R. Kincaid and Albert J. Kuhn, 168–96. Columbus: Ohio State University Press, 1983.

Block, Andrew. *The English Novel, 1740–1850.* 1939. Rev. ed. London: Dawsons, 1961.

Booth, Wayne. *The Rhetoric of Fiction.* Chicago: University of Chicago Press, 1961.

Boumelha, Penny. *Charlotte Brontë.* New York: Harvester/Wheatsheaf, 1990.

Brooks, Peter. *Reading for Plot: Design and Intention in Narrative.* New York: Vintage Books, 1985.

Bruner, Charlotte H. "A Caribbean Madness: Half Slave and Half Free." *Canadian Review of Comparative Literature* 11 (June 1984): 236–48.

Burns, Wayne. "Critical Relevance of Freudianism. *Western Review* 20 (Summer 1956): 301–14.

. . . .

Cambridge Bibliography of English Literature. Edited by F. W. Bateson. Cambridge: Cambridge University Press, 1940–57.

Cecil, Lord David. *Victorian Novelists.* 1935. Chicago: University of Chicago Press, 1961.

Chase, Karen. *Eros and Psyche: The Representation of Personality in Charlotte Brontë, Charles Dickens, George Eliot.* New York: Methuen, 1984.

Chase, Richard. "The Brontës: A Centennial Observance." *Kenyon Review* 9 (Autumn 1947): 487–506. Reprinted as "The Brontës: or, Myth Domesticated." In *Forms of Modern Fiction,* edited by William Van O'Connor. Minneapolis: University of Minnesota Press, 1948.

Clayton, Jan, and Eric Rothstein, eds. *Influence and Intertextuality in Literary History.* Madison: University of Wisconsin Press, 1991.

Cohn, Dorrit. *Transparent Minds: Narrative Modes for Presenting Consciousness in Fiction.* Princeton: Princeton University Press, 1978.

Colby, Robert A. *Fiction with a Purpose: Major and Minor Nineteenth-Century Novels.* Bloomington: Indiana University Press, 1967.

Colby, Vineta. *Yesterday's Woman: Domestic Realism in the English Novel.* Princeton: Princeton University Press, 1974.

Cunningham, Valentine. *Everywhere Spoken Against: Dissent in the Victorian Novel.* Oxford: Clarendon Press, 1975.

Dalziel, Margaret. *Popular Fiction a Hundred Years Ago.* Philadelphia: Dufour, 1957.

Dessner, Lawrence Jay. *The Homely Web of Truth.* The Hague: Mouton, 1975.

Donaldson, Laura E. "The Miranda Complex: Colonialism and the Question of Feminist Reading." *Diacritics* 18 (Fall 1988): 65–77.

Dry, Florence Swinton. *The Sources of "Jane Eyre."* 1940. Folcroft, Pa.: Folcroft Library Editions, 1973.

Eagleton, Terry. *Criticism and Ideology: A Study in Marxist Literary Theory.* London: New Left Books, 1976.

———. *Myths of Power: A Marxist Study of the Brontës.* New York: Macmillan, 1975.

Ewbank, Inga-Stina. *Their Proper Sphere: A Study of the Brontë Sisters as*

. . . . . .

Early-Victorian Female Novelists. 1966. Cambridge, Mass.: Harvard University Press, 1968.

Feltes, N. N. "Phrenology: From Lewes to George Eliot." *Studies in the Literary Imagination* 1 (1968): 13–22.

Fish, Stanley. "Commentary: The Young and the Restless." In *The New Historicism,* edited by H. Aram Veeser. New York: Routledge, 1989.

————. *Is There a Text in This Class? The Authority of Interpretive Communities.* Cambridge, Mass.: Harvard University Press, 1980.

Fleishman, Avrom. *Figures of Autobiography: The Language of Self-Writing in Victorian and Modern England.* Berkeley: University of California Press, 1983.

Friedman, Susan Stanford. "Spatialization: A Strategy for Reading Narrative." *Narrative* 1 (January 1993): 12–23.

Gallagher, Susan VanZanten. "*Jane Eyre* and Christianity." In *Approaches to Teaching Brontë's "Jane Eyre,"* edited by Diane Long Hoeveler and Beth Lau, 62–68. See Hoeveler and Lau.

Gates, Barbara. "*Jane Eyre* and Poverty." In *Nineteenth-Century Women Writers of the English-Speaking World,* edited by Rhoda Nathan, 79–87. See Nathan.

Genette, Gérard. *Narrative Discourse.* Ithaca, N.Y.: Cornell University Press, 1980.

————. *Narrative Discourse Revisited.* Ithaca, N.Y.: Cornell University Press, 1988.

Gérin, Winifred. "Byron's Influence on the Brontës." *Essays by Divers Hands* 36 (1972): 47–62.

————. *Charlotte Brontë: The Evolution of Genius.* 1967. Reprint. London: Oxford University Press, 1969.

Gilbert, Sandra M., and Susan Gubar. *The Madwoman in the Attic: The Woman Writer and the Nineteenth-Century Literary Imagination.* New Haven: Yale University Press, 1979.

Griffin, Gail B. "Once More to the Attic: Bertha Rochester and the Pattern of Redemption in *Jane Eyre.*" In *Nineteenth-Century Women Writers of the English-Speaking World,* edited by Rhoda B. Nathan, 89–97. See Nathan.

. . . .

Grudin, Peter. "Jane and the Other Mrs. Rochester: Excess and Restraint in *Jane Eyre.*" *Novel* 10 (Winter 1977): 145–57.

Harrison, G[race] Elsie. *The Clue to the Brontës.* London: Methuen, 1948.

———. *Haworth Parsonage: A Study of Wesley and the Brontës.* London: Epworth Press, 1937.

Heilman, Robert B. "Charlotte Brontë, Reason, and the Moon." *Nineteenth-Century Fiction* 14 (1960): 283–302.

Hobsbawm, E. J. *The Age of Capital, 1848–1875.* New York: New American Library, 1979.

Hoeveler, Diane Long, and Beth Lau, eds. *Approaches to Teaching Brontë's "Jane Eyre."* New York: Modern Language Association, 1993.

Hunter, J. Paul. *The Reluctant Pilgrim.* Baltimore: Johns Hopkins Press, 1966.

Iser, Wolfgang. *The Act of Reading: A Theory of Aesthetic Response.* 1976. Translated 1978. Baltimore: Johns Hopkins University Press, 1980.

James, Louis. *Fiction for the Working Man.* 1963. Harmondsworth, Middlesex: Penguin, 1974.

Jauss, Hans Robert. "Literary History as a Challenge to Literary Theory." In *New Directions in Literary History,* edited by Ralph Cohen, 11–41. Baltimore: Johns Hopkins University Press, 1974.

Jay, Elisabeth. *The Religion of the Heart: Anglican Evangelicalism and the Nineteenth-Century Novel.* Oxford: Clarendon Press, 1979.

Kaplan, Cora. *Sea Changes: Culture and Feminism.* London: Verso, 1986.

Kristeva, Julia. *Desire in Language: A Semiotic Approach to Literature and Art.* Edited by Leon S. Roudiez. New York: Columbia University Press, 1980.

Kucich, John. "*Jane Eyre* and Imperialism." In *Approaches to Teaching Brontë's "Jane Eyre,"* edited by Diane Long Hoeveler and Beth Lau, 104–9. See Hoeveler and Lau.

———. *Repression in Victorian Fiction: Charlotte Brontë, George Eliot, and Charles Dickens.* Berkeley: University of California Press, 1987.

Lankford, William T. "The Parish Boy's Progress: The Evolving Form of *Oliver Twist.*" *PMLA* 93 (January 1978): 20–31.

· · · · · · ·

Leavis, Q. D. Introduction to *Jane Eyre*, by Charlotte Brontë. Baltimore: Penguin Books, 1966.

Lerner, Laurence. "Bertha and the Critics." *Nineteenth-Century Literature* 44 (1989): 273–300.

Lubbock, Percy. *The Craft of Fiction*. 1921. New York: Viking, 1957.

Maison, Margaret. *The Victorian Vision: Studies in the Religious Novel*. New York: Sheed and Ward, 1961.

Martin, Robert Bernard. *Charlotte Brontë's Novels: The Accent of Persuasion*. 1966. New York: W. W. Norton, 1968.

Medvedev, P. N./M. M. Bakhtin. *The Formal Method in Literary Scholarship*. 1928. Translated by Albert J. Wehrle. Baltimore: Johns Hopkins University Press, 1978.

Mink, JoAnna Stephens. "The Emergence of Woman as Hero in the Nineteenth Century." In *Heroines of Popular Culture*, edited by Pat Browne. Bowling Green, Ohio: Bowling Green University Popular Press, 1987.

Nathan, Rhoda B., ed. *Nineteenth-Century Women Writers of the English-Speaking World*. Contributions in Women's Studies, no. 69. New York: Greenwood Press, 1986.

Nestor, Pauline. *Charlotte Brontë's "Jane Eyre."* New York: Harvester Wheatsheaf, 1992.

Peterson, Linda. *Victorian Autobiography: The Tradition of Self-Interpretation*. New Haven: Yale University Press, 1986.

Phelan, James. *Reading People, Reading Plots*. Chicago: University of Chicago Press, 1989.

Pollard, Arthur. "The Seton-Gordon Brontë Letters." *Brontë Society Transactions*, pt. 92 (1982): 101–14.

Poovey, Mary. "The Anathematized Race: The Governess and *Jane Eyre*." In *Uneven Developments: The Ideological Work of Gender in Mid-Victorian England*, 126–63. Women in Culture and Society, edited by Catharine R. Simpson. Chicago: University of Chicago Press, 1988.

Praz, Mario. *The Romantic Agony*. 1933. New York: World Publishing Co., 1963.

Qualls, Barry V. *The Secular Pilgrims of Victorian Fiction*. Cambridge: Cambridge University Press, 1982.

· · · · · · ·

Rabinowitz, Peter J. *Before Reading: Narrative Conventions and the Politics of Interpretation.* Ithaca, N.Y.: Cornell University Press, 1987.

Reed, John. *Victorian Conventions.* Athens: Ohio University Press, 1975.

Rich, Adrienne. "*Jane Eyre:* The Temptations of a Motherless Woman." *Ms.* 2 (October 1973): 68–72, 98, 106–7.

Rinehart, Keith. "The Victorian Approach to Autobiography." *Modern Philology* 51 (February 1954): 177–86.

Roudiez, Leon S. Introduction to *Desire in Language,* by Julia Kristeva. New York: Columbia University Press, 1980.

Schorer, Mark. Introduction to *Jane Eyre,* by Charlotte Brontë. Boston: Houghton Mifflin, 1959.

Somervell, D. C. *English Thought in the Nineteenth Century.* 1929. New York: David McKay, 1962.

Spens, Janet. "Charlotte Brontë." In *Essays and Studies by Members of the English Association,* vol. 14. Oxford: Clarendon Press, 1929.

Spivak, Gayatri Chakravorty. "Three Women's Tales and a Critique of Imperialism." *Critical Inquiry* 12 (1985): 243–61.

Sternberg, Meir. *Expositional Modes and Temporal Ordering in Fiction.* Baltimore: Johns Hopkins University Press, 1978.

Stevick, Philip. *The Chapter in Fiction: Theories of Narrative Division.* Syracuse, N.Y.: Syracuse University Press, 1970.

Stone, Donald D. *The Romantic Impulse in Victorian Fiction.* Cambridge, Mass.: Harvard University Press, 1980.

Thomson, Patricia. *The Victorian Heroine: A Changing Ideal, 1837–73.* London: Oxford University Press, 1956.

Thorslev, Peter. *The Byronic Hero.* Minneapolis: University of Minnesota Press, 1962.

Tillotson, Kathleen. *Novels of the Eighteen-Forties.* Oxford: Clarendon Press, 1954.

Todorov, Tzvetan. *Mikhail Bakhtin: The Dialogic Principle.* Minneapolis: University of Minnesota Press, 1984.

Tompkins, Jane. *Reader-Response Criticism.* Baltimore: Johns Hopkins University Press, 1980.

. . . .

Trombley, Annette. *The Cover of the Mask: The Autobiographers in Charlotte Brontë's Fiction*. Victoria, B.C.: English Literary Studies, University of Victoria, 1982.

Tush, Susan Rowland. "George Eliot's Review of 'The Silly Novels by Lady Novelists' and Her Own Fictional Practice." Ph.D. diss., Emory University, 1990.

Vargish, Thomas. *The Providential Aesthetic in Victorian Fiction*. Charlottesville: University of Virginia Press, 1985.

Veeser, H. Aram, ed. *The New Historicism*. New York: Routledge, 1989.

Volosinov, V. N. *Marxism and the Philosophy of Language*. Cambridge, Mass.: Harvard University Press, 1973.

Watt, William W. *Shilling Shockers of the Gothic School*. 1932. New York: Russell and Russell, 1967.

West, Katherine. *Chapter of Governesses: A Study of the Governess in English Fiction, 1800–1949*. 1949. Folcroft, Pa.: Folcroft Library Editions, 1974.

"Where the Brontës Borrowed Books." *Brontë Society Transactions* 11 (1951): 344–58.

Winnifrith, Tom. *The Brontës and Their Background*. New York: Barnes and Noble, 1973.

Wise, T. J., and J. A. Symington. *The Brontës: Their Lives, Friendships and Correspondence*. 4 vols. Oxford: Shakespeare Head Press, 1934.

Wolff, Robert Lee. *Gains and Losses: Novels of Faith and Doubt in Victorian England*. New York: Garland, 1977.

INDEX

Gallagher, Susan VanZanten, 210–11, 235 n. 7
The Gallant Glazier; or, the Mystery of Ridley Hall, 58
Gaskell, Elizabeth, 204, 216; on origin of mad wife, 4
Gilbert, Sandra M., and Susan Gubar, *The Madwoman in the Attic,* 74; on Bertha's role, 148, 149–51; on Jane as revolutionary, 155–56; on the red-room experience, 233 n. 12; on St. John, 177–78
Godwin, William: *Caleb Williams,* 16, 17, 23; *Deloraine,* 16; *Enquiry Concerning Political Justice,* 16; fictional autobiographies, 16–17; *Fleetwood,* 16; *Mandeville,* 17; mix of rebel-novel and Gothic, 60; revolutionary Romanticism, 17; *St. Leon,* 16
Godwinism: in *Jane Eyre,* 47, 51, 57, 61, 78–79, 81, 92; in *Memoirs of Emma Courtney,* 79–80
Goethe, Johann Wolfgang von, *Braut von Korinth,* 120, 121
Gothic novel, xiii, 5–6, 219; deserted wing motif, 4–5, 65–71, 76; and *Jane Eyre,* 57–66, 76, 88, 94–95, 227 n. 5; morality of love, 161; problematic ontology, 143–44; stiles in, 64, 126; vampirism in, 119–21, 143–44
Governesses' Benevolent Institution, 49
Governess novel, 5, 49–57, 77, 219, 225 n. 5; chastising of Godwinian passions in, 81; governesses as orphans, 230 n. 1a; gypsy fortune-teller topos, 117; and *Jane Eyre,* 46, 49–57, 61–62, 94, 117; marriage to clergyman as reward in, 180; prevalence of providence in, 172–74; sexual harassment in, 54–56; social humiliation topos, 112–14; unknown uncle topos, 126, 188

Gubar, Susan. *See* Gilbert, Sandra M.

Hall, Anna Maria, "The Governess, a Tale," 56, 112, 159; "Our Governess," 114
Hays, Mary, 130, 234 n. 3; *Memoirs of Emma Courtney,* 79–80, 81, 88
Hobsbawm, E. J., *The Age of Capital, 1848–1875,* 194
Hofland, Barbara, *Ellen, the Teacher. A Tale for Youth,* 28–30, 37, 44, 226 n. 9
Hook, Theodore, *Fathers and Sons,* 146
Howitt, Mary, 118
Hunter, Paul, 171

Ideologemes, xiii, 5, 219
Ignis fatuus (false lead), 135–36, 234 n. 3
Imperialism, 235 n. 8; and *Jane Eyre,* 192–95
Iser, Wolfgang, xiv, 154–55, 183, 223 n. 2; on reader's participation in producing meaning, 184–85; on recombining of conventions in literature, 72, 180; on the text vs. the work, x–xi

Jack, A. A., 72–73
Jack, Jane, ix
James, Louis, 58, 120, 143–44, 225 n. 8
Jane Eyre: acknowledgment of sexuality, 130–31; anticipatory cautions regarding Jane's character, 30, 32, 47, 110, 125; anticipatory cautions regarding Jane's relationship with Rochester, 92; anticipatory cautions regarding St. John, 176, 179–80, 187; asceticism of St. John, 182–83, 192; authorial reading of, 105, 107, 125, 151, 201, 203, 208, 211, 214, 216; Bertha's role, 148–54;

Novel, nineteenth century
(*continued*)
219; prevalence of providence in,
172–74; reader of, 7–9; romantic creole topos, 116–17; scenic
topoi, 4, 23, 42, 69, 112; silver-fork
novel, 112; telepathic experience
in, 204–5; tree as emblem of
lovers, 135; vampirism in, 119–21,
140–44; women's novels, 80–81.
See also Gothic novel; Governess
novel

Observer, 155
Ong, Father, 7
Orphan (foundling) novel, 219

Peacock, Thomas Love, *Nightmare
Abbey*, 64
People's Journal, 155; review of *Jane
Eyre*, 28
Perrault, Charles, 58
Pitt, G. D., 225 n. 8
Poems by Currer, Ellis and Acton Bell,
12, 73
Polidori, John, *The Vampyre. A Tale*,
120–21, 144, 230 n. 2
Politi, Jina, "*Jane Eyre* Class-ified,"
152, 192–93, 210
Postformalism, xi–xiii; pre-
postformalism, xii, 7
Poststructuralism (post-
modernism), xi, 223 n. 2
Praz, Mario, 120, 145, 230 n. 4
Primacy effect, ix–x, 26–27, 215–16

Qualls, Barry, 184, 233 n. 2

Rabinowitz, Peter J., 11, 229 n. 2b;
concept of "authorial audience"/reader, 8, 9, 105, 203, 211,
263
Radcliffe, Anne, *The Mysteries of
Udolpho*, 147, 161–62; *Sicilian
Romance*, 66

Ratchford, Fanny, 204
Reader, x, 7–9; defining of, 107;
Victorian, 107–8
Reading: authorial, 8–9, 105, 229
n. 2b; formalist, x; as misreading,
107, 217–18, 229 n. 2b; spatialized,
x–xi, 101–2
Reed, John, 236 n. 4
Reeve, Clara, *Fatherless Fanny*, 58–
59, 110, 145, 165–66, 227 n. 6, 228
n. 10
Revue des deux mondes, review of
Jane Eyre, 28
Reynolds, G. W. M., *The Mysteries of
London*, 226 n. 3
Rhys, Jean, *The Wide Sargasso Sea*,
152
Richardson, Samuel: *Clarissa*, 54,
95, 129–30, 160, 234 n. 3; *The
History of Sir Charles Grandison*,
139–40; *Pamela*, 54–55, 117
Rigby, Elizabeth, review of *Jane
Eyre*, 13, 49–50, 92, 155, 226 n. 2,
229 n. 2a
Ross, Mrs., *The Governess; Or, Poli-
tics in Private Life*, 56, 77, 114
Roudiez, Leon S., 224 n. 1a
Rymer, James Malcolm, *Varney the
Vampire*, 120, 141–42, 143–44, 230
n. 3

Sand, George, 80, 204; *Consuelo*, 128
Sargent, John, *A Memoir of the Rev.
Henry Martyn, B. D.*, 183
Scenic topoi, 4, 23, 42, 69, 112
Scenic units, 1–2
Schorer, Mark, 205
Scotsman, 43
Scott, Sir Walter: *The Heart of Mid-
lothian*, 231 n. 3; *A Legend of
Montrose*, 145; *Waverley; or, 'Tis
Sixty Years Since*, 65, 67, 206
Sewell, Elizabeth, 183; *Amy Herbert*,
41, 44, 112–13

· · · · · ·

. . . .

THE THEORY AND INTERPRETATION
OF NARRATIVE SERIES

*James Phelan and
Peter J. Rabinowitz,
Editors*

Because the series editors believe that the most significant work in narrative studies today contributes both to our knowledge of specific narratives and to our understanding of narrative in general, studies in the series typically offer interpretations of individual narratives and address significant theoretical issues underlying those interpretations. The series does not privilege any one critical perspective but is open to work from any strong theoretical position.